The Muslim World

Edited by Geoffrey Orens

The Reference Shelf
Volume 75 • Number 1

The H. W. Wilson Company
2003

The Reference Shelf

The books in this series contain reprints of articles, excerpts from books, addresses on current issues, and studies of social trends in the United States and other countries. There are six separately bound numbers in each volume, all of which are usually published in the same calendar year. Numbers one through five are each devoted to a single subject, providing background information and discussion from various points of view and concluding with a subject index and comprehensive bibliography that lists books, pamphlets, and abstracts of additional articles on the subject. The final number of each volume is a collection of recent speeches, and it contains a cumulative speaker index. Books in the series may be purchased individually or on subscription.

Library of Congress has cataloged this title as follows:

The Muslim world / edited by Geoffrey Orens.
    p.cm
    Includes bibliographical references and index.
    ISBN 0-8242-1019-0 (alk. paper)
    1. Islam 2. Islam—Essence, genius, nature 3. Islam—Doctrines, 4. Islam—Relations. 5. Muslim. I. Orens, Geoffrey.

BP161.3.M87 2003
297—dc21   2002041476

Cover: A Muslim praying at a mosque, by Tim Hall (PhotoDisc).

Visit H.W. Wilson's Web site: www.hwwilson.com

Printed in the United States of America

Contents

Preface

Islam, which is practiced by about 1.3 billion people, is the world's second largest religion and is growing faster than most other faiths. Muslims inhabit six continents, can be found among all races, and embrace various orientations, ranging from strict Wahhabism to mystical Sufism. Nevertheless, few religions are as misunderstood by the West as Islam. Years of terrorism by Muslim extremists have led many in the West to develop a mistakenly homogeneous portrait of the Islamic world. While the terrorist attacks on the United States on September 11, 2001, revealed in the starkest terms the vast gulf between Western democratic capitalism and Islamic fundamentalism, a greater desire to understand Islam and the Muslim world has followed.

The complex sphere of the Muslim world raises many difficult questions for Muslims and non-Muslims alike. The majority of Islamic nations are authoritarian states where most of the population has little political power or freedom and no great love for many aspects of Western culture, which they perceive as lacking ethics. Islamic law (shariah) is followed to one degree or another by most Muslims, but its often harsh interpretations appear to Western eyes as fostering sexism and lacking humanitarianism. The propagation of Wahhabism and its followers' lack of tolerance for other forms of Islam make reform difficult both in the West and in Muslim nations.

However, to approach Islam by attending to only cultural and political trends is to lose sight of its rich spiritual dimension. The Qur'an is one of the world's most remarkable texts and amazes many non-Muslims with its beauty and directness. Chanted in its original Arabic throughout the Muslim world, it is a constant reminder to Muslims of the universal and timeless word of God. At least 17 times a day the devout Muslim will recite the Fatiha, the first sura, or chapter in the Qur'an, as part of his or her daily prayer ritual, which relates God's mercy and compassion and his dominion over all while intoning each Muslim to follow faithfully the path of Islam.

The first section of this book explores Islam's various practices and principles. Terry C. Muck concisely describes the orthopraxy and orthodoxy of Islam, while Imam Feisal Abdul Rauf elaborates on the heart of the religion and what it means to be Muslim. Reshma Memon Yaqub describes the hajj, the pilgrimage to Mecca that all Muslims are expected to perform once in their lifetimes, and Scott Peterson looks at the small but extremely important and powerful Islamic sect of Wahhabism, which has influenced such people as Osama bin Laden. Richard Vara then provides an introduction to Islamic mysticism known as Sufism.

The book's second section looks at some of the controversy surrounding Islamic law throughout the world. Jerry Useem discusses the role Islamic law plays in financial dealings. Caryle Murphy then considers the recent debate among Muslims around the world concerning the nature of Islam. Franklin Foer relates the difficulties faced by one of the rare liberal Islamic scholars, and Francis Fukuyama and Nadav Samin discuss the global repercussions of Islamism.

Section three examines the role women play in Muslim society and in the religion of Islam. First, Lisa Beyer and others writing for *Time* magazine describe the hurdles women face in achieving equality in the Muslim world. Madeleine Bunting addresses many aspects of Islam that Muslim women find liberating, while Katherine Millett examines why some American women have converted to Islam.

The fourth section considers the question of whether or not a democratic system of government is viable for Muslim nations in the near future. David Lamb examines the close ties between religion and politics in the Muslim world. Next, John L. Esposito and John O. Voll explore whether or not Islam is compatible with democracy, while Ray Takeyh ponders whether or not Islamic democracies will be able to significantly alter their societies and their relations with the West. Mark R. Woodward's article on Islam and the government of Indonesia examines the young and fragile democracy that exists in that nation.

The next section explores the way Muslims view Jews and Christians, referred to in the Qur'an as "people of the book." Kenneth L. Woodward compares the Qur'an with Jewish and Christian scripture, with particular emphasis on the Qur'an's views on violence. Next, Ali S. Asani defends Islam as a peaceful and tolerant faith that is misunderstood by militants. Susan Sachs then tackles the difficult issue of anti-Semitism among Muslims. In Sara Miller's article, the relationship between Muslims and Jesus is examined.

The book's final section looks at Muslims living in Western nations. Jane Lampman examines the ways American society has affected the lives of many Muslims who live here. The successes and tribulations of the African-American Muslim community are next discussed by Michelle Cottle, while Alexander Stille considers the controversial world of Qur'anic scholarship. Finally, Aleksei Malashenko explores the complex relationship between Muslims and non-Muslims in Russia.

I would like to extend my thanks to all the authors and publications that granted their permission to use their work for this compendium. I would especially like to thank Lynn Messina, Sandra Watson, Gray Young, Norris Smith, Rich Stein, Jennifer Peloso, and Clifford Thompson at H. W. Wilson for their role in the book's production. In addition, I would like to thank Frank Vriale, John and Elizabeth Orens, and Sheikha Fariha al-Jerrahi for their helpful advice during the research for this project.

Geoffrey Orens
February 2003

I. Introduction to Islam and Its Practices

Editor's Introduction

In the Western world there is much confusion and misinformation about the nature and practices of Islam. While the terrorist attacks of September 11, 2001, led many Americans to educate themselves more about the Muslim world, there remains a great deal of ignorance about the fundamentals of the religion. Some believe Muslims worship the prophet Mohammed, or that the Qur'an is filled with little else but incitements to violence. Their lack of knowledge about Islam stems partly from the fact that, until the Arab-Israeli wars in the second half of the twentieth century, the media largely ignored the Muslim world. As tensions rise between Muslim nations and the West at the beginning of the twenty-first century, much can be gained from even a basic understanding of Islamic culture. In this section we shall look at Islamic practice and faith through the eyes of both Muslims and journalists from outside of Islam.

In his article "An Introduction to Islam: One God, Many Believers," Presbyterian minister and professor of religions Terry C. Muck gives an overview of Islam and points to the common scriptural history that Jews and Christians share with Muslims. Muck encapsulates the life of the prophet Mohammed, who brought monotheism to the polytheistic Arabic peninsula in the seventh century A.D. He discusses the five pillars of Islamic faith that tie Muslims together and provides an overview of the moral and theological beliefs of Muslims on such current issues as abortion and jihad, often defined as "holy war." Muck also points out the difference between Shiite and Sunni Muslims, who together compose roughly 98 percent of all Muslims.

In an interview for the PBS television program *Frontline*, Imam Feisal Abdul Rauf, who is the imam of the Masjid-al-Farah in New York City and the founder of the American Sufi Association, considers the fundamental beliefs of Islam through the eyes of someone who was born in the Muslim faith. Rauf offers an insider's view of the Muslim belief system and asserts that, in Islam, the purpose of human existence is to realize and acknowledge the divine aspect of humanity. Rauf's explanations add color to Muck's outline of Islam, as the imam addresses some of the subjects that this book will explore at greater length, such as the role of women in the Muslim world; shariah, or Islamic law; and what it means to be a Muslim in Western society.

The hajj, or pilgrimage to Mecca, is an Islamic practice that is unique in the grandeur of its scale and in the fundamental obligation placed on the faithful to participate at least once in their lifetimes. Millions each year perform the pilgrimage to Mecca, described by many Muslims as an astounding experience of spiritual clarity, and many who cannot afford it are often sponsored by other Muslim families. In his article "Hajj: The Journey of a Lifetime," Reshma Memon Yaqub describes the pilgrim's experience from a Muslim perspective.

In his article "Wahhabi Roots in Saudi Desert," Scott Peterson examines the origins of the Wahhabi Sunni sect of Islam. Although only a small portion of Muslims worldwide adhere to Wahhabi beliefs, the influence of Wahhabism is wide-ranging. The extreme wealth of many Wahhabis—the majority of whom are Saudi—has enabled them to open mosques, fund charities, and pay for the wide distribution of books on Islamic law. It is from the Wahhabi school of thought that Osama bin Laden and many members of al Queda have developed their rationale for terrorist activity, a source of great tension between Wahhabi clerics and more-liberal Muslims in the United States.

At the other end of the spectrum of Muslim belief is Sufism, adhered to by only about 3 percent of Muslims worldwide. Nevertheless, just as Wahhabism has made a large impact on the world, so have the Sufis, with their music (made popular by recording artist Nusrat Fateh Ali Khan) and their mystical poetry, which has become immensely popular in the West through the work of the 13th-century Persian poet Rumi. Richard Vara's essay "They're Muslims, But Sufis Still Go Own Way" reflects on the Sufis' mystical relationship to God as divine love and Sufism's ability to attract both traditional Muslims and non-Muslims. Since their ceremonies are filled with music and singing, Sufis are often looked down upon by other Muslims, but Vara shows how Sufism, with its openness to dialogues with other religions and acceptance of all paths, could play a significant role in its future, especially as it attracts more attention in the West.

An Introduction to Islam: One God, Many Believers[1]

By Terry C. Muck
The Columbus Dispatch, September 30, 2001

For the past 50 years, Islam has been one of the world's fastest-growing religions—so much so that the United States has more Muslims than Episcopalians or Presbyterians.

One of the three monotheistic religions with roots in the Middle East, like Judaism and Christianity, Islam traces its history to worship of the one God (Allah, in Arabic) instituted by Abraham in the second millennium B.C. Muslims claim for this common history the traditional prophets and leaders of Jewish and Christian history such as Adam, Noah, Moses, Abraham and Jesus, but believe that this line of genuine prophets ends with Muhammad, a man born in Mecca, in present-day Saudi Arabia, in 570.

Muhammad is called the "seal of the prophets," the one to whom God revealed that last and most authoritative of his revelations, the Quran, the Muslim holy book. While wandering in the rocky hills outside Mecca, Muhammad began to receive the revelations that eventually made up the chapters of the Quran. A voice from the heavens, the angel Gabriel, gave him the revelation, commanding him to learn and recite the message to others. After receiving each of these audible revelations, a process that lasted many years, Muhammad would then return to the streets of Mecca and preach them to his compatriots. His standard sermon had three points: the uniqueness of Allah; the need to care for the poor, orphaned and widowed; and the inevitability of a final judgment. Each of these points, however, seemed to alienate segments of the Meccan populace. By stressing the uniqueness of God, Muhammad threatened the various tribal and clan gods, a threat that had not only religious but economic overtones in a city that had become something of a religious pilgrimage site for followers of those many deities. By advocating the need to care for the poor, Muhammad was calling for social welfare at a time when the trading fortunes of Mecca had taken a downturn and money was tight. By predicting a judgment at the end of time, Muhammad alienated whomever he had not alienated with the first two points; no one likes to be told his or her lifestyle could lead to the fires of hell.

---

1. Reprinted, with permission, from *The Columbus Dispatch*.

After several years of reciting these revelations and interpreting them for the Meccans, Muhammad had only a handful of followers and was in danger of losing his life.

At this crisis point, a delegation from Medina, a town 200 miles northeast of Mecca, came to town looking for a leader. Medina was divided by rivalry between a fairly large Jewish population and an indigenous population that held to the belief in tribal gods. Muhammad's message proved to be a bridge between the two. Largely rejected in Mecca, he was welcomed in Medina. After building a secure base there, Muhammad began extending his influence into surrounding areas, eventually incorporating all of western Arabia, including Mecca. Many have seen his political skills as being as important as his religious message.

Essential Practices

Muhammad's message has often been summarized as five basic duties, sometimes called the Five Pillars:

- The creed (Shahada).
- Prayer (Salat).
- Alms-giving (Zakat).
- Fasting (Sawm).
- Pilgrimage (Hajj).

The creed: The basic requirement for calling oneself Muslim is to be able to say the creed with conviction of its truth: "There is no god but God, and Muhammad is his messenger."

Prayer: An observant Muslim uses a standardized set of prayers five times a day: at dawn, noon, midafternoon, dusk and evening. The prayers are said either alone or in community. Friday noon is the traditional time for a communal service at the mosque, the Muslim building of worship, facing Mecca, with accompanying physical postures and movements. The prayer content is almost exclusively praise of Allah taken from various chapters of the Quran.

Alms-giving: Zakat is a mandatory annual "loan" to God of charity in an amount based on one's net worth. However, Muslims are also encouraged to give regularly throughout the year to the mosque for the support of the poor in the community.

Fasting: During the lunar month of Ramadan, observant Muslims practice a daylight fast: no food, drink, smoking or sexual activity. Between sunset and dawn, the fast may be broken.

Pilgrimage: Every Muslim, if physically and financially able, should make one pilgrimage to Mecca's holy sites during the official three days of the Great Hajj.

The Five Pillars are the basic practices of Islam, and most of the theology of the faith is readily apparent in them: the oneness of God, the praiseworthiness of God, the importance of the Prophet Muhammad and the requirements of membership in both the local and the larger Islamic community.

Other key theological tenets include a belief in spiritual beings (both angels and more ambiguous beings called jinn); the centrality of the Quran and the importance of its purity in the Arabic language; a literal belief in heaven and hell; and the importance of establishing sharia law in order to unite the secular and religious communities.

Sharia, or the "Islamic Way," is the legal code of Islam and is derived from the teachings of the Quran and other Islamic religious texts.

This last tenet—the importance of sharia—has shaped much of the interaction of modern Islam with the non-Islamic world. Muhammad himself set the tone for this debate in that he was as much a political leader as a spiritual one. By incarnating both roles in his singular leadership style, Muhammad managed to unite, or set the stage for his immediate followers to unite, much of one of the most politically fractious geographies on Earth, the Middle East.

In the early days of Islam, from the eighth to the 19th centuries, this took the form of a number of waxing and waning dynasties. With the coming of the colonial powers—Britain, France and the United States—and the peace accords after World War I, this dynastic structure gave way to the nation-states of the 20th century.

> *The importance of sharia ... has shaped much of the interaction of modern Islam.*

Sunni and Shiite

Although Muhammad was a marvelously skilled political leader, he died without naming either a successor or establishing a process by which his successor should be named. As a result, two opinions developed among his followers regarding who should lead this increasingly powerful religious community. Some thought the leader should come from Muhammad's family. Others thought that the leader should be elected through consultation and consensus. The second opinion carried the day, perhaps in part because Muhammad had no sons survive him, and the only viable candidate from his family was a son-in-law, Ali, husband of one of Muhammad's daughters, Fatima.

The three leaders who directly followed Muhammad, then, were called successors or caliphs: Abu Bakr (632–634), Umar (634–644) and Uthman (644–656). The party advocating that leadership come from Muhammad's family finally succeeded in getting their candidate appointed in 656 when Uthman was assassinated and Ali was named head of the Islamic community. Controversy continued, however.Ali was considered the fourth caliph by those advocating that process of choosing a leader, but was considered the only rightful heir of leadership, an imam, by those who considered the first three caliphs usurpers. The controversy raged and eventually led to the assassinations of Ali and his son, Husayn.

The importance of this controversy for understanding modern Islam cannot be overestimated. It represents both the historical and ongoing division between the two largest Muslim sects, the Sunni and the Shiite. Sunnis, who make up about 95 percent of all Muslims, were the champions of the caliphate system. Although the caliphate per se no longer exists, the principle of choosing leaders through consultation and consensus was adapted to the dynastic structures that ruled Islam through the Ottoman Empire in the 19th century.

Shiite Muslims, accounting for perhaps 3 percent of the worldwide Muslim community, still advocate the imanate, the descendants of Muhammad as the rightful heirs of the leadership mantle.

The important point to remember is that this modern division is largely over polity: how the community should be led. It is not primarily a division of belief or religious practice, except where these relate to theories of leadership and political questions. Otherwise, both Sunnis and Shiites practice the same Islam taught by Muhammad. It does account, however, for much of the division that exists in the Muslim world, especially surrounding the difficult questions of sharia. Both Sunnis and Shiites agree that some form of Islamic law should be established but differ widely over the means to accomplish it.

Questions and Answers

As a result of this history, Muslims in today's world present the non-Islamic population with several difficult questions.

- Politics: Are Muslims democratic or authoritarian? In a sense, the Islamic world is out of step with the current political trend of moving toward pluralistic democracies. These democracies, fashioned largely after the United States model, have as one of their key characteristics the separation of church and state. This is not a congenial model for Muslim countries where the ideal is not separation of church and state but the identification of the two under a single, Muslim-dominated leadership structure. In other words, in the Muslim world, President Bush and Pope John Paul II would be the same person. Given this difference in viewpoint, the question is whether a form of political leadership congenial to Islamic theological views and nonantagonistic to democratic ideals can be developed.

- Jihad: Why are Muslims so intense about their religion? Muslims, like Christians and Buddhists, have a very powerful missionary tradition, a theological mandate to spread the influence of their religion worldwide. This practice is included in a wider mandate to fully realize the injunctions of the Quran called jihad. Because Muslims do not have a strict separation between the theological and political spheres, this missionary mandate is often indistinguishable from the political aims of Islamic governments. In practice this means some of the tools of statecraft—

political negotiation, economic leverage and military might—have sometimes been employed in the spreading of religion. In practice this is not much different from some of the methods used by Christians and Buddhists. In Islam, however, the theological warrant for such practices is much clearer and less controversial.

- Pluralism: Do Muslims respect other faiths? Traditional Islamic teaching has no place for secularism and polytheism but tolerates the other monotheistic religions: Judaism, Christianity and Zoroastrianism. This religious/political exclusivism is at odds with the notion of different religions enjoying equal freedoms under secular pluralistic democracies.

- Liberty: How much for the individual? Islam has often been called a communitarian religion, not an individualistic one. This means that when it comes to balancing individual rights with community responsibilities as defined by religious teaching, the community responsibilities usually win out. This puts many Islamic moral and ethical emphases at odds with Western individualism.

Islam and U.S. Life

Muslims find themselves in agreement with many features of American culture:

- Human rights: Despite their communitarian emphases and drive to extend the sway of Quranic teaching, Muslims are not anti–human rights. They believe all humans are created by God and as such deserve respect. This is particularly true of the disadvantaged of society. One of Muhammad's main points in his preaching was the need to take care of widows, orphans and the poor.

- Drug abuse: Observant Muslims do not use any mood-altering drugs, including alcohol.

- Family values: Muslims have very high ethical ideals, particularly where they relate to family members. One of the difficulties immigrant Muslims in the United States have, for example, is the relaxed mixing of the sexes in schools and the unchaperoned dating common to most teen-agers.

- Monotheism: Thinking of God in the singular is natural to Muslims. This is a point of contact with Americans, many of whom are strongly influenced by the Judeo-Christian tradition of monotheism.

Calendar and Holidays

Muslims follow the lunar calendar. This means they have 12 months of 29 days, 12 hours and 44 minutes each. The Muslim year is 11 days shorter than the solar year. As a result, Muslim months and holidays are not seasonal and rotate through the solar calendar year. The Muslim calendar is dated from the time of Muhammad's move from Mecca to Medina—the Hegira—and is designated by the letters A.H. (After the Hegira). Muslims living in Western countries that follow the solar Gregorian calendar usually keep both sets of dates.

Muslims celebrate two major holidays: Eid ul-fitr is the celebration at the end of Ramadan, the month of daylight fasting. It lasts three days. Eid ul-adha is the celebration at the end of the Great Pilgrimage to Mecca. Those who do not go on the pilgrimage celebrate at home with a four-day feast. Both of these major feasts are times of joy and praise of God.

Muslims also celebrate several minor holidays. They celebrate a New Year's Day on the first day of the first month (Muharram) of the year. The 10th of Muharram is a day of fasting, commemorating creation, the birth of Adam, the end of Noah's flood, the birth of Abraham and the birth of Jesus, and anticipating the Day of Judgment.

Perhaps no feature of modern Islam is more publicly evident than the way some Muslim women dress.

Customs and Rules

Perhaps no feature of modern Islam is more publicly evident than the way some Muslim women dress.

What is not required in Islam: The full-length chador and face veil. These are cultural expressions that actually have their roots in Persian culture. They are worn in some Muslim cultures, for example Saudi Arabia and Iran. In those cultures they express the Muslim abhorrence of adultery—an offense punishable by death—and the desire that clothing not be a temptation to men.

What is required in Islam: the general principles of modesty and cleanliness. For women, these principles mean that covering the hair in public is required. They also mean the neck to knees should be covered; thus, the hemlines of dresses should fall below the knees.

Islam has two kinds of food: halal, or allowable, and haram, or prohibited.

Haram foods fall into two categories. The first prohibits foods based on the way they were killed. Animals killed by any means other than the single approved way of killing are not allowed, nor are animals that kill: birds of prey, animals with claws and fangs, rodents, reptiles and insects (except locusts) are all haram. The second category prohibits foods because of what they are. The two main groups here are pork and the blood of any animal.

Allowable food animals are those not haram, killed by a single knife stroke across the jugular while saying a prayer. The carcass is then left upside down to be drained completely of blood. Muslim halal killing is the same as Jewish kosher killing; Muslims may buy meat from a kosher shop. All fish, fruits, vegetables, grains and root crops are allowable.

Worship and Ceremonies

The primary worship service is Friday noon prayers.

Shoes are removed at the door of a mosque. Most mosques have an entryway with racks for shoes. The main room of a mosque is the prayer room. Men and women pray separately. Different mosques divide them differently. In some, men are on one side of the prayer hall, women on the other. In others, men are in front, women in back. In still others, women might be in a separate prayer hall altogether.

After a ritualized purifying washing, worshippers enter the prayer room and sit in rows facing a mark on the wall that signifies the direction of Mecca. The service is made up of regular prayers, a series of memorized texts done in a standing, bowing and prostrate series of bodily positions. Prayers will be followed by a sermon or homily on a Quranic passage, perhaps followed by announcements. The entire service will take less than an hour.

Muslims have customs for celebrating the major events of life:

- Birth. Some Muslims hold a ceremony called aqiqa, a short, informal celebration of the birth of an infant. The elements of the ceremony vary from culture to culture and might include a naming ceremony, recitation of the Quran and a ceremony where the infant's hair is shaved and weighed and the parents give an equivalent amount of silver to the mosque as alms.

- Adult initiation. At any age from about 15 upward, a Muslim may declare his or her faith in the Shahada or witnessing ceremony. The initiate publicly repeats the creed— "There is no god but God, and Muhammad is his messenger"—in the presence of at least two male Muslims or eight female Muslims. This ceremony is the official joining of the Muslim religious community. Guests are often invited to this 15–30 minute service.

- Marriage. Marriage is very important to Muslims; everyone should get married unless physically or financially unable. The ceremony at the mosque lasts from 30 minutes to an hour, and guests are invited.

Death. Muslims have a strong belief in an afterlife: heaven for the righteous, hell for the unrighteous. The funeral ceremony is held two or three days after death, usually in a funeral home. The service is simple, less than an hour with interment following. There will be no open casket. Muslims bury their dead; no cremation is allowed. Mourning may not exceed 40 days.

An Interview with Imam Feisal Abdul Rauf[2]

FRONTLINE, MARCH 2002

What are the fundamentals of Islam? What does it teach to be a Muslim?

The fundamental idea which defines a human being as a Muslim is the declaration of faith: that there is a creator, whom we call God—or Allah, in Arabic—and that the creator is one and single. And we declare this faith by the declaration of faith, where we . . . bear witness that there is no God but God. And that we are accountable to God for our actions.

And that's the bottom line?

That is the universal Quranic definition of a person who is a Muslim. Because God says in the Quran that there is only one true religion, God's religion. It's the same theme that God revealed to all of the prophets, even before Muhammad. They all came to express the truth about ultimate reality: that the ultimate reality, with a capital "R" is God; that God created this universe; and God created humanity for a very specific purpose and mandate, which is to recognize what he or she truly is—a being created, as we say in the Judeo-Christian world, in the image of God. The Quran uses a different language. It says, created out of a divine in-breathing, because the Quran says when God created the shape, the form of Adam from clay, God says, "When I shall have breathed into him from my spirit." Then he announced to the angels, "Fall in prostration to Adam."

So the defining aspect of a human being is that the human being has within its envelope a piece of the divine breath. This is the Quranic definition of what you might call the quote, unquote, "divine image in the human envelope." And the human mandate is to recognize this essential definition of self, and to acknowledge the very special relationship that exists between that self and the creator.

It doesn't sound so different from Christianity or Judaism.

The Quran does not speak about Christianity or Judaism. You will not find that word once mentioned in the Quran. But you'll find many, many instances of Christians and Jews, because the definitions the Quran uses are human-based definitions. Not conceptual

---

2. Article from *Frontline* March 2002. Copyright © *Frontline*. Reprinted with permission.

definitions; very much it speaks about the realities. So God, for example, is creator. God is seeing. God is knowing. God is all-powerful. You don't have words of concepts as much. God is beautiful. So the ascriptions or the descriptions or the adjectives are what are used to describe the creator. Religion is defined by the relationship between God and man. And Islam is the submission and the acknowledgment of the human being to the creator.

Could you just give me a short version on how these two religions are related to one another?

God says in the Quran that there is not a single community on earth to whom we did not send a messenger. So the same message, the same truth, was revealed to all of humanity through a series of prophets; whose complete number, we don't know. The Quran mentions 25 of them by name.

But the message is one: that God is one; that the creator is single; that the creator has no partner; that the creator is described by the perfection of a number of attributes, which Muslims call the divine

---

Islam is the submission and the acknowledgment of the human being to the creator.

---

names. So God is one; God is almighty; God is all-seeing; God is all-knowing; God is all-hearing. God is compassionate, merciful, forgiving, loving. God is just. And so forth.

So we are forbidden to ascribe to God attributes of weakness or imperfection. So we cannot say God is one, but God is poor; God is one, but God is blind, for instance, or doesn't have the attribute of seeing. It is equally important for Muslims to assert, not only the oneness of God, but the perfection of his attributes.

And the message, in its substance, embodies what Jesus said were the two greatest commandments. When Jesus was once asked, "Rabbi, or Rebbe, what are the greatest commandments?" he said, "To love the lord your God with all of your heart, with all of your soul and all of your mind." And the second, which is co-equal with it: that you love your neighbor as you love yourself. Love for your brother or your sister, what you love for yourself. Not to harm them in a way that you do not wish to be harmed.

That again embodies these two principles: A, that you have to acknowledge the creator correctly. And B, that you are going to be held accountable for your ethical decisions and choices. And the particular form of revelation was a function of society. So every prophet or messenger spoke in his own language to his own community. Some words were spoken in Hebrew, or in ancient Egyptian. Every revelation was given in the language of the community to whom it was sent. The rituals may have been a little bit different, but the essence of the rituals were there: prayer, charity, and fasting.

If the message is the same, then how come the people don't agree with each other?

Well, God's perennial lament—not only in the Quran, but in other scriptures as well—is that people generally do not follow God's dictates and the guidance and the mandate that God has offered to humanity to follow. We tend to be recalcitrant. We tend to be disobedient to divine guidance. And if you look at human conflict, it has even existed within people of the same religious tradition. I don't need to remind you that even among those who call themselves Muslims there has been a lot of bloodshed.

We're finding that it's very hard to define who Muslims are. Every time we figure, oh, that's what it is, or that's who they are, there's an exception to the rule. There's a very traditional housewife-looking lady in Malaysia who's also an OB/ Gyn who ministers to unwed mothers. We have girls in Turkey who are saying, "Look, we want to express ourselves as Muslims. We want to cover our hair." And we have a secular government that's discriminating against them—women who want to cover, women who don't. Men who want to keep women in the house; men who agree that women have absolute opportunity to do what they need to do in society. How does this all fit?

The definition of the faith of Islam that I gave you before is the Quranic universal definition of the human being vis-a-vis the creator. There is a narrower definition of Islam which is used, which is those who follow the teachings of the prophet Muhammad. Now, according to that definition, their Islam is defined by what was commonly called the five pillars of faith. This is what theologians call the orthopraxy, or the orthopraxis. It means the practices which define you as a Muslim.

There are also five articles of creed, of belief, which theologians call the orthodoxy. That which defines you as a Muslim, if you adhere to these beliefs, [parallels] to, say, [Christianity] and Judaism, that in the Jewish faith, there is an orthopraxy, not much of an orthodoxy. As long as you abide by the rituals, the dietary laws, male circumcision, et cetera, et cetera, there is flexibility within the Jewish tradition on what you might choose to believe in to be considered as a member of the Jewish faith community. So there is flexibility in whether [you] believe in an afterlife, heaven and hell and so forth.

In the Christian faith, you have the opposite situation. You have a fundamental orthodoxy, which is, you have to believe that Jesus Christ is savior. If you believe wholeheartedly that Jesus Christ is savior, you are saved; you receive salvation. And there's a great flexibility on the ritual end. What you do in terms of prayers or dietary laws, circumcision, et cetera, there's flexibility on that.

In Islam, we have both an orthodoxy and an orthopraxy. The orthodoxy of the Islamic faith is defined as a belief in the oneness of God and the right attitude, the right understandings of God, as I mentioned earlier. A belief in the angels, beings created of light, who convey the divine commandments. The belief that God communicated to humanity via scriptures. And these scriptures are considered to be both oral and written form. . . . And the belief that God also communicated his guidance and messages and teachings to humanity via human intermediaries, human messengers, we call them prophets, or messengers.

And the last item of the Islamic orthodoxy is the belief in the last

---

> *The orthodoxy of the Islamic faith is defined as a belief in the oneness of God and the right attitude, the right understandings of God.*

---

day. The last is a compound concept which means that this creation will, in fact, come to an end. So those of us who believe in the big bang theory, there will be a big implosion, in other words, at the end of time, so to speak, followed by a day of resurrection, where all the souls shall be resurrected; followed by a day of judgment, where all souls will be judged; followed by the obtaining of divine approval or divine disapproval. A pass grade or a failing grade. Those who get a passing grade will be in paradise. Those who get a failing grade will be in what we call hell. And the underlying theme of the last day is that we are all accountable for our ethical actions. . . . That's the orthodoxy.

The orthopraxy of Islam is a declaration of faith: the statement that there is no God but God; that Muhammad is the messenger of God; the five-time daily prayer; the giving of alms, typically 2.5 percent of one's income or assets; the fasting of the month of Ramadan; and the going to pilgrimage, or hajj, once in one's lifetime, if one can afford it, financially and physically. Anybody who does these things is within the box of Islam.

There are other things, secondary things. Rules of dress and rules of behavior and rules of what may be considered right or wrong. And these come from cultural norms and from secondary sources of jurisprudence. But anybody who believes in these things and practices these things is a Muslim. . . .

[Who decides the rules of Islamic jurisprudence?]

The thing about the Islamic situation is we don't have a church. We don't have an ordained priesthood, which makes it a little complicated. But we do have a tradition of scholarship, and rules of scholarship. It's very much like any field of knowledge.

The prophet, for his times, was a feminist.

Take any field of knowledge, like physics or biology or chemistry. Anybody can become a chemist or a biologist or a physicist. But there are rules [developed], and a kind of a growing consensus of opinion on how one should think correctly to arrive at what would be deemed a right, a correct decision.

Analogously, there is, in Islam, a tradition of theological interpretation, of [juridical] understanding and knowledge. And as long as you abide by these, the consensus of understanding on how you arrive at a decision, certain differences of opinion are considered equally valid.

What about interpretations regarding women, in particular? We find, in many parts of the world that tend to be populated by Muslims, it seems that women are getting the short end of the stick.

Well . . . the prophet, for his times, was a feminist. And there are certainly voices within the Muslim world who believe and argue very strongly for the rights of women. But gender relationships really deal with the cultural norms of a particular group and the times in which they live. If one were to say, for instance, that American women are behind Muslim women—and I pick the fact that there have been five Muslim women heads of state, and that the United States is behind the Muslim world in this regard—that would not be considered to be an accurate assessment of how women are regarded in a particular society. One has to look at the sum total . . . of the norms and the relationships and the understandings that exist in a given society in a given time. . . .

Some of what we see may be considered to be inequities. But we have to remember that when Islam spread from Arabia to what we consider the Muslim world today, it spread through countries and societies which had very ancient traditions. Egypt had an ancient tradition, Iran, another ancient country, Persia before that. The subcontinent of India: another ancient culture. Same thing with current-day Turkey, the Byzantine Empire. . . .

Through that, many cultural norms became to be considered by societies as being Islamic, but they're really cultural. So in matriarchal societies, which you will see some matriarchal societies like in West Africa or in Egypt, you'll find women very, very influential.

Women hold the purse strings; women determine a lot of what happens, because ancient Egypt had a tradition of having women kings, women queens, queens of Egypt.

Whereas in some societies, which tended to be nomadic, it was very much more male-oriented, and the patriarchal and very strong male orientation became predominant. So as you go across much of the Muslim world, you will see this diversity, which really entered into Muslim life through custom, and not through the Quran and the hadith itself.

Can you define "hadith" for an American audience?

The word "hadith" means any report of something the prophet either said or did. That's hadith with small "h." Hadith with capital "H" is the collection of all these reports.

Which have been carefully substantiated or authenticated?

There are all kinds of grades of hadith, from the most authentic to those that have been forged, and various degrees in between. Islamic hadith scholarship actually is a very fascinating study, because through the different hadith you get a slice of Islamic history. The politics of what happened at different periods of time are all manifest in the hadith.

And the Sunna, similarly.

The word "Sunna" is used to mean the normative practice of the prophet. In fact, the jurists have defined the general Sunna of the prophet to mean everything the prophet did or said. The hadith is the report of the Sunna. And of the practice of the prophet, there's a certain class of actions that are normative for Muslims to follow, Sunna which has legal value, has a precedent value. And there is Sunna which has no Sharia value. For instance, the prophet prayed a certain way. This has Sharia value, we're supposed to pray that way. The prophet went to hajj on a camel—doesn't mean that we have to ride a camel from Medina to Mecca for our hajj to be valid. We can take a car. We can take a plane, because that Sunna has no Sharia value.

Can you explain Sharia?

The word "Sharia" is the term given to define the collectivity of laws that Muslims govern themselves by. And there is a presumption that these laws recognize all of the specific laws mentioned in the Quran and in the practice of the prophet, and do not conflict with that. So any law, anything studied in the Quran or the hadith, is definitely [Sharia]. The idea is that it is divinely legislated, that the creator also has legislated certain things for us.

But in the community of Muslims, it was recognized very early on that the Quran and the hadith do not speak to all issues. And there are many issues which are not necessarily addressed in the Quran and the hadith, that the Quran is silent on. . . . There is a recognition in the [science] of Islamic jurisprudence that there are issues which have to be obtained by analogy, by consensus, and other [subsidiary] sources of jurisprudence. But as long as they don't conflict with the Quran and hadith of the prophet, it's considered to be, quote, unquote, "Sharia."

> ### You do not define Sharia law by just a couple of penalties.

The flexibility built in there, you know, the using of your own common sense, is that what allows different places to apply Sharia differently?

Well, I wouldn't phrase it quite that way. The correct phrasing would be that when people think about Islamic law, there's a presumption that all of Islamic law is Quranic, or emanates from the Quran and the hadith. The point is, and the truth of the matter is, what really defines Islamic law [is] the sum total of Islamic law as has been practiced by Muslims throughout the last 14, 15 centuries. . . . Generally, it emanates from the Quran and the hadith. The Quran and the hadith are a limiting factor and a shaping factor. But any body of laws that includes and embodies the specific commandments and prohibitions mentioned in the Quran and the hadith, that does not violate any of these things, has been considered as Sharia, as Islamic. And this allows a lot of variation of opinion, in things which the Quran and the hadith are relatively silent on as long as the principles are maintained, of justice, et cetera.

My understanding of [the Sharia] rules about punishment for matrimonial infidelity [is that] you have to have four eyewitnesses, or several eyewitnesses to the [act] in order to demand the death penalty. It's almost inconceivable to me that you could ever produce that kind of eyewitness or evidence. But we hear that these kinds of punishments are meted out fairly regularly. Is the law being followed the way it's set [out]?

You cannot judge a whole body of law by one instance of criminal law. When people think about Sharia law, they often think about the penalties for certain crimes. They don't think about the sum total of Islamic law and its jurisprudence, which means the underlying structure and philosophy and understanding of how you arrive at what we call the Islamically correct decision. You do not define Sharia law by just a couple of penalties. . . .

Islamic law has a few penalties for certain crimes. But the rules of evidence, as you mentioned in the case of adultery, require either the free confession by the individual and/or the existence of four witnesses who are of sound mind and who fit the description of qualified witnesses, which is very rare to obtain.

Much of what we see when we hear of events that apply Sharia law, what we see in Nigeria, for instance, or even in Pakistan, is a desire by much of the people to see the general principles of justice followed. . . . It is a desire by the people to see their system of laws be more equitable. It is a call for correction of the overall system of social justice, of economic justice, which the Quran calls for, and the example of the prophet calls for.

You see, Muslims have an ideal. Part of their ideal is to follow what they call the example of the prophet, the Sunna of the prophet. So at an individual level, a human being who wants to perfect himself or herself looks to the tradition of the prophet, his individual practice, and tries to emulate the prophet as much as possible.

There is also a collective subliminal ambition that Muslims have, that at a collective level, they also embody the ideals of the community that the prophet developed in Medina. So when Muslims today speak of the attempt to establish an Islamic state, what they are really saying is that they would like to have a community that lives in accordance with the ideals, the relationships, the social contract, which the prophet had developed in Medina with his companions and how they had this amongst each other. . . .

In what ways do Western values, morals, and cultural practices intrude upon, and [in what ways] are they at variance with Islamic ideals?

I think there are two aspects to this question, in the broader sense of the word. There is Western values regarding governance; Western values regarding separation of powers; Western notions regarding what the role of government is in society; Western notion in terms of democratic institutions and principles and ideas. And to a large extent, Muslims are very enamored of these systems, and would like to implement them in their own societies . . . because these principles and norms are completely in sync with the principles of the Quran and the teachings of the prophet. Muslims would like very much to implement these norms within their societies.

When you come to speak about things like behavioral norms, gender relationships, or the kind of things that people will do, this is a separate issue. And there is another aspect of the West, and that is the attitude of the West towards the non-Western countries, in terms of trying to be presumptuous in telling them how they should even live their lives in ways that they are not accustomed to—like modes of dress, for instance. In the 1930s, when the first shah of Iran forced his soldiers at bayonet point to force Iranian women to take off the chador, for instance.

People don't like to be told how to dress. This is a matter of personal individual conscience. Even we here in the West do not insist that our students in public schools wear uniforms. We give them that level of freedom. People do not like to be told how to do certain things in their personal lives.

What are the key differences between being a Muslim in America and being a Muslim in the Muslim world?

There are many aspects to that. There is the political aspect, the sociological aspect, the social and family aspect, the economic aspect. So there are many aspects to the difference between living in a Muslim country, as a native especially, and living in this country. . . .

If I were to look at maybe the broadest difference: there is a sense of freedom in the United States. So one practices one's faith in the United States as an act of deliberate choice. If you are not [doing so, it's] not so much because of social pressure. There may be a certain

---

There are many aspects to the difference between living in a Muslim country, as a native especially, and living in the U.S.

---

amount of social pressure. But at a certain point in one's life, one is relatively free to live one's life as one chooses in this country.

And that sense of freedom makes one's religiosity or the defining lines of one's religiosity much sharper. Religion is a much more personal thing here. It is also a deeper experience within the personal envelope. One is forced to attach oneself to one's religion in a personally deeper way in terms of the existential issues—it has to be anchored on a much deeper existential foundation.

Another aspect about living in the United States is that one experiences a lot of negative media attention to one's Islamicity. And that has resulted, and can result in a reaction one way or the other by many people. Many Muslims feel in this country like the Christians did in Rome when they were fed to the lions. And here the lions are the media. We hope that perhaps things will change in the United States, as they did in Rome, as well.

It seems there is a societal dimension to being a Muslim, in terms of the ways one would like one's society to be organized. Are there conflicts in that sense between how one would like society to be, and the realities of American society?

I would say that Muslims in America, especially those who come from other countries, experience both an attraction, a strong attraction, to the positive things that America offers: freedom, political freedom; economic mobility and well-being, the ability to live a materially comfortable life. These are all the things that draws people from all over the world, Muslim and non-Muslim, to this country.

However, there are certain things that people, even when they come from their own country, don't like to give up. They don't like to give up certain aspects of their cultural norms. Their practices of family relationships they try to maintain. Their cuisines they like to maintain. Those values, which they consider to be their ethics, they like to maintain.

And so Muslims who have come to this country generally believe that the democratic principles, the political principles, the economic structure of this country really resonates with the faith of Islam, and draw them to this country.

To the sense that, let's say, American social norms or values are not supportive of the families—in those issues, Muslims may hap-

---

The American Muslim community will be an interlocutor and important intermediary between the West and the Muslim world.

---

pen to have a different opinion. [On] those values which violate their sense of decency, they may have a different opinion.

In a certain sense, much of the ethical and moral issues which Muslims feel strongly about in this country is shared by what you might call the Christian majority in this country—more of the moral mooring, or the sense of decency, which is commonly shared in other faith traditions.

. . . I also believe that, as the American Muslim community matures in this country, that the American Muslim community will be an interlocutor and important intermediary between the West and the Muslim world. And more so today, because today, we have much more much easier communications between the immigrant Muslim population and their extended families in the Muslim world. . . . Unlike those who immigrated a century ago from Europe, there is maintained contacts with the Old World and the New [World]. And this phenomenon will give rise to a much different sense of what it means to be a Muslim in the world.

Tell me more about that. What is an American Muslim—if there is such a thing as "an American Muslim"?

I think it is very much a work in progress. If you look at what happened to the Muslim-American community over the last, say, 40 years, it is a mosaic; it is a cross-section of the Muslim world.

We look at the Muslim centers, or mosques, starting with the early 1970s as waves of immigration began to occur from the Muslim world. You found, as certain ethnic groups reached critical mass, that mosques sprouted with a very ethnic complexion. So we have a Turkish mosque in Brooklyn, an Albanian mosque. You will find a West African mosque, mainly from French-speaking West Africans from Senegal and Mali [in] the Bronx, for instance.

You have also always had African-American mosques. You have Arab mosques, Hindu, Pakistani mosques, Bangladesh mosques.

However, what we are seeing is that these mosques tend to be maintained in terms of their cultural complexion and their general collective psychology by the continued immigration from the Old World. The second generation, the children of these immigrants, are finding themselves with a different psychological complexion. And I see a development of an American Islamic identity, which is currently a work in progress, which will be kind of the sum total of these influences.

But amongst those who are born in this country, or came very early into this country at a very early age, they grew up with a sense of belonging to the American scene, which their parents did not have. The immigrants tend to come here with a little bit of a guest mentality. But those who are born and raised here feel they are Americans. We have to define ourselves as Americans. And just as I said earlier, when Islam spread to Egypt, and Iran, and India, it restated its theology and its jurisprudence within the cultural context of those societies. It also anticipated that Islam will restate itself within the language constructs, within the social constructs, within the political constructs of American society, as well. . . .

[What do you think will come of the American influence on Islam?]

I think the major lesson that will come out of it is the increased democratization of our societies, our Islamic societies. The increased democratization of Islamic societies, and the sense of greater equality amongst people, whether on the basis of gender, the elimination of any vestiges of a class society. . . .

Do you think we have witnessed a period of reactionary-ism against the Western influence within the Muslim world in the past 50 or 100 years?

The 20th century was a century in which the Muslim world experienced the hands of the West in the perception of the Muslim world—a dismantling of some of its important constructs. The most significant of that was the dismantling of the Ottoman caliph. Because for the first time in the collective consciousness of Muslims, there is no caliph anywhere. And it was replaced—especially in major population centers of the Muslim world, those that were important at the turn at the beginning of the 20th century: Turkey, Egypt, Iran—the traditional forms of rulership were replaced by militantly secular regimes. Not only secular regimes, but militantly secular regimes, which did not even support traditional values which were cherished by the people. In Turkey, for instance, Ataturk himself forbade the calling of the prayer in the Arabic language. They changed the script of Ottoman Turkish from Arabic script to the Roman script.

So the Muslim world felt that there was a deliberate attempt to create a split in that bond which Muslims had. . . . So what happened created a split between Arabs and Turks . . . and refigured the map and created new identities of people.

People [had] thought of themselves as part of a group. You had the family, the clan, the tribe and extended notion of a tribe, a people, a nation. So for example the Uzbekis were split geographically. So you have some Uzbekis in Uzbekistan, some in what we call Afghanistan.

The Pashtun people were split: some in Pakistan, some in Afghanistan. The Hazaris were split between Iran and Afghanistan. We tell these people, this segment of Uzbekis, Pashtuns and Hazaris, now think of yourself as a completely new identification based upon geography, which people did not have before. And this seeded conflict. . . .

We did the same thing in Iraq, and the Kurds lost out. They are split between Iraq and Turkey. So the West planted the seed for some grave problems in the Muslim world. But at the same time, they robbed the Muslim world in the minds of the Muslims, from a sense of identity that was based upon people, and also a sense of pluralism that existed within the Muslim dialectic. So within, let's say, the Ottoman caliphate, they had a principle of different peoples.

So they had the notion that the sultan had political power over these different people. But these peoples had their different cultural norms, different religions. They had their different religious leaders, as long as political homage was paid to the sultan, and they didn't act in a way which was treasonous politically. They had their own court system, dealing with matters of religious affairs and so forth.

All was part of this grouping of people. So we had a method of pluralism which worked, which was successful. And there were instances of intermarriage between the people and so forth, but people lived harmoniously. It created what Samuel Huntington calls "torn societies.". . . Samuel Huntington describes a torn society as "a society whose leadership, those who hold the reins of the power, identify with a different set of cultural norms than the people on whom they govern."

And what would be the key implications that came of this fracturing, tearing apart, in the way Islam has been lived?

I think the major thing is that Muslims have been taught to think in certain ideas that are peculiarly Western—the idea of nationalism, the idea of nation-states. And in their attempt to fulfill their natural urge to perfect themselves as Muslims individually and collectively, they therefore try to create some peculiar hybrids.

Like the notion of an Islamic state, for instance. Several generations of Muslims now have been educated in ways that their mindset and ways of thinking, if not their language even, is very much Westernized. So they think in terms of Western ideas and concepts, even if they speak their own native languages.

So the urge therefore to develop an Islamic nation-state—a concept which some people may regard as being an oxymoron, because the nation-state is not something which developed out of the Islamic tradition . . . that the Islamic philosophical tradition was based upon identification of grouping of peoples, who had governed themselves according to living in certain ways and structured in a slightly different way. . . .

There seems to be a growing conservatism, or conservative interpretation of Islam taking hold. Is that something you have seen, or agree with?

I think that in the 20th century there are certain waves that occurred. There was, at one point in time, a feeling—in fact, when you go back to the first part of the 20th century, there were some well-known voices who grew out of Islamic tradition but who were exposed to the West . . . who felt the need to restate what it means to be a Muslim in the 20th century. They found many aspects of Western society to be highly admirable, and wanted to bring it to their own countries.

In fact, in the 1920s the Wafd party was founded in Egypt to introduce democracy into Egypt. And the Wafd party had on its platform Egyptians—not only Egyptian Muslims but Egyptian Jews and Egyptian . . . Christians from the Coptic Church on the platform.

So there was an attempt to meld the best of the of the East with the best of the West. These movements . . . were interrupted by events of World War II and the rise of militant dictatorial regimes, which completely changed the sociological complexion, the political complexion of much of the Muslim world. During that period of time, I would say 1950s and 1960s, there was a time when these regimes had the upper hand. And they felt that the way to fast-forward as societies, in terms of the industrial development, was to emulate the West in all of its aspects.

Their policies didn't succeed. And this resulted in a reaction to much of these policies, because this newfangled way of doing things didn't work. Let's go back and revisit our traditions, and let's find comfort in those traditions. . . .

Could you just explain to us the key things that Islam, Christianity and Judaism have in common—what they share?

They share geography. They share Jerusalem, which is important to all. We share a common ancestor, Abraham, who was really the founder and the patriarch of all of us. And I think if we can revert back to the Abrahamic foundation, that is [where] we will find our common ground. Our languages are very similar—Arabic and Hebrew and Aramaic. . . . The ideas are very similar; and the fundamental impulse of belief in God, that God is the creator, that we are obliged to act in a way that is ethical and just and right. These are certainly among the important aspects of kinship between these three faith traditions. And I would even go further and say—apart perhaps from some differences in the notion of God—but as far as the idea of the common good, the idea of social justice—[that] is shared with all faith traditions.

Hajj: The Journey of a Lifetime[3]

By Reshma Memon Yaqub
The Seattle Times, February 20, 2000

My husband keeps a map of the world on the wall in the den of our Maryland home. Every place we travel, he marks with a thumbtack. You can barely see the paper anymore.

But this trip would be different. This wasn't for the sights or the sunshine or family or work.

This was hajj—for a Muslim, the journey of a lifetime.

Hajj is a pillar of Islam, a spiritual and physical journey to the core of my faith.

It's a five-day sojourn across Saudi Arabia to the city of Mecca and the holy sites of Mina, Arafat and Muzdalifah, places where the word of God was revealed to mankind 14 centuries ago.

It's a series of rites and rituals that follow in the footsteps of Prophet Abraham and Prophet Mohammed.

The pilgrimage is required, once in a lifetime, of every Muslim who is physically, mentally and financially able.

The reward for a properly completed hajj is monumental: the wiping clean of your slate of bad deeds accumulated over a lifetime. You emerge without sin, as on the day you were born.

Hajj is said to be one of the largest annual gatherings of humans on the planet, each year drawing up to 2 million of the world's 1.2 billion Muslims to southwest Saudi Arabia.

The odyssey begins on the eighth day of Dhul-Hijjah, the 12th month of the Islamic lunar calendar (in mid-March this year). Last year it began on March 25.

And when it began, I was there.

March 18, 1999—Though we left home today, our hajj began long before the first steps are taken. I have spent months reading, planning, saving.

There is no Fodor's guide, no *Let's Go Hajj*. But there are books, Web sites, people who have already done hajj.

Typically, Muslims go on hajj with large groups organized by specialty travel agencies, or are led by people who have been on hajj many times.

My husband, Amer, his sister Sajeela and I each pay nearly $5,000 to go with a New York travel agency recommended by friends. We see ads for hajj programs for as little as $2,000, but the cheaper pro-

---

grams require you to share rooms with same-gender strangers. And the hotels wouldn't be within walking distance of the mosques that we're already traveling across the world to be near.

Amer jokes that our package is Hajj-Lite—all the prayer, none of the pain.

Not only is hajj the most important journey of a Muslim's life, it's also the most celebrated. Within the local Muslim community, word quickly spreads of who will become a hajji each year. Well-wishers call and visit and tell me what prayers to say when I'm prostrating to God in the holiest of mosques. I'm asked to pray for people's marriages, people's children, people's jobs, for their long, healthy lives, for their entrance to Paradise.

On the flight, I reflect on the Talbiyah, the supplication that Muslims repeat en route to and throughout hajj, telling God that we are coming to Him. Hajj is considered partly a rehearsal for the Day of Judgment.

> ### *Not only is hajj the most important journey of a Muslim's life, it's also the most celebrated.*

March 19—As I step off the plane in the Saudi city of Medina, my lips parch. Buildings, mountains, desert, palm trees, people suffer in the heat. Everything here is beige. There are no lakes, beaches or resorts.

It's immediately clear that there is little for us to do here but to worship—and that's why God chose this place for this purpose. This is to be nothing but a spiritual sabbatical.

On the bus to the hotel, a guide for our American hajj group leads us in reciting the Talbiyah. The words, in Arabic, are still unfamiliar on my tongue:

Labbayk Allahumma Labbayk (Here I come, oh Lord, here I come). . . .

The next few days in this holy city, I recite my five daily prayers at the Prophet's Mosque, a majestic house of worship that contains the simple, green-domed mosque that Prophet Mohammed built. It also contains the grounds of his home, where he is buried.

Prophet Mohammed informed Muslims that the divine reward for praying in this mosque is 1,000 times more than praying in any other mosque—except the Sacred Mosque in Mecca, where the reward is 100,000 times greater. He also told Muslims that in the area between his house and his pulpit—perhaps a few hundred square feet of empty space—lies a garden of Paradise, the only earthly manifestation of Heaven.

I pray there. It's simple and it's peaceful.

And it's crowded.

March 20—Praying five times a day is, like hajj, a pillar of the faith. Each prayer takes about five or 10 minutes.

Between prayers we hide from the heat and rest at our Medina hotel.

In the evenings, we walk around the marketplace near the mosque. Many varieties of dates are sold everywhere, from street vendors and from fancy glass cases in glitzy stores.

At 2 A.M., at 3 A.M., at 4 A.M., I watch from my hotel window as worshipers float through the streets toward the Prophet's Mosque. At 5, I walk the two blocks to join them for dawn prayers.

Several hundred thousand worshipers already are there, so I pray outside on the cool marble. I am touched when the woman next to me turns her prayer rug sideways and pushes half of it in front of me. This happens every time I pray outside. I'm moved to tears a few days later when a stranger praying next to us places her prayer rug in front of us and proceeds to pray on the bare ground herself. That, my heart tells me, is the spirit of hajj and the spirit of my religion. That is the kind of person I have come here to become.

I recite the Talbiyah under my breath, and pray.

March 23—Medina and Mecca are Islamic sanctuaries, cities only Muslims can enter. There is no hunting allowed, no cutting of trees. The streets are safe.

I walk alone in the middle of the night without fear. At the Kentucky Fried Chicken outlet down the block from the mosque, the cashiers often stack money on the counter instead of putting it in the register, and no one touches it when they turn around. The stores close at every prayer time so the merchants can hurry to the mosque.

March 24—Today I will enter the state of ritual purity called Ihram—and officially declare to God my intention to perform hajj.

First I take a ritual bath at the hotel. I'm acutely aware that this same step-by-step washing will be done to my body when it's buried, when I return again to God.

I slip on a jilbab, a loose, ankle-length dress, and cover my hair with a scarf. It's what I've been wearing over T-shirts and drawstring pants since I left home, and what I'll keep wearing, like most women here, throughout this journey.

My husband Amer, like every male hajji, wraps two large towel-like pieces of white cloth around his body. That and sandals are all men can wear for the next few days.

These white cloths—great equalizers that make it impossible to distinguish between a doctor and a street sweeper—are what Muslims are dressed in for burial. Many hajjis save their Ihram cloths for that purpose.

We leave by bus for Mecca. En route, the chanting of the Talbiyah is loud. It consumes the 12-hour overnight bus ride, a 280-mile trip south that would take a third the time if there weren't 2 million people following this route.

To avoid the crowds, we travel at night throughout this journey. It saves time, but we lose all sense of day and night and sleep. Luckily, patience is a condition of our Ihram. We're not allowed to get angry: You must accept what you cannot alter.

The several dozen American Muslims on my bus are drawn from every corner and ethnicity of America's 6 million Muslims.

There's a sprightly 68-year-old jazz musician from Detroit; Pakistani-American doctors; an Albanian man who has brought his aging mother; a board member from the Neutrogena Corp.; two Iranian brothers who own a U.S. carpet store.

We are so very different. But we become intensely attached and interdependent. We share our food, we carry each other's bags, we help lift wheelchairs over steps, we track each other in the crowds, we take old people to the bathroom. We become an integral part of each other's hajj experience.

March 25—We are in Mecca. No Muslim can forget the first sight of the Kaaba—a brick cube the size of a tiny house, the object that Muslims face as they bow in prayer five times every day.

The Kaaba—first built by Prophet Abraham and surrounded by the open-air Sacred Mosque—stands empty. It is draped with a black cloth, which is covered with Koranic verses embroidered in gold and silver thread.

The Kaaba is not an object of worship; it simply signifies a direction, imposed by God to maintain unity and uniformity among worshipers.

Still, it's nearly other-worldly to be in the first 10 rows of worshippers facing the nucleus of my faith, knowing there are 1.2 billion Muslims worldwide who are praying, in concentric circles, behind me.

Every Muslim family, no matter where they live, knows what direction the Kaaba is from their house. In Saudi Arabia, the hotels have direction markers on the ceiling. Even our Saudi Arabian Airlines flight had a curtained-off prayer room with a digital direction marker.

When I first see the Kaaba, it doesn't seem real. It looks as if somebody has taken the picture of the Kaaba on my parents' mantel and flipped an "on" switch, turning it into a living diorama.

I slip into the slow-moving crowd to walk around the Kaaba seven times—a ritual called Tawaf. In this mass of bodies, Tawaf takes two hours. If the space were empty, which it never is, it would take 15 minutes.

Because it's so crowded, we stop halfway through and walk up the stairs to the second level of the open-air mosque and continue our Tawaf there. The path around is longer, but it's much less crowded.

Later I walk from the huge courtyard that surrounds the Kaaba back into the covered area of the mosque to drink holy water from the Zamzam well. It's a well that has miraculously flowed ceaselessly in this desert land since the time of Prophet Abraham. It sprung up to provide water to his wife, Hagar, as she ran back and forth between two hills in desperate search of water for her baby.

The Day of Arafat is the core of hajj.

Zamzam is bottled and given away free throughout Saudi Arabia. Trucks full of it slowly roll through the streets with cups attached to the back—people walk behind the trucks, filling the cups and drinking. As a foreigner here, I stick to bottled water, except for Zamzam. This water isn't just safe, it's history. It's healing.

March 26—The bus has brought us to the Arafat area 12 miles southeast of Mecca. We are here for the Day of Arafat, the most important day of hajj.

The plain is empty year-round, save for this one day, when believers descend and congregate in tents. There's also a huge mosque here, Masjid Namira, which stands empty except for today.

Nearby is the Mount of Rahmah, a rocky hill where Prophet Mohammed stood and delivered his last sermon, during his hajj.

Because our group leaders are afraid we will get lost in the crowd, we don't go to the mosque to hear the afternoon sermon. Instead, scholars in our midst deliver a sermon to our group, and we stay in our carpeted and air-conditioned tents.

I stand and bow in prayer from noon until sunset, counting my blessings, listing my sins, praying for forgiveness, reciting the Talbiyah. I pray for God to accept my hajj, and for my life to change as a result of it.

This is the time and the place where, God willing, the sins I have accumulated in 27 years will be forgiven. This is the time and place where God says to his angels, "Why have they come?" and the angels reply, "They have come to establish the oneness of God." To which God commands, "Let them go, for I have forgiven them all."

The Day of Arafat is the core of hajj. Any other missed step can be made up for, but if you miss being at Arafat on this day, you have missed hajj.

March 26—This night is spent in the valley of Muzdalifah, five miles north of Arafat. The pedestrian traffic from Arafat to Muzdalifah is horrific.

I peer out the window of my air-conditioned bus. People who don't have $5,000 to pay for a tour like mine, people who have saved their whole lives for this trip, are crammed into cars, vans and buses. And on top of cars, vans and buses. Rooftop luggage racks have somehow become seats. Those who can't afford even that luxury are walking.

As my bus lurches forward, I count 30 human beings inside and atop a nearby minivan that would normally seat nine. I watch their lips move as they recite the Talbiyah. Somehow, through the closed window, through the congested traffic, I can hear their recitation.

It's some time before I realize that the voice I'm hearing is my own.

March 27—Today is Eid, commemorating the Day of Arafat. At home, I usually spend this day feasting with family, visiting friends, exchanging gifts. Today, I spend the early morning hours in a bus to Mina, where I will stay in a tent for three nights.

Mina, three miles east of Mecca, is a temporary city of tents. There are miles and miles of them. Most tents look big enough to fit a family, but I wonder how many people are actually squeezed in. The streets are filled with people who don't have tents and who just lay down a blanket or a newspaper on the dirt to mark their territory; maybe they sling a sheet over a branch to fashion a roof.

Our group's air-conditioned tents seem barely large enough to hold our few dozen people. There's a dirt floor covered by rugs. Men and women are in separate tents. In our women's tent, we peel back a foot of the Velcroed seam that connects us to our spouses' tent, a makeshift communication portal.

March 28–29—We have come to Mina to perform a ritual stoning of the Jamarats. The Jamarats—three round, walled basins, chest-high, a few dozen feet in diameter and about 500 feet apart—mark the spots where Satan appeared to Prophet Abraham when he was on his way to Mecca after completing his hajj. The Prophet stoned Satan at each of the three points before Satan gave up.

On this day, thousands of years later, I re-enact Prophet Abraham's trials, throwing seven pea-size pebbles into the largest basin, shouting "Allahu akbar!"—"God is great!"—with each toss.

The crowds at the Jamarats can be overwhelming. The year before, 150 people died in a stampede here.

We are lucky because a 23-year-old Islamic scholar who's with us, and who is on his sixth hajj, knows exactly what times we should go to be safest from the crowds and the flying pebbles. He knows what the surging crowds don't know—that the backs of the basins are empty. We walk right up to the edge of the basins and drop our stones in.

Ihram, the state of ritual purity, ends after the first of the three days of stoning, and to signify it, hajjis cut a bit of their hair. It's preferred for men to shave their heads. We clip a lock from each other's hair with little manicure scissors.

On the bus ride back to Mecca, I see crowds of men on the sidewalks, having their heads shaved with straight razors in makeshift barber shops. Afterward, these brothers, these strangers, hug and congratulate and laugh as they pat one another's bald heads.

On the afternoon of the third day that we prepare to leave Mecca to spend the night in Mina, I break down crying, sick from a vicious flu and exhausted from the physical exertion, from not sleeping through a night from walking for hours with my belongings in hand.

But to my surprise, my internal reserves don't dry up. I keep myself level with the thought that the physical hardships endured by early Muslims, as well as by so many people of all faiths today, are something that I should be compelled, at least once in my life, to better understand. Even on this Hajj-Lite, I am learning how much I can live without.

Later, in our two-room hotel suite, I turn on CNN and watch Albanian Muslim refugees fleeing Kosovo. After a 1 1/2-hour walk with all their belongings, there is no bus waiting to take them to a hotel. There is nothing awaiting them, except maybe another 1 1/2-hour walk. For the first time, I understand a little bit.

March 30—My last act of hajj is to perform a Farewell Tawaf around the Kaaba. The crowd is so thick that it takes 20 minutes just to walk the five-minute path from my hotel to the Sacred Mosque.

The tide of people inside is so strong, and I am so jostled that by the end, I feel as though I've survived a car accident.

This evening, difficulty awaits me at Jeddah airport. My ticket says Dulles airport near Washington, D.C., but the computer says JFK in New York. I recite the Talbiyah and remind myself that I've come here for God, and he'll send me home when it's time. My patience has been tested so much in the past two weeks that I am now used to, even expect, this kind of random test.

Peace replaces panic. Take me anywhere in America, I tell them. I'll find my way.

Twenty-four hours later, I am home.

Wahhabi Roots in Saudi Desert[4]

BY SCOTT PETERSON
THE CHRISTIAN SCIENCE MONITOR, AUGUST 11, 1999

The Wahhabi sect of Islam is most firmly established in Saudi Arabia, where it determines law and the strict rules of daily life.

Wahhabism first sprang from the central Arabian desert in the mid-18th century, when its zealous and puritanical founder, Muhammad bin Abdi al-Wahhab, made a political pact with ancestors of the ruling Saud family.

In exchange for the support of Wahhabi followers in expansionist wars, Muhammad Saud promised to promote Wahhabism in his territory. Most Saudi Arabians today are Wahhabi Muslims.

Based on a rigorous—and in the early days, uncompromising—interpretation of Islam, the Wahhabi creed accepted no other teaching but that of the 7th-century Prophet Muhammad and the following generation of disciples.

Al-Wahhab branded all those who disagreed with him heretics and apostates, thereby justifying the use of force in imposing his doctrine. This way he could declare a jihad, or "holy war," on fellow Muslims.

Followers were once so strict that, after the capture of Mecca, the playing of a trumpet caused a riot among Wahhabis, who forbade music. Minarets, a post-Prophet innovation, were also once forbidden. Police could raid a home and beat its owner if they caught a whiff of tobacco. In line with the Prophet's direction not to "make of my grave a place of pilgrimage," Wahhabi zealots nearly destroyed the Prophet's tomb in 1926.

Wahhabism is noted for compelling strict observance of the rules of Islam, such as prayers five times a day—punishment for such a violation was once flogging—and public enforcement of morals that is rare in the Muslim world today.

Women are not allowed to drive in Saudi Arabia and must cover themselves completely in public. Tough Islamic law—including beheadings for drug dealers and murderers—are common. Many Islamic countries, including Iran, look down on Wahhabi rules as backward and un-Islamic. But hard-line rules have relaxed some over time. Music, minarets, and smoking tobacco from water pipes today are common across Saudi Arabia.

---

4. This article first appeared in *The Christian Science Monitor* on August 11, 1999, and is reproduced with permission. Copyright © 1999 The Christian Science Monitor (*www.csmonitor.com*). All rights reserved.

They're Muslims, But Sufis Still Go Own Way[5]

By Richard Vara
The Houston Chronicle, October 19, 2002

It was the peace and contentment on the faces of friends and relatives that enticed Nahid Ghanimi to check out Sufism after she arrived in Houston from her native Iran more than a decade ago.

"They had gained a lot of peace and self confidence," said Ghanimi, now a Houston Community College teacher. "They had found that harmony that everyone looks for."

She began attending Saturday evening Sufi classes and soon experienced the love and peace she had long sought. "Sometimes I am so full of joy, I can fly," Ghanimi said excitedly. "I feel quiet and peaceful and relaxed and enjoy my peace."

Sufism is described as the mystical dimension of Islam, emphasizing spiritual union with God (Allah) or the Divine Beloved through prayer, music, poetry and a singing, swaying meditation known as *zikr* (pronounced *zek*). Sufis believe that the path to divine union or enlightenment begins with an inward journey to discover the divine presence that exists within every individual.

"Sufism is a spiritual discipline that assists one in ascending to a higher spiritual level so you can come to know God who is seen as the Divine Beloved," said Lynn Wilcox, a Sufi meditation teacher and professor at California State University in Sacramento, Calif. Wilcox conducts meditation seminars in Houston and participated at a recent Sufi presentation at Rice University.

But Sufis' goal of enlightenment or divine union is not accepted by most of the other Muslim theologies practiced around the world, according to Qamar-ul Huda, an assistant professor of Islamic and comparative theology at Boston College.

The basic principles of Sufism have been known and practiced for centuries through such enlightened prophets and saints as Adam, Noah, Buddha, Moses, Jesus Christ and Muhammad, Wilcox said. It blossomed under Muhammad's Islamic teachings and that of his successors. Sufis believe there has been an unbroken succession of 42 Sufi masters or teachers who have attained divine union since the time of Muhammad.

"They have been to the mountaintop and they know the way," Wilcox said.

Sufism restored Ghanimi's Muslim faith.

"I was tired of the fanatic ways of Islam," said Ghanimi, who grew up Muslim and moved here in 1989.

"I was really reluctant to go to anything that had the name of Islam on it because of what I had seen in my country," she said. The Islam she saw in Iran was mixed with political activism, local superstition and cultural practices. Women were not considered equal to men and were regulated on their dress and behavior.

> *Sufis have to purify themselves spiritually to attain the divine union.*

She was inspired by Sufism's emphasis on love and its practical application on a daily basis. "The basis of Sufism is to do whatever you do with love and passion," Ghanimi said.

Wilcox said Sufis have to purify themselves spiritually to attain the divine union.

"You have to let go of envy, jealousy, greed and all other negative things," Wilcox said.

Sufis can invoke the spiritual through *zikr*, a meditation that involves music and swaying, Wilcox said. Participants sit crosslegged and the upper body sways as they sing rhythmic chants of divine love poems set to Persian-style music.

The *zikr* is reminiscent of "whirling dervishes," a religious practice introduced in the 13th century by Sufis. Dancers evoke a divine presence or trance by whirling to music and chanting.

But the divine presence can also be evoked by instrumental solos and by poetry. The most famous of Sufi poets, Wilcox said, is Rumi, who found the divine presence in everyday experiences such as silence, death, grief and music.

"Rumi is a major intellectual and social figure especially in Turkish Islam," said David Cook, an assistant professor in Rice's department of religious studies. Although Rumi did not originate spiritual poetry, he was a popularizer of the form.

Cook said Sufism was born in the 9th century as a reaction to the rationalism and legalism of early Islam. It is similar to the Chabad Lubavitch movement in Judaism and Pentecostalism in Christianity in emphasizing a personal experience of the divine and underscoring personal joyful and positive feelings expressed in nontraditional ways such as dancing and music.

There are about 50 major orders (schools or denominations) of Sufism and numerous sub-groups within the orders, Cook said. The Houston center, Maktab Tarighat Oveyssi Shamghsoudi School at 5645 Hillcroft, is a Persian order.

There are no estimates of the number of Sufis worldwide or in the United States because membership counts are foreign to Islam. But the impact of Sufism has been tremendous over the centuries.

"Every Muslim leader between 1000 and 1900 was Sufi," Cook said. "I would personally assume that between 70 and 80 percent of Muslims get their sense of spirituality from (Sufism)."

Sufism is characterized by a very intense, internal spirituality, said Huda, the Boston College professor. Sufis want to go beyond the traditional five daily prayers and fasting at Ramadan.

"They are involved with intense meditation, intense studying of the self, reflecting on the self and are guided by a teacher or master," Huda said.

More conservative elements within Islam, such as the Wahabis, reject Sufism as incompatible with Islam and even refuse to allow Sufis to enter their mosques. But Sufism is still present in many Islamic countries such as Iran and Pakistan, complete with mosques and centers, Huda said.

"Sufis have been the main missionary branch of Islam," Cook said. "Practically all converts to Islam have converted through Sufism."

Wilcox, who teaches counselor education, was introduced to Sufism 18 years ago by a psychologist who kept mentioning Sufism. She was later introduced to Sufi master Saladheddin Ali Nader Shah Angha.

"There was an immediate spiritual connection when I met the Sufi master," said Wilcox, who is now Muslim. "I knew I was in the presence of something that was totally unfamiliar and very powerful and very positive."

Wilcox described herself as a seeker who grew up Methodist, tried Christian Science and was Unitarian briefly before moving to the Presbyterian Church.

"I was looking for God but couldn't find him," she said. "When I came here, I found him."

II. Islamic Law

Editor's Introduction

The complexities of Islamic law have often been reduced to headlines about executions in such places as Saudi Arabia, Afghanistan, and Nigeria. Known as shariah, Islamic law is often discredited in the West as an arcane and repressive code. Shariah runs the gamut from regulating how one dresses to setting the punishment one faces for participating in criminal activity. However, the actual language in the Qur'an and in hadith regarding law often leaves a large amount of room for interpretation and has resulted in the development of four schools of thought about shariah. Today it is often the harshest interpretation that has the widest influence, with extreme sentences such as death by stoning being carried out in several countries with little explicit justification and no point of reference in the Qur'an. Many citizens seeking justice in Islamic countries welcome Islamic courts, where they can receive judgements within the day, instead of having to endure a legal system that could take months to grant a hearing.

In Jerry Useem's article "Banking on Allah," the author discusses a lesser-known but very important aspect of Islamic law in the modern world that dictates that no Muslim should make money on money–i.e., earn or pay interest. Useem relates how the Islamic financial system works, showing that it is not based on fixed savings accounts but on investments on various ventures that are far more unpredictable. The prohibition to deal with interest was very useful in Muhammad's day, when loan sharking, which could lead to enslavement for those who defaulted, was a major problem. Useem explains how even today banks avoid dealing with interest when they lend money and screen stocks so as not to trade with companies whose conduct might violate Islamic law through, for instance, the selling of alcohol.

The debate raging among many Western Muslims over meaning in Islam is discussed in Caryle Murphy's article "In the Throes of a Quiet Revolution," which focuses on Muslims in the West who, with more freedom of thought and speech, have begun to question many aspects of their religion, especially interpretations of shariah. Though not necessarily a shift towards drastically liberalized Islamic thinking, this critical tendency reveals a new willingness to examine whether or not the authoritative statements of Muslim clerics can withstand the scrutiny of scholars and debate. This process of attempting to reach a true understanding is known in Islam as *itjihad*, and it is being driven by the Internet, where new ideas can be exchanged within seconds. Murphy points out that this search for new understanding in Islam has taken root most avidly among women, many of whom long for greater openness in modern Islamic thought.

Given the vast amount of interpretation needed for the majority of decrees in the Qur'an and in hadith, as well as the predominance of extreme Islamic jurisprudence, one would think that a liberal Islamic scholar would be welcome, especially among Muslims in the West. In "Moral Hazard: The Life of a Liberal Muslim," Franklin Foer explains why this is not the case, as he examines the experience of Khaled Abou El Fadl, a progressive Muslim scholar living in the United States whose liberal yet scholarly interpretations of Qur'an and hadith have drawn fire from fellow Muslims. According to Foer, Fadl's difficult and often dangerous decisions to comment on Islamic law demonstrate the enormous influence of Saudi Arabia's wealthy Wahhabi sect throughout the Muslim world.

In Francis Fukuyama and Nadav Samin's article "Can Any Good Come of Radical Islam?" the authors probe the development of Islamism, which combines strict interpretations of shariah and a condemnation of Western culture with political goals. The authors point out that this radical strain of Islam is not a return to earlier practices but a wholly modern approach to the religion. Fukuyama and Samin compare Islamism with the European fascist movement of the 1930s, with its use of religious symbols as a means to incite people to adhere to common political goals. They note that in the increasingly poor Arab world, where political freedoms are lacking, the strict code of Islamism provides a form of self-identity for many. The authors also ask whether radical Islam could be the transitional stage through which Muslim societies could transform themselves.

Banking on Allah[1]

By Jerry Useem
Fortune, June 10, 2002

There's nothing in Osman Abdullah's bearing to suggest an Islamic fundamentalist. He's a businessman, sober in dress and political outlook. Ask him about America, and he'll talk fondly of his time at the University of Wisconsin, where he earned his MBA. But when it comes to his banking habits—and the Koran's ban on giving or receiving interest—Abdullah turns deadly serious. "Allah gave us very clear instructions: Don't make money on money," he says. The words from Chapter 2, Verse 278 of the Koran are, in fact, quite specific: "O you who believe! Have fear of Allah and give up what remains of what is due to you of usury. . . . If you do not, then take notice of war from Allah and His Messenger." "If I break that," says Abdullah, "I'm dead sure that I'm going to get very bad results in the hereafter. I believe it as I believe in talking to you now."

We are talking, just now, outside Shamil Bank in the tiny Persian Gulf state of Bahrain. It's the bank where Abdullah keeps his money, and, except for the tellers' untrimmed beards and the section for ladies' banking, it looks much like any other: customers standing in line, an ATM machine, a hum of efficiency.

But Shamil is not like any other bank. For starters, Abdullah's savings account isn't really a savings account at all, but something called a *mudarabah* account: Instead of earning fixed interest, his savings are invested directly in a range of ventures, such as construction projects and real estate. "In Islam, money has to work," Abdullah explains. "If it works, we have to share the profits. If it doesn't, you don't owe me anything else." That means his nest egg could shrink if enough of those ventures fail. But, he says, "I'm willing to take the risks."

So, it turns out, are an increasing number of Muslims. At a time when the words "Islam" and "finance" are more likely to conjure the association "terrorist money laundering," the Muslim world has quietly embarked on a very different sort of jihad: building a financial system where interest—a phenomenon as old as money itself—does not exist.

Spread across the Middle East and beyond are more than 200 Islamic financial institutions: banks, mutual funds, mortgage companies, insurance companies—in short, an entire parallel economy in which Allah, not Alan Greenspan, has the final say. Industry growth has averaged 10% to 15% a year. Sniffing opportunity, conventional banks like Citibank and HSBC have opened Islamic "windows" in the Gulf. And while the industry's market share is still modest—about 10% in Bahrain—its very existence challenges the modern assumption that global capitalism flattens all before it.

Which leaves just one question: How on earth can it work?

This spring, Shamil Bank helped Abdullah buy a car through a transaction known as *murabaha*, which is more distinct from *mudarabah* in function than in spelling. In a deal you'll never see from GMAC, Abdullah identified the Toyota Corolla he wanted, then asked the bank to buy it from the dealer for roughly 3,600 dinar (about $9,500). At the same time he agreed to buy the car from Shamil for 4,000 dinar, to be paid in monthly installments over three years. The two sales were executed almost simultaneously, but because Shamil Bank took possession of the car for a brief period of time, everything was kosher. Or rather, *hilal*.

The result looked a lot like interest, and some argue that *murabaha* is simply a thinly veiled version of it; the markup Shamil charges is very close to the prevailing interest rate. But bank officials argue that God is in the details. For example, any late fees Shamil collects must be donated to charity, and the bank cannot penalize a borrower who is genuinely broke.

Mortgages, meanwhile, are out of the question for Abdullah. That's why a house he's building in his native Sudan sits unfinished near the Nile River. "I started it four years ago," he says. "Sometimes I stop the construction until I collect enough money."

Given the inconveniences, you might ask: What's the point? Can earning a little interest really be such a big deal? Bahrain's most eminent Islamic scholar provided some answers.

I found Shaykh Nizam Yaquby at the back of his family's store in Bahrain's humming market—a diminutive, robed figure partly obscured by the piles of papers and books on his desk. They include both the *hadiths*, or sayings of the Prophet, and *Inside Secrets to Venture Capital*, which more or less capture Yaquby's eclectic background. He is trained in both economics (at McGill University in Canada) and in Islamic sharia law (in Saudi Arabia, India, and Morocco). During its heyday many centuries ago, sharia was the world's most vibrant body of commercial law, its contracts recognized from the Arabian peninsula to the Iberian peninsula. Then it fell into a long decline, which Yaquby and other Islamic scholars are doing their best to reverse.

As a member of Shamil Bank's five-member sharia board, Yaquby issues *fatwas*, or opinions, on which transactions are Islamically acceptable and which are forbidden. On the day of my visit he was dispensing advice to a steady stream of callers. Was it sinful, a 15-year-old boy wanted to know, to continue living in his father's house while his father was receiving interest?

"There is a *hadith*: 'The body that is nourished from nonpure sources is bound to go to hellfire,'" Yaquby declared with a somewhat incongruous grin. But his advice to the boy was milder. "My answer to him was that he should advise his father politely and gently. However, the boy was not committing any sin, because his father is responsible in the sight of Allah."

Just how serious a sin is paying or receiving interest? Yaquby noted that Christianity and Judaism got over their hangups about it sometime during the Middle Ages. (The Old Testament offers several stern warnings about interest.) But Islam never really budged. Back in the days of Mohammed, the reasons for deploring interest were pretty self-evident. Loan-sharking was rampant, and failure to repay a loan could mean slavery. By outlawing interest, Islam advocated an economy based on risk-sharing, fair dealing, and equity—in both the financial and social-justice senses of the word.

Islamic scholars believe this system is superior on several counts.

> ## *By outlawing interest, Islam advocated an economy based on risk-sharing, fair dealing, and equity.*

It leads to more prudent lending, they say, by encouraging financiers to invest directly in an entrepreneur's ventures. ("A financial system without interest is more interested," says Shaykh Yusuf DeLorenzo, a Virginia-based Islamic scholar.) If adopted fully, say the scholars, interest-free finance would also prevent future Enrons and Argentinas. "One reason for prohibiting interest is to keep everybody spending according to his limit," says Yaquby. "This consumerism society was only created because of the banking system, because it encourages 'buy today, pay tomorrow.' You also have poor economies in debt to rich ones. This is because of borrowing and lending with interest. So this is creating big economic chaos in the world."

Fourteen centuries after these principles were laid down, their application can be a tricky matter. Needless to say, ancient texts are mute on such matters as derivatives and stock options, meaning scholars like Yaquby must extrapolate. Currency hedging, for instance, is prohibited on the basis of *gharar*, a principle that says you shouldn't profit from another's uncertainty. Futures contracts? Not allowed, since Mohammed said not to buy "fish in the sea" or dates that are still on the tree. Day trading? Too much like gambling. Credit cards? Not cool, though debit cards are.

Bonds? Well, that's where the disagreements start. Malaysian scholars have approved the issuance of specially designed "Islamic bonds." But Middle Eastern scholars, who take a harder line than their Far Eastern counterparts, have roundly criticized them. "Playing semantics with God is very dangerous," warns Yaquby. "Calling fornication 'making love' doesn't make it any different."

Everybody can agree on one matter, though: It's okay to buy and sell stocks, since stocks represent real assets. And now they can be traded safely using the Dow Jones Islamic index.

Launched in 1999 with the help of Yaquby, the index offers a pre-screened universe of stocks for the devout stock picker. One screen removes companies that make more than 5% of their revenues from sinful businesses. That expels such notables as Vivendi (alcohol), Citigroup (interest), Marriott (pork served in hotel restaurants), and FORTUNE's parent company, AOL Time Warner (unwholesome music and entertainment). A second screen eliminates companies with too much debt, the cutoff being a debt-to-market-capitalization ratio of 33%. A third screen applies the same standard to a company's cash and interest-earing securities, while a fourth makes

---

Nostalgia for the lost golden era of Muslim power has been a strong impetus for Islamic banking.

---

sure that accounts receivable don't exceed 45% of assets. "Islamic investing is low-debt, nonfinancial, social-ethical investing," explains Rushdi Siddiqui, who manages the index at Dow Jones.

Of the 5,200 stocks in the Dow Jones global index, 1,400 make the cut—yet even those may not be entirely pure. If a company makes, say, 2% of its money from selling pork rinds, an investor must give away 2% of his dividends to charity, a process known as "portfolio purification." Then, too, he should urge management to exit the pork-rind business.

So what does a typical Islamic portfolio look like? Actually, a lot like the Nasdaq 100, since technology companies tend to carry acceptable levels of debt. That made for a rough 2001, as favorites like Microsoft and Intel sputtered. But demand for Islamic mutual funds is booming. There are now more than 100 funds worldwide, including three based in the U.S., while a clutch of Internet companies position themselves as the Muslim E*Trade (iHilal.com), the Muslim Morningstar (Failaka.com), and the Muslim Yahoo Finance (IslamiQ). The latter offers members a feature called "Ask the Scholars."

All of which raises another question: How high a price must investors pay for following the rules? "Some people say you have to apply the COBM—the Cost of Being Muslim," says Yaquby. But he and others insist that no such tradeoff exists. Obey God's rules, in other words, and your portfolio will prosper.

It is an argument that holds great appeal in the Arab world, where moral decay is frequently blamed for the region's millennium-long material decline. Nostalgia for the lost golden era of Muslim power has been a strong impetus for Islamic banking. "The Islamic economy covered half the world," says Jamil Jaroudi, Shamil Bank's head of investment banking. "How do you think Islam reached Indonesia and Malaysia? It was through traders, not jihad." Indeed, Mohammed himself was a trader who early in his life led a caravan from Mecca to Syria.

The golden era gave way to a period of colonial domination in which Western-style banking was imposed on much of the Islamic world—a source of resentment to this day. (Individual Muslims handled this dilemma differently. Some opened interest-bearing accounts under the principle of darura, or overriding necessity. Others opened accounts but refused the interest. Still others opted for their mattresses.) It was mostly that resentment that gave rise, in the 1940s, to the quasi-academic field known as Islamic economics.

As an attempt to build a "third way" independent of capitalism and communism, Islamic economics was never long on scientific rigor; one contemporary academic calls it "bad moral philosophy with a little Keynes thrown in." But it produced a voluminous critique of Western capitalism and its attendant evils, notably speculation, consumerism, volatility, inequality, "unnecessary" products, large corporations, and of course usury. Whereas conventional economics was built on Adam Smith's notion of harnessing human nature ("Every man working for his own selfish interest will be led by an invisible hand to promote the public good"), Islamic economics proposed to reform human nature. "The intended effect," the University of Southern California economist Timur Kuran has written, "is to transform selfish and acquisitive *Homo economicus* into a paragon of virtue, *Homo Islamicus*."

For decades this vision remained just that—a vision. It was the oil boom of the 1970s that turned it into a movement. In 1973, flush with petrodollars and keen to reassert their Islamic identity, Muslim nations formed the Islamic Development Bank, a sort of interest-free version of the World Bank. Two years later the first Islamic retail bank began accepting deposits in Dubai.

Not everyone welcomed the phenomenon. While Malaysia promoted Islamic banks as a constructive outlet for religious fervor, Saudi Arabia would not allow them, lest they imply that the kingdom's existing banks were un-Islamic. (The Saudi royal family, not incidentally, subsists largely on income from conventional investments.) The government finally allowed one to open in 1987, though the word "Islam" was nowhere in its name. At the radical end of the spectrum, Iran, Pakistan, and Sudan officially Islamicized their entire banking systems—in theory anyway. In practice, their fundamentalist clerics had little interest in economics—the

Ayatollah Khomeini famously scoffed that the Islamic revolution was not about "the price of watermelons"—and settled for changes that were mostly cosmetic.

Elsewhere, scandal threatened to capsize the whole enterprise. The 1989 collapse of several nominally Islamic investment houses in Egypt led to disclosures about some very un-Islamic practices, such as fraud. And last year's failure of a Turkish Islamic bank, Ihlas Finans, panicked depositors at Turkey's other Muslim banks.

But in banking centers like Kuwait, Dubai, and especially Bahrain, which is known for its strict regulatory oversight, Islamic banking is serious business. A respected group known by the acronym AAOIFI (Accounting and Auditing Organization for Islamic Financial Institutions) has codified sharia rulings into a set of industry standards. The early zealots have given way to more pragmatic professionals. Even the sharia scholars—once recruited from the local mosque and barely fluent in English, much less financial statements—now come toting advanced degrees in economics. "In the last five years," says Shamil Bank's Jaroudi, "the industry has accomplished more than it did in its first 20."

Now it is making inroads in the U.S., home to seven million Muslim-Americans. Here the most pressing issue is home ownership. Since buying a house usually requires a mortgage, many Muslims end up renting their whole lives, thus missing out on a crucial component of the American dream. Azmat Siddiqi was one of them. A manager at Applied Materials who immigrated from Pakistan 22 years ago, he hoped to circumvent the problem by making an all-cash purchase. After years of saving, he, his wife, and their two daughters finally had enough for their dream property: a $1.3 million plot of land facing the mountains in Saratoga, Calif. But then Siddiqi's stock holdings plummeted, leaving him $275,000 short. "I thought, 'By golly, should we let go of it?'" he says. "I looked at the Koran for guidance."

He also looked on the Web, where he discovered a Pasadena-based company called Lariba, which offers a lease-to-own arrangement for Muslim homebuyers. Lariba bought the property in partnership with Siddiqi, who agreed to pay rent to Lariba while buying out its $275,000 ownership share over ten years. Unlike interest, the rental price could fluctuate as market conditions changed. "There was a very high premium," says Siddiqi, 45. "But to me this was like a godsend opportunity to achieve my real estate objective and not incur the negatives of interest."

Lariba is still tiny in relative terms; it closes 15 to 30 mortgages a month. But it recently struck a deal with Freddie Mac that could vastly increase its volume. "We are like ants among the giants," says Lariba's founder, Dr. Yahia Abdul-Rahman. "*Insha'allah*, we will catch up." Meanwhile, HSBC has begun offering Islamic mortgages in the New York City area.

Despite growing acceptance of Islamic banking, supporters concede that it has a long way to go. The basic problem, they say, is that *Homo Islamicus* keeps acting a lot like *Homo economicus*. Take the idea of profit-and-loss sharing. For the concept to work, a bank must know how much profit, or loss, there is to share. Yet in countries with widespread use of double bookkeeping—one for the tax collector, one for the safe—business owners can easily understate profits or overstate losses. "If someone is using [an Islamic bank], it doesn't mean that he is guaranteed to be moral," says Saiful Azhar Rosly, an economics professor at the International Islamic University in Malaysia. "Good Muslims are still tempted by the devil."

Another problem is that profit-and-loss sharing tends to attract entrepreneurs with dimmer prospects, who are looking to share losses in the event of failure. Entrepreneurs with the best prospects are more likely to seek out fixed-interest financing to maximize the returns on their presumed success. The "adverse

---

> ### *Despite growing acceptance of Islamic banking, supporters concede that it has a long way to go.*

---

selection" problem saddles Islamic banks with bad risks.

Perhaps not surprisingly, then, profit-and-loss sharing deals constitute only 15% of Shamil Bank's transactions, while the *murabaha* double-sale, considered the most gimmicky of techniques, accounts for more than 30%. "We are very careful because [profit-and-loss sharing deals] are very risky," acknowledges Shamil's CEO, Dr. Said Al-Martan. "You have to be involved in the company, which is not easy in this part of the world. It's much easier to do leasing or *murabaha*."

Such admissions have left the industry open to charges that it has opted for pragmatism over purity—something Islamic hard-liners have pounced on. "And so the core Islamic concepts sit neutered, no longer a different paradigm but instead just another member of the product range," writes one firebrand on the Website islamic-finance.com. "What a humiliation this is for a great body of law." Another writer is even more strident: "The 'Islamic Bank' is a Trojan horse which has been infiltrated into *Dar al-Islam*. . . . [It] is a totally crypto-usurious institution and like all other usurious institutions must be rejected and fought."

When I read some of these passages to Yaquby, he smiled patiently. "These are very sincere people, but they are not realistic people," he said. "Of course we would like Islamic banking to have more activities with benefit to society, and also to have more courage in sharing risk. But if you're saying that until we reach this ideal state, we should do nothing, this is where we object. Because until then, me and you have to do banking. We have to purchase our homes. We have to invest our wealth."

These days, Islamic banking faces another challenge: the lingering suspicion that it is connected to terrorism. So far, there is little evidence that its activities are any more suspect than those of conventional Arab banks. (The U.S. government's list of terrorist organizations includes one small Islamic bank, Al-Aqsa Al-Islami in the West Bank.) Islamic finance has always had more to do with conservative, devout Islam than radical, political Islam. Nonetheless, September 11 has put the industry on the defensive, with some depositors withdrawing money for fear it would get caught in an anti-terrorism dragnet. "A lot of investors were frightened, to be honest," says Atif Abdulmalik, CEO of First Islamic Investment Bank in Bahrain. "'Collateral damage,' I call it."

Even if those fears prove unfounded, there's the question of how Islamic finance fits into the broader issues raised by September 11. Could it reduce the Muslim world's isolation by serving as an intermediary between pure belief and pure capitalism? Or will its litany of rules merely build the walls higher? Should it be seen as an innovative force? Or a reactionary one?

Among the optimists is Frank Vogel, a Harvard Law School professor who helps organize the university's annual conference on Islamic finance and has co-written a book on the topic. "It's very much in our interest that it succeed," he told me, "yet I'm afraid that we're going to be against it, that we're going to make all these snotty remarks. Time is running out for healthy, happy experiments like this. The radicalization, the desire to make yourself as ugly to the West as you can—that rage isn't only at us, it's at the secular forces in their own societies. We need Islamicization, because they're not going to stop being Muslims overnight."

Oddly, Vogel's co-author, Harvard Business School finance professor Samuel Hayes III, gave me a different slant. In his view, literalist interpretations of the Koran threaten to choke off Muslim participation in the global economy. "Prophet Mohammed's teachings take very practical account of commerce in the seventh century," says Hayes. "It's not up to me to say, but if he were living today, I think he would find some accommodation. [Otherwise], there's no way a business can operate competitively."

In the end, even Islamic scholars concede that Hayes might have a point. "Once you face reality," Yaquby said shortly before I left his store, "it's not possible to isolate yourself from the whole economic system of the world."

In the Throes of a Quiet Revolution[2]

By Caryle Murphy
The Washington Post, October 12, 2002

As the 21st century gets underway, more Muslims than ever before are reexamining their faith in light of the political, economic and intellectual challenges of contemporary life.

This global undertaking is a far more important enterprise for Islam's future than the headline-grabbing events of Political Islam. For it holds out the promise of a new Islamic theology as it plumbs the toughest questions: How should the Koran be read? What is the proper relationship of religion and the state in Muslim countries? What role, if any, should religious scholars have in political governance? Who holds authority in Islam? Should the rules of Islamic jurisprudence be modified? Is there such a thing as "Islamic secularism?" If intellectual freedom is a right, how far can a modern Muslim go in expressing doubts about his faith?

Similar questions, of course, have riveted Muslim minds since Islam began in the 7th century. But in recent decades, the search for new answers is unfolding on a scale never before seen in Islamic history.

It is a quest propelled by a deep yearning among many Muslims for new thinking in Islam, which they deem essential for political reform, cultural vitality and even the survival of their faith.

"The most urgent problem facing us, the Muslims, is neither political nor economical, but a crisis of our thinking and learning process in relation to ourselves, Islam, Muslims and humanity at large," wrote Laith Kubba, an Iraqi-born Islamist thinker. "Without an objective, relative and rational Islamic discourse, our relationship to Islam will remain as that of a sentiment to the past or a mere slogan at present but it will not become an alternative towards a better future."

The craving for new thinking has led to an explosion of *ijtihad*, the Islamic practice of "exerting one's utmost to understand." Bubbling up in universities, newsrooms and Koranic study groups, ijtihad is recharging Islam as never before.

Ijtihad springs from the root word *jhd*, meaning to struggle, strive or exert. Its provenance makes ijtihad a cousin to jihad, a word of many meanings, but known in the West mainly as "holy war" or "holy struggle." Ijtihad is the intellectual counterpart of

---

jihad—the struggle to resolve a problem or reach a new understanding of some issue through serious reflection on Islamic teachings and scripture.

Traditionally, ijtihad was a competence reserved to Islam's ulema, the religious scholars who for centuries have been looked to by Muslims to interpret their sacred scriptures. The ulema typically spent years committing the Koran and Sunna to memory and mastering Arabic grammar and *sharia* (Islamic law) rulings. But nowadays, Muslims with no classical theological training are claiming the right to do ijtihad.

So great is the impulse for ijtihad that the word has taken on new meaning, often denoting any individual's effort to apply the moral message of Islam to contemporary problems guided by his or her own conscience, experience and knowledge. It is ijtihad in this more expansive meaning—a sort of grass-roots, mass effort beyond the traditional ulema ranks—that is proliferating.

The reexamination of Islam is significant first of all because of its sweep, drawing in all social ranks and professions.

The reexamination of Islam is significant first of all because of its sweep, drawing in all social ranks and professions. Among its most avid enthusiasts are women, ones like Heba Raouf Ezzat, the Islamist writer and political scientist in Cairo. Ezzat has a special interest in promoting women's participation in politics but has had to fight what she considers outmoded thinking on women by other Islamists.

"God in the Qur'an never put restrictions on a woman in a ruling position," she wrote. "Contrary to what the traditional Muslim scholars teach, a woman in a leading political position is not against God's system or against the Qur'an. It might be against the chauvinistic views of some men."

Ezzat believes that Islamists have not always dealt adequately with women's issues, sometimes leaving the impression that women are inferior to men. So she did her own ijtihad, finding Islamic texts on women not usually mentioned in current Islamic discourse. Assisted by these, she said, "I have been trying to develop an Islamic approach to women's issues."

Her arguments have a ring of legitimacy with other Islamists because they are bolstered by Islamic texts interpreted by the same rules that male scholars have long used. "I'm doing my ijtihad according to the same lines of the classic methodological rules of interpretation," Ezzat said wryly, "but, amazingly, reaching different conclusions."

The tools now available to Muslims facilitate the contemporary interest in ijtihad. Just as Gutenberg's printing press helped spread the ideas of the Protestant Reformation, the Internet, e-mail and jet travel are now giving Muslims unprecedented access to knowledge of their religion and the world.

A mere generation ago, ulema had to tap their memories or delve into thick, yellowed volumes to find relevant Koranic citations when asked for advice. Today, the Koran and commentaries on it are instantly accessed on CD-ROMs at the click of a mouse. Muslims can debate different interpretations of Koranic verses in digital chat rooms, exchange ideas with Muslims around the world or even become authorities themselves, giving online advice to other Muslims. The Internet has allowed a thousand ijtihads to bloom.

The contemporary zest for ijtihad is also exceptional because it involves millions of Muslims living permanently in the West, a relatively new development in modern history. Turkish guest workers in Germany, second-generation Pakistanis in Britain, long-time Algerian immigrants in Paris and recent Afghan and Iraqi refugees in the United States are all part of Islam's expanding presence in the West. Most of them regard Europe and North America as home and are raising children and grandchildren who will do likewise. All live in secular societies where religion and politics occupy separate compartments and their faith has no place of privilege, as it often does in their homelands. These experiences cannot but affect the conclusions they reach in their ijtihad.

Some of the most innovative thinking in Islam is coming from those who live in the West.

Muslims in the West also have greater freedom to debate the future of their faith. It is no surprise, then, that some of the most innovative thinking in Islam is coming from those who live in the West. While they have only a limited impact in their native lands for now, their ideas are affecting the future of Islam.

Still, the expectation is not that this period of questioning and introspection will result in a uniform new understanding of Islam around the globe. Islam has always been a pluralistic, versatile faith with a diversity of views on how divine revelation should be understood and applied. Sharia, for example, developed four different schools of thought.

Moreover, those who sincerely exercise ijtihad can differ in their conclusions. The fruit of ijtihad depends on one's life experiences, knowledge of Islamic teachings and sense of how Islamic values should be manifested in social and political life. Moreover, Muslims of all stripes—Islamists and secularists, liberals and conservatives—are all engaging in ijtihad. So there will be disagreements.

What is significant, however, is that all of them are stirring the pot of intellectual and theological inquiry that now is simmering on the stove.

"The sheer abundance of people actively seeking answers to religious questions," observed Richard Bulliet, an expert in the history of Islam, "affords a better augury of the future of the Islamic world than the specific teachings or political policies of particular religious leaders." And while "a new Islamic synthesis will be achieved" out of all this questioning, Bulliet adds, "the final shape of 'modern' Islam is still too distant to discern."

Muslims are only at the beginning of their latest communal journey. Decades of ijtihad lie ahead before "modern-friendly" ijtihad achieves critical mass. Along the way, there is likely to be messiness, experimentation and discombobulations. Some Muslims will distort the process of ijtihad, producing warped versions of their faith for personal and political ends. Osama bin Laden comes to mind. And in many Muslim countries, including Egypt, the winds of orthodoxy still blow strong.

Resistance to new thinking in Islam comes from several quarters. Authoritarian governments restrict public debate and tradition-bound religious establishments, allied to the state, reject new interpretations of Islamic scriptures. Political opportunists who prefer religious slogans to genuine reform are another barrier. As are orthodox Islamists who read the Koran in a literal way and maintain that theirs is the "correct" version of Islam and all others heretical. Finally, extremists threaten new thinkers in Islam with violence.

These conservative forces are likely to remain powerful for some time to come. In a world shaken by terrorism in the name of Islam, it is often difficult to even notice, never mind heed, those who are working to modernize their faith with ideas instead of debasing it with bombs. Like a giant forest fire, terrorists easily draw the most attention. Closer scrutiny is required to see the stubbly mushrooms of new thinking sprouting all over the forest floor.

Moral Hazard

The Life of a Liberal Muslim[3]

By Franklin Foer
The New Republic, November 18, 2002

The death threats began shortly after September 11, 2001. Every few days, for about four months, Khaled Abou El Fadl would receive an angry, anonymous phone call at either his San Fernando Valley home or his UCLA office. In his e-mail inbox, he found ominous messages from obscured sources with warnings such as, "You know what we're capable of." At first, the pudgy, 39-year-old professor of Islamic jurisprudence dismissed the calls as harmless outbursts at a tense moment. But, as the fall of 2001 progressed, Abou El Fadl began suspecting that the threats were more serious than he had initially assumed. Twice in November, he noticed a van that inexplicably lingered outside of his relatively isolated home but then disappeared after he called the police. A few months later, he found the windows of his family's SUV smashed at a crowded movie theater parking lot. Neither the radio nor the cash in the car had been stolen; no other vehicle in the lot had been touched. When he brought these incidents to the attention of police, they requested—and he granted—permission to tap his home phone. Ucla installed a red panic button next to his desk, ensuring that campus cops could respond within minutes to any crisis in his office. The FBI even assigned an agent to track down his tormenters. (To date, they have not been found.) All of this might sound like the prelude to a textbook hate crime, but the Abou El Fadl case has a twist: The callers weren't angry white men accusing him of terrorist sympathies; they were fellow Muslim Americans accusing him of selling out the faith.

On September 14, 2001, Abou El Fadl had published an op-ed in the *Los Angeles Times*. Many Muslim Americans had condemned the week's attacks as un-Islamic. But Abou El Fadl felt this response amounted to an evasion. The attacks, he worried, didn't represent a deviation from mainstream Islam; they reflected a crisis at the core of the faith, the logical conclusion of "a puritanical and ethically oblivious form of Islam [that] has predominated since the 1970s." Centuries of Islamic intellectual development had been destroyed by the "rampant apologetics" of Muslim thinkers, which had "produced a culture that eschews self-critical and introspective insight and embraces projection of blame and a fantasy-like level of confidence and arrogance."

---

3. Reprinted by permission of *The New Republic*, © 2002 The New Republic, LLC.

Abou El Fadl had, for years, made essentially the same argument in his scholarly writings, particularly the books *And God Knows the Soldiers* (1997) and *Speaking in God's Name* (2001). With imams justifying suicide bombings in Israel and elsewhere, Abou El Fadl had voiced concern that Islam had been "rendered subservient to political expedience and symbolic displays of power." And he'd railed against the ascendance of Wahhabism, a rigidly puritanical brand of Islam exported and subsidized by the government of Saudi Arabia. The Wahhabis insist that Islam must recover the practices of the "golden age"—the decades that followed the prophet's death—and dismiss subsequent centuries of interpretation and intellectual exploration as devilish sophistry. It is that thoughtful, pluralist tradition that Abou El Fadl wants to recover, an "ethos where the numerous traditions . . . emphasiz[ed] that pursuit of knowledge is an act of permanent worship."

The Wahhabis insist that Islam must recover the practices of the "golden age."

Whereas the thrust of modern Christian history has been toward decentralization, Sunni Islam has undergone a rapid period of theological consolidation. In the faith's first century and a half, Abou El Fadl estimates that 135 legal schools competed to influence the religion. Even up until the last part of this century, Greek-inspired rationalists (*mu'tazila*) argued against puritanical literalists (*ahl-al-hadith*) and strict constructionists (*usulis*). But with Saudi money, and in the guise of Wahhabism, the *ahl-al-hadith* have of late won the upper hand. And, unlike other traditions that accommodate dissenting views, the Wahhabis claim to possess an undebatable vision of "true Islam." Abou El Fadl, by contrast, comes from the ever-shrinking *usuli* school. As he describes *usulism*, it is a conservative tradition. To protect the Koran's integrity, *usulis* impose a stiff test for the derivation of God's laws. For edicts to carry divine imprimatur, they must be unambiguously stated in the Koran or *sunna* (the body of literature that includes the sayings and biography of the prophet). "You have to be willing to bet your soul that law is God's will," he argues. "Otherwise you might be guilty of arrogance in the eyes of God."

Paradoxically, the *usulis*' theological conservatism makes them quite liberal relative to much of the current Muslim world. While Wahhabis assert the necessity of veiling women, for example, Abou El Fadl and other *usulis* point to texts casting doubt on God's intention that women's faces be constantly covered. (The Koran urges the veil specifically to protect against molestation, notes Abou El Fadl; if there's no threat of molestation, there's no need for the veil.) Likewise, the *usulis* reject many of the Wahhabis' other proscriptions—guidelines for sex, prohibitions against keeping pet dogs and women attending funerals—as passages plucked from context that ignore vast chunks of the holy books. But what bothers Abou El Fadl most about Wahhabism isn't simply its textual distortions. It is the tradition's denigration of morality, which the Wahhabis argue shouldn't affect the implementation of Koranic law. Abou El Fadl insists that his usuli tradition naturally leads Islam to an ethical humanism—a set of ideas about justice and beauty that help to achieve God's will. "If the intent and moral vision do not exist, then the rules become meaningless pedantry," he argues. Indeed, he considers much of modern Islam to be a tyranny of the picayune. As he wrote in the introduction to his 2001 collection of essays *Conference of the Books*, "I pray that this is a passing phase in the history of Islam and that Muslims will regain their intellectual vigor and enlightened spark."

Abou El Fadl is part of an international movement of Muslim intellectuals who oppose the extremism of the Wahhabis. It includes the Syrian theorist Mohammad Shahrour, the Italian imam Abdul Hadi Palazzi, and the Egyptian jurist Muhammad Imara. Abou El Fadl has his own informal cluster of American dissident scholars, which self-deprecatingly calls itself the "consolation club"—in e-mail and phone calls, they console each other. They trade stories of receiving death threats, being protested by their own radical students, and being constantly tempted by the enticements of Saudi emissaries who offer grants and endowed chairs in exchange for their theological conformity. Even in the West, dissident thinkers like Abou El Fadl have been shut out of mainstream Islamic institutions. To find an intellectual home, they reside in secular academia, where they grow even further removed from potential constituents. It's a condition that breeds depression and deep cynicism. When I ask Abou El Fadl about his hope for the future of Islam, he pulls a Diet Coke from the mini-refrigerator next to his desk

> *Even in the West, dissident thinkers like Abou El Fadl have been shut out of mainstream Islamic institutions.*

before lighting a cigarette and smoking it out his window. "The chances are that I would be appreciated by a rabbi interested in interfaith discussions far more than I will be by a leader of a Muslim organization," he says. After a few puffs, he rubs the cigarette into the sill and throws it from the window. "It's very disheartening and discouraging. The reason I'm speaking so openly is that I'm fed up to the core."

For centuries, the Abou El Fadl family included jurists who studied in the schools affiliated with Cairo's Al Azhar mosque, the venerable epicenter of Sunni Islamic thinking—Islam's Oxbridge. But for the epicenter of Sunnism, it had a strange history: The mosque had been founded by Shia from Tunisia in the tenth century. Perhaps, because of this lineage, Al Azhar tolerated dissident sects long after the Shia vacated the mosque in the twelfth century. Proponents of nearly all varieties of Islamic legal thinking—*mu'tazila*, *ahl-al-hadith*, and *usuli* alike—found intellectual homes in Al Azhar. To be sure, Al Azhar shifted with the politics of the times. After Napoleon conquered Egypt in 1798, the mosque's leaders made slandering the French occupiers a religious crime; during the

Ottoman era, the school excelled at producing pliant scholars versed in the empire's favored *hanafi* legal school. But, for the most part, Al Azhar's acceptance of intellectual diversity continued regardless of fluctuations in Egypt's political leadership.

At least up until the post-colonial era, that is. In 1961, Egyptian president Gamal Abdel Nasser nationalized the school. Sheiks at Al Azhar became government-paid functionaries—and were expected to conduct themselves as such, promoting Nasser's vision of a secular pan-Arab socialism. As Gilles Kepel, the French historian of political Islam, writes in his book *Jihad*, "By linking the reformed Azhar institution too directly to the state, Nasser's regime deprived it of credibility. . . . A vacuum had been created, to be filled by anyone ready to question the state and criticize governments in the name of Islam."

The vacuum was filled by proponents of radical Islamism—first by theorist Sayyid Qutb (who was hung by Nasser in 1966) and his comrades in the Muslim Brotherhood and then, more gradually, by Wahhabi clerics supported by Saudi Arabia. In 1962, Saudi Arabia founded the Muslim World League to fund the distribution of Korans, the production of Wahhabi scholarship, and the building of mosques throughout the globe. And, over the course of the next four decades, the Saudis steadily purchased the ideological direction of Al Azhar. It started subtly, with cushy Gulf sabbaticals for scholars. "In six months on sabbatical, they would earn twenty years' salary," says Abou El Fadl. As these contributions became more customary—and scholars became increasingly eager to supplement their $40-a-month salaries—the Saudis expanded their influence. Through the Muslim World League, they began endowing chairs for scholars and funding departments. By the late '90s, it was growing difficult to find an Azhari who hadn't benefitted from Saudi largesse—and who hadn't returned the favor with pro-Wahhabi scholarship.

When Abou El Fadl began studying with the Azhari sheiks, in 1969 at the age of 6, the mosque was in the midst of this transition from religious diversity to Wahhabi predominance. Signs of moderation still existed: Following Abou El Fadl's adolescent flirtation with Islamism—during which he destroyed his sister's Rod Stewart tapes and fulminated against mixed gatherings—the sheiks persuaded him to adopt a more moderate path. But, over the years, Abou El Fadl noticed the increasing presence of Saudi money and of Wahhabism. For years, one of his most beloved teachers, Muhammad Jalal Kishk, had mocked the ignorance of Wahhabi Islam. But, in 1981, after Kishk received the $200,000 King Faisal Award and the $850,000 King Fahd Award from the Saudi government, he published a pro-Wahhabi tome called *The Saudis and the Islamic Solution*.

Today, the takeover of Al Azhar is largely complete. The highest-ranking sheik in the once-moderate institution, Muhammad Sayyed Tantawi, endorses suicide bombings. And Al Azhar has bullied the

Egyptian government into granting it power to censor all books on Islam. As the university's president told *Al-Ahram Weekly* last year, "Freedom is restricted by respect for God, his prophet and all religious values." Many Azharis who refused to toe the Wahhabi line have been purged from the institution. Abou El Fadl tells the story of another of his teachers, Muhammad al-Ghazali. Even though al-Ghazali was among the more conservative Azharis, he grew impatient with the rising anti-intellectualism at the school. In 1989, he published a book called *The Sunna of the Prophet: Between the Legists and Traditionalists*, accusing the Wahhabi of justifying fanaticism and defiling Islam's reputation. Within two years, the Saudis subsidized the publication of seven books trashing al-Ghazali. At three Muslim World League-sponsored conferences in Saudi Arabia, scholars lined up to dismiss his arguments. Even the Saudi newspaper, *Al-Sharq al-Awsat,* issued its own lengthy rebuttals. But, what most pained al-Ghazali, according to Abou El Fadl, was not the Saudi smear campaign but watching his old students—many of whom had received Saudi fellowships and book advances—remain silent amid the uproar. At the time, al-Ghazali told Abou El Fadl, "I never realized how bad it has become until this instance. I realize that the foreseeable future is lost." After years of suffering polemics, Abou El Fadl told me, "al-Ghazali died of a broken heart."

In May 1985, after Abou El Fadl completed his junior year at Yale, he returned home to Cairo for the summer. A few weeks earlier, Yale had named him "Scholar of the House," an award that *Al-Ahram* celebrated in its pages. In addition to his academic work, Abou El Fadl had spent the year studying for certification in a top-level field of Islamic jurisprudence called *hadith* authentication. Now, at home with his Azhari teachers, he put the final touches on his preparation. One evening, as he left his study circle, however, two plainclothes Egyptian policemen approached him. Without explanation, they shoved him in a truck and blindfolded him. Abou El Fadl later discovered that they had taken him to the basement of a detention center called Lazoughli. "You think that you're scholar of the house," his interrogators declared sarcastically as they beat him. Next, the police transferred him to a notorious desert prison called Tora, rumored to be surrounded by the make-shift graves of torture victims. Abou El Fadl was suspended from the ceiling by his left arm for six-hour intervals; guards shocked him with electricity and pulled out his fingernails. After three weeks, and without a conviction, they released him.

This was not the first time Abou El Fadl had been targeted by police. As a teenager, he had published antiregime poetry and stories in the opposition dailies and had twice been taken in for beatings. But, whereas many of Abou El Fadl's contemporaries responded to such police-state tactics by embracing militant Islamism, the abuse only magnified his desire to find a community where he could speak his mind without fear of retribution from either secular or religious authorities. And so, after his 1985 visit, Abou El Fadl returned to the United States in self-imposed exile. He had high hopes for the Muslim community in the United States. Unlike the scholars at Al Azhar, they didn't have to contend with government censorship and Wahhabi oppressiveness, he imagined. "Naively, I had assumed that the freedoms afforded in the United States, and the relative absence of political persecution, would allow for a Muslim intellectual rebirth," he writes in the introduction to *And God Knows the Soldiers*. He even daydreamed that American Muslims might form a diaspora movement that would return to remake the Middle East.

But, instead of tolerance, Abou El Fadl found a community that wasn't significantly more open than the one he'd left behind. Where he expected vibrant intellectual debate, he found rigid conformity to Wahhabi-like practices. "As I move from mosque to mosque, I encounter Muslims who seem to think that the harsher and the more perverse the law, the more it's Islamic," he says. He noticed

---

"As I move from mosque to mosque, I encounter Muslims who seem to think that the harsher and the more perverse the law, the more it's Islamic."—Abou El Fadl

---

that American imams often lacked even the rudiments of Islamic education. And he noticed that community leaders worried more about combating criticism of their organizations than about building educational institutions. "Despots," he calls them.

After finishing graduate school at Princeton in 1995, Abou El Fadl began publicly criticizing mainstream Islam, and it was not long before it got him in trouble. In 1997, while teaching at the University of Texas, he was driven from his mosque, the Islamic Center of Greater Austin. Finishing Friday supplications, he was interrupted by a man who "kindly invited" him into the building's boardroom. Entering the room, he found 15 men sitting around a long table. They took turns condemning his scholarship as heretical. A board member stood up and pronounced him "the great Satan." Abou El Fadl left the room. But congregants began to trail him on the street. One took off his shoe and began swinging it at him. The attack only stopped after the intervention of a passing graduate student.

But the post–September 11 backlash was much greater. The criticism that followed his *Los Angeles Times* op-ed was not limited to anonymous threats; it came from good friends, too. This past summer, he was banned from *The Minaret* magazine, a publication to which he had contributed a monthly column for nearly 20 years. "Good luck with your career that is based on self-promotion and self-aggrandizement," the magazine's editor wrote in an e-mail. The Los

Angeles–based Muslim Public Affairs Council (MPAC) posted condemnations of Abou El Fadl on the American Muslims Intent on Learning and Activism (AMILA) Internet site. And, several days after he published another contentious op-ed this summer, a lawyer with ties to MPAC began representing Abou El Fadl's ex-wife of ten years in a custody battle. "My son has been living with me for the past ten years. Suddenly, their lawyer is representing her in her lawsuit filed against me," he says. "They've made it personal." In an e-mail to Abou El Fadl, MPAC denied all involvement in the custody suit.

Last month, Abou El Fadl had been scheduled to lecture at the University of Kuwait on the subject of Islam and democracy. He'd been looking forward to the talk, a rare opportunity to address Islamic intellectuals in the Middle East. But, a week before the lecture, he caught wind of a disturbing rumor. A dissident within the Saudi government told a friend of his that the Saudis planned to pick him up and make him disappear. "The Kuwaitis would say,

---

Even within the confines of Western academia, the Saudis have attempted to impose their Wahhabist interpretation of Islam.

'We don't know what happened,'" he explains. "Everyone would be interested for a while; then, it would be forgotten like everyone else." Abou El Fadl canceled the trip.

Even within the confines of Western academia, the Saudis have attempted to impose their Wahhabist interpretation of Islam, to re-create their takeover of Al Azhar. And, just as with the Azharis, their primary inducement has been monetary. There's no better way to gauge the Saudi effort than by reading off the names of prominent Middle Eastern studies departments and the gifts they have received from the Saudi royal family. Five years ago, King Fahd gave Oxford University more than $30 million to its Islamic Studies Center. In 1994, the University of Arkansas received a $20 million grant to begin the King Fahd Program for Middle East Studies. Thanks to a $5 million gift, U.C. Berkeley now houses the Sultan Bin Abdel Aziz Program in Arab Studies. Even Harvard has a chair, currently occupied by legal scholar Frank Vogel, called the Custodian of the Two Holy Mosques Adjunct Professor of Islamic Legal Studies—and subsidized by at least $5 million from the Saudis.

Ever since Abou El Fadl's days as a graduate student at Princeton, the Saudis have plied him with similar offers of wealth. In 1991, before he'd finished his dissertation, the Muslim World League offered him $100,000 to write a book on Islam; in return, however, it demanded "final editorial control." Abou El Fadl rejected the offer. Seven years later, the Saudis offered to nominate him for the $200,000 King Faisal award. After a preliminary phone call, Abou El Fadl stopped returning the Saudis' messages; they'd made him uncomfortable with too many leading questions about the "enemies of Islam." But, despite his past rejections, the Saudis have kept trying. Last year, they offered Abou El Fadl and his "guests" an all-expenses-paid "VIP" trip to Mecca for Hajj.

Abou El Fadl has rejected the offers because he's seen what Saudi patronage has done to the scholarship of his colleagues. He calls Vogel's book on Saudi law, *Islamic Law and Legal System: Studies of Saudi Arabia*, "an embarrassment." (Vogel says he has no qualms about accepting Saudi money. "I saw it as something very much in the greater good of the Muslim world and particularly of Saudi Arabia," he told NPR in 1993.) In Abou El Fadl's view, the Saudi contributions have exacerbated the shift in Middle Eastern studies away from critical, secular analyses of modernization toward celebrations of Islamist "civil society." As the Washington Institute for Near East Policy's Martin Kramer puts it, "The last places to look for anything critical are Berkeley and Harvard. There's nothing out there on opposition trends in Saudi Arabia. Because even if you aren't getting money, you're trying to get in the game."

To give me a sense of the Saudi advantage on the intellectual battlefield, Abou El Fadl took me on a tour of his massive home library. First, he showed me a Saudi-published fivevolume set listing Islamic texts that good Muslims should never read. According to Abou El Fadl, the Saudis have even banned some of the works of their most important *ahl-al-hadith* jurist, the thirteenth-century Syrian Ibn Taymiyyah. Next, he pulled several books from the shelves. One, a volume from Riyadh, is leather-bound with a gold-leaf pattern on the spine that, when lined up with other books on the shelf, makes up a lovely mosaic. Next, he showed me the work of an important moderate jurist from Cairo. The pages have a quality a bit higher than toilet paper, and the printing looks like it was run off a mimeograph machine. Only 100 copies of the book exist, and, despite its low quality, it is expensive. The Wahhabi texts, by contrast, are not only beautiful, they're cheap, thanks to heavy subsidies from the Saudis.

"Islam is about the subjective engagement," Abou El Fadl told me, neatly encapsulating how his theological vision differs from the strident absolutism of Wahhabism. But, because he believes the true meaning of Islam should be continually debated, hashed out in arguments between jurists, he finds himself rhetorically disadvantaged when facing opponents who lay claim to ultimate truth. This asymmetrical warfare was on display last month, when Abou El Fadl went to Qatar to debate the morality of suicide bombings with Islamist Sheik Youssef al-Qaradawi, who preaches on the TV network Al Jazeera. (Al-Qaradawi had previously announced that those who shook hands with Shimon Peres should wash their hands "seven times, one time with dirt.") Abou El Fadl only agreed to the trip because the State Department had helped organize it and guaranteed his safety. Bodyguards maintained a constant watch over his hotel room.

In a conference room at the Doha Ritz Carlton, Abou El Fadl pointed out the logical inconsistencies in al-Qaradawi's defense of suicide bombing and cited pre-modern Islamic jurists on the ethics of revenge. But such details were of no interest to al-Qaradawi. According to Abou El Fadl, al-Qaradawi told the crowd of Muslim intellectuals and foreign journalists, "I don't know why brother Abou El Fadl keeps needlessly complicating things; Islam is against such complications," before going on to cite statistics about the murders of Palestinian children. By the end of the debate, Abou El Fadl felt that he'd been mocked, ignored, and rhetorically run over. Al-Qaradawi stopped addressing him by his proper title—sheik—and, as he left the stage, refused to shake hands. "It wasn't a fair fight," one participant told me later.

Two weeks after he returned from Qatar, Abou El Fadl got a visit from the FBI. The State Department, the agents told him, had asked them to set up a meeting: It wanted to ensure that his criticism of al-Qaradawi didn't result in any physical harm. Already, al-Qaradawi had mentioned their debate on his website, and it had unleashed a torrent of response. A group of social scientists in Egypt had e-mailed Abou El Fadl to tell him that they "prayed God would return him to a straight path." And he received similar messages from Jordan and elsewhere. A few days before the FBI visited, we had discussed the debate and the consequences of challenging popular imams. As he spoke, he stroked his blind terrier, Lulu. With a resigned tone, he told me, "There may need to be sacrificial lambs. I'm going to play this role and speak my conscience."

Can Any Good Come of Radical Islam?[4]

By Francis Fukuyama and Nadav Samin
Commentary, September 2002

What is going on in the Muslim world? Why does it produce suicide hijackers on the one hand and, on the other, lethargic and haphazardly capitalist societies that have delivered neither economic development nor democracy? A good if partial answer to these questions—partial because it is limited to the Arab region of that world—can be found in a United Nations "development report" issued in July. As the UN assessment concludes, the entire Arab sector, with all its oil wealth, is "richer than it is developed." Its economies are stagnant, illiteracy is widespread, political freedom is hardly to be found, and its inhabitants, especially its women, are denied the basic "capabilities" and "opportunities" of the modern world.

The UN report—written, significantly, by a group of Arab intellectuals—was commissioned well before last fall's attacks on the U.S. But its pertinence to those attacks has seemed clear enough to commentators. Thomas Friedman of the *New York Times* called it the key to understanding "the milieu that produced bin Ladenism, and will reproduce it if nothing changes." An editorial in the *Wall Street Journal* found "little wonder" in the fact that "such an isolated culture became a breeding ground for the Islamic fundamentalism that spawned September 11."

The Islamism of Osama bin Laden and his followers is indeed inseparable from the developmental failures of the world's Arab societies. All the same, however, it would be a mistake to conceive of the Islamist movement as nothing more than an expression of those failures. The phenomenon of radical Islam is more complicated than that, and in all sorts of surprising ways its long-term effect on the entire orbit of Islamic society may turn out to be more complicated still.

Last September's attacks against the United States were carried out by a group of Muslims led by a gaunt, bearded ascetic sitting in a cave in Afghanistan and spouting unfathomable rhetoric. So all-consuming was the hijackers' hatred of America that they were willing to blow *themselves* up for their cause—something that set them apart from earlier generations of terrorists. Where did this zeal, so foreign to the modern democratic temperament, come from?

---

4. Reprinted from *Commentary*, September 2002, by permission; all rights reserved.

On the part of many observers, the immediate impulse was to attribute it to deep cultural factors, and in particular to the teachings of fundamentalist Islam. And of course there was, and is, much to be said for this view. In particular, the fact that, far from repudiating bin Laden, Muslims and Westerners tended to line up on opposite sides in their interpretation of the events of September 11 gave credence to the paradigm of the Harvard political scientist Samuel Huntington, who predicted a number of years ago that the post-cold-war world would give rise to a "clash of civilizations."

Still, foolish as it would be to downplay the role of religious or "civilizational" factors, it will not do simply to call Osama bin Laden an Islamic fundamentalist. For the Islamism of which he is a symbol and a spokesman is not a movement aimed at restoring some archaic or pristine form of Islamic practice. As a number of observers have argued, including most recently the Iranian scholars Ladan and Roya Boroumand in the *Journal of Democracy*, it is best understood not as a traditional movement but as a very modern one.

Groups like al Qaeda . . . owe an explicit debt to 20th-century European doctrines of the extreme Right and Left.

Groups like al Qaeda, the Boroumands write, owe an explicit debt to 20th-century European doctrines of the extreme Right and Left. One stream of influence can be traced to Hassan al-Banna, the schoolteacher who founded the Muslim Brotherhood in Egypt in 1928. From Italy's Fascists, al-Banna borrowed the idea of unquestioning loyalty to a charismatic leader, modeling the slogan of his paramilitary organization—"action, obedience, silence"—on Mussolini's injunction to "believe, obey, fight." Taking a cue from the Nazis, he placed great emphasis on the Muslim Brotherhood's youth wing and on the marriage of the physical and the spiritual, of Islam with activism. Unsurprisingly, al-Banna also taught his followers to expect not encouragement but repression from traditional Islamic authorities.

A second European source of Islamism can be traced to Maulana Mawdudi, who founded the Jamaat-e-Islami movement in Pakistan in the early 1940's. A journalist well-versed in Marxist thought, Mawdudi advocated struggle by an Islamic "revolutionary vanguard" against both the West *and* traditional Islam. As the Boroumands observe, he was perhaps the first to attach "the adjective 'Islamic' to such distinctively Western terms as 'revolution,' 'state,' and 'ideology.'"

These strands of the radical Right and Left eventually came together in the person of Sayyid Qutb, the Egyptian who became the Muslim Brotherhood's chief ideologist after World War II. In his most important work, *Signposts Along the Road*, Qutb called for a monolithic state led by an Islamic party, advocating the use of every violent means necessary to achieve that end. The society he envisioned would be classless, one in which the "selfish individual" of liberal societies would be abolished and the "exploitation of man by man" would end. This, as the Boroumands point out, was "Leninism in an Islamist dress," and it is the creed embraced by most present-day Islamists.

Though developed among Sunnis, this virulent ideological mix reached the Shiite world as well, most notably through its influence on Ayatollah Khomeini in Iran. Indeed, the Iranian revolution of 1979 conferred on Islamism a degree of religious respectability that it had never before possessed. But the fact that the movement could so easily bridge the bitter Shiite-Sunni divide also suggests just how sharply divorced it is from Islamic history and custom. As the Boroumands conclude, the key attributes of Islamism— "the aestheticization of death, the glorification of armed force, the worship of martyrdom, and 'faith in the propaganda of the deed'"—have little precedent in Islam but have been defining features of modern totalitarianism. The seeming rigor of Osama bin Laden's theology belies the reality of his highly heterodox beliefs.

> *The key attributes of Islamism ... have been defining features of modern totalitarianism.*

So much for the ideological side of things. On the sociological side, there is still another close parallel between Islamism and the rise of European fascism. Though Hitler was a great entrepreneur of ideas, the roots of his movement, as described in classic analyses like Fritz Stern's *The Politics of Cultural Despair* (1974), lay in the rapid industrialization of central Europe. In the course of a single generation, millions of peasants had moved from tightly-knit village communities to large, impersonal cities, losing in the process a range of familiar cultural norms and signposts.

This rapid transition—captured in Ferdinand Tönnies's famous distinction between Gemeinschaft (community) and Gesellschaft (society)—was perhaps the most powerful impetus behind modern nationalism. Deprived of local sources of identity, displaced villagers found new social bonds in language, ethnicity, and—ultimately—in the mythopoetic propaganda of Europe's extreme Right. Though the various right-wing parties pretended to revive ancient traditions—pre-Christian Germanic ones in the case of Nazism, Roman ones in the case of the Italian Fascists—their doctrines were really a syncretic mishmash, old symbols and new ideas brought together by the most up-to-date forms of communications technology.

Islamism, as the late Ernest Gellner was among the first to note, has followed a similar path. Over the last several decades, most Muslim societies have undergone a social transformation not unlike that of Europe in the late 19th century. Large numbers of villagers and tribesmen have moved to the vast urban slums of Cairo, Algiers, and Amman, leaving behind the variegated, often preliterate Islam of the countryside. Islamism has filled the void, offering a new identity based on a puritanical, homogenized creed. Syncretist in the manner of fascism, it unites traditional religious symbols and rhetoric with the ideology of revolutionary action.

Some observers, especially after September 11, have suggested that the real engine of Islamism's growth is poverty, but this is not the case. According to the recent UN report, for example, the Arab world actually compares favorably to other developing regions when it comes to preventing abject want. Rather, like European fascism before it, Islamism is bred by rapid social dislocation. More often than not, its leaders and propagandists are newcomers to the middle or upper classes. Islamism introduces these educated but often lonely and alienated individuals to a larger *umma* (community) of believers, from Tangier to Jakarta to London. Through the magic of the cassette tape recorder (in Khomeini's case) or video (for bin Laden), they become members of a vibrant, if dangerous and destructive, international community.

Seeing Islamism for what it really is goes beyond correct taxonomy. It also points us in the direction of an important, if seemingly perverse, question: could it, like both fascism and Communism before it, serve inadvertently as a modernizing force, preparing the way for Muslim societies that can respond not destructively but constructively to the challenge of the West?

The question is not as absurd as it may sound. Comparisons are especially tricky here, but the Bolsheviks succeeded in creating an industrialized, urbanized Russia, and Hitler managed to get rid of the Junkers and much of the class stratification that had characterized prewar Germany. Through a tortuous and immensely costly path, both of these "isms" cleared away some of the premodern underbrush that had obstructed the growth of liberal democracy. There are, of course, much safer and more peaceful routes toward modernization, like those taken by countries like Korea or Britain or the United States, and less expensive paths to modernity were surely available to Russia and Germany. But one has to deal with what one has, and in Islamic cultures, in any case, there is arguably much more underbrush to be cleared away. If Islamism is directed as much against traditional forms of Islam as against the West, could it, too, be a source of such creative destruction?

There are myriad ways in which not only Islamic practice but the rigid legal framework within which it is encased has obstructed change. The economic historian Timur Kuran has documented in painstaking detail a series of traditional Islamic institutions whose inflexibility and legalism have served as immense barriers to development. Interest rates are fixed by religious authorities, schooling focuses on rote learning of religious texts and discourages critical thinking, women are kept out of political and economic life, and so on. Even an institution like the *waqf*, or traditional Islamic charity, which could serve as a bulwark of civil society in a reformed Islamic order, fixes the bequests of wealthy individuals in perpetuity, with no opportunity for adaptation to changing circumstances.

Many of these same constraints existed historically in the Judeo-Christian West, and were eliminated or ameliorated only after long struggle. All of them continue to exist in the Islamic present, and can only be removed through the exercise of political power. Islamism has already demonstrated the capability of doing this, and even of accommodating Western norms when it has to: though Khomeini brought back the chador, or veil, for women, he also reluctantly sanctioned women's right to vote in Iranian elections, a practice (won under the Shah) that he had once likened to prostitution.

In Egypt, the Muslim Brotherhood as well as other, even more radical Islamist organizations have created a layer of voluntary associations standing between the family and the state. It was, for example, Islamist charities that stepped into the breach at the time of the 1992 Cairo earthquake, providing important social services unavailable from the inept and corrupt Egyptian state. The Islamists clearly hope to reunite religion and political power one day, which would be a disaster. But they are learning—and inculcating—habits of association and independent action that, if somehow divorced from their radical ideology, might yet help lay the groundwork of a true civil society.

There is another area in which the reactionary ideas of the Islamists may play a potentially progressive role, and this has to do with the fundamental sources of authority and legitimacy in the Islamic world.

The traditional system of Islamic jurisprudence—with its rigid rules and hierarchies—has been under attack, in one way or another, since at least the 19th century. The most important early figures in this effort were modernizers, like the Iranian Jamal al-Din al-Afghani (1839–1897) and his student, the Egyptian reformer Muhammad Abduh (1849–1905). Abduh was among the first to depart from the rigidly textual form of interpretation that had characterized the Sunni world since the earliest caliphates. In his view, human reason was the only appropriate tool for applying the fundamental truths of the Qur'an and the Sunna (the traditions of the Prophet). Appointed mufti of Egypt toward the end of his life, Abduh issued rulings reflecting, in the words of one scholar, his desire "to render the religion of Islam entirely adaptable to the requirements of modern civilization."

The implications of this turn were profound. Though the institutional base of orthodox Sunni Islam remained intact, the long-sealed gates of doctrinal explication were unhinged. Like a Muslim Luther, Abduh shook up the clerical establishment by reviving, under the influence of his mentor al-Afghani, the possibility of independent legal interpretation. His example gave unprecedented latitude to all

subsequent construers of Islamic tradition, whether saints or demagogues—the latter including anti-Western radicals like the Muslim Brotherhood's Sayyid Qutb and, eventually, Osama bin Laden.

In the battle for interpretative power, it is no coincidence that the
primary breeding ground for Islamism has been the brittle oligar-
chies of Saudi Arabia and Egypt. Both regimes have co-opted the
traditional clergy, forcing the populist current of Islam into back
alleys and store-front mosques and turning it into an ideological
guerrilla movement. Detached from the moorings of tradition, the
Islamists have proved adept at manipulating the symbols of faith
and appropriating them for their own revolutionary purposes.

Osama bin Laden's famous 1998 *fatwa*, in which he declared
jihad on the United States and any American fair game for his followers, is a case in point. Though the content of this declaration is
itself contrary to traditional Islamic moral teachings—as the eminent Middle East scholar Bernard Lewis has observed, "At no point
do the basic texts of Islam enjoin terrorism and murder"—the most
notably radical thing about it is the identity of its author. Osama

---

> ### *Osama bin Laden has no credentials as a religious authority and no right, under traditional Islamic practice, to issue a fatwa.*

---

bin Laden has no credentials as a religious authority and no right,
under traditional Islamic practice, to issue a *fatwa*. It is a bit like
Hitler issuing a papal encyclical, or Lenin a decree in the name of
the Russian Orthodox church. The mere fact that bin Laden was
willing to cross this line shows the extent to which Islamism has
undermined traditional Islamic legal authority. But a line crossed
in the name of waging all-out war against the West may yet be
crossed in the name of healthier purposes.

We should not kid ourselves. The modernization of Islam is hardly immi-
nent, and it will not occur without enormous struggle. There are several
deeply imbedded obstacles in Islamic society, not least the often-noted lack
of a tradition of secular politics. To many Muslims, what may simply seem
more "natural" is a totalizing ideology that seeks to unite society and the
state within a single revolutionary whole. Nor is it clear, despite the UN's
recent report, that the Muslim world is capable of the realistic
self-appraisal necessary for a modernizing shift to occur.

Many non-Western societies, after all, have tried the path of violent resistance to the enormous military, economic, and cultural power of the West.
It was only when faced with defeat and domination that nations like China
and Japan undertook a serious study of what, in Lewis's phrase, "went
wrong." Joining the West when they could not beat it, they adopted a variety of Western institutions while retaining a core of their own culture. This

process of social learning has been much slower in Muslim societies; for Arabs in particular, it has been all too convenient to blame Israel and the United States for their own lack of progress.

If the wait for Muslim modernization is likely to be a long one, how, then, should the West respond in the short term as it faces the continued prospect of terrorism, suicide bombings, and weapons of mass destruction? The determined application of military power is certainly part of the answer. European fascism did not fall because of the inherent wickedness of its animating ideas; having brought havoc to the societies that embraced its doctrines, it lost legitimacy because it was crushed on the battlefield. Just as Osama bin Laden and his cause gained status and support with the successful attacks of September 11, so the rout of al Qaeda from Afghanistan and continuing U.S. operations against radical Islamic terrorism are absolutely key to dampening Islamist fervor.

But the more important struggle must take place within the Islamic world itself. For too long, genuine Muslim modernizers have sat in the wings while traditionalists and Islamists battled one another on center stage. The great need now is for Western-oriented Muslims to take advantage of the turmoil created by September 11 to promote a more genuinely liberal form of their religion.

There is reason to think that such an opening exists. Though many Muslims continue to favor Islamism in the abstract, the movement has left a disastrous record everywhere it has come to power. Saudi Arabia, home of the extremist Wahhabi strain of fundamentalist Islam, is one of the most corrupt and mismanaged regimes in the contemporary world. Even with the country's vast oil wealth, per-capita income fell in real terms from $11,500 in 1980 to $6,700 in 1999. As for Afghanistan under the Taliban, ordinary Afghans were overjoyed to be liberated from their yoke, and eagerly returned to such simple modern pleasures as watching cheesy Indian movies on their long-buried VCR's.

It is the Iranians, who, having lived under Islamist rule for the past generation, are most likely to lead the Islamic world out of its current impasse. Though Western hopes for the seemingly reform-minded President Khatami have proved misplaced, there is one basic demographic fact working in favor of eventual liberalization: 70 percent of Iran's population is now under the age of 30, and from all reports these young people tend to abhor the Islamic theocracy. Having brought the first Islamist regime to power, Iran would set a powerful example for the rest of the Middle East—and beyond—if it were to move toward liberalization on its own steam.

In the end, it is as important not to overestimate the strength of Islamism as it is fatal to underestimate it. It has little to offer Arabs, much less the rest of the Muslim world. Its glorification of violence has already produced a sharp counterreaction, and—provided it is defeated—its "successes" may yet help pave the way for long-overdue reform. If so, this would certainly not be the first time that the cunning of history has produced so astounding a result.

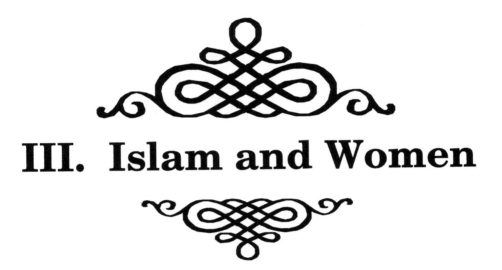

III. Islam and Women

Editor's Introduction

One of the most polarizing issues confronting Muslims and their relations with Western society is the role of women in Islam. With the rigid application of Islamic law under the Taliban regime in Afghanistan, in Saudi Arabia, and parts of Nigeria, most Western nations have the impression that women in Islamic nations are repressed, both sexually and legally. The imposition in Afghanistan of the burkha—the dress that covers the entire female body except for a slit for the eyes—has become for the West a symbol of sexual discrimination and repression in the Muslim world. Yet there are many Muslim women, particularly in Western nations, who feel Islam offers them more freedom than other religious systems and who point to the many Qur'anic passages that explicitly call for equality among the sexes, more so than holy texts of the Western traditions.

In "The Women of Islam" by Lisa Beyer and others writing for *Time* magazine, the authors point out that "nowhere in the Muslim world are women treated as equals." They also note, however, that the Prophet Muhammad was something of a feminist for his time, and that the Qur'an allowed women more rights than they had been given in 7th-century Arabia. Nevertheless, under shariah women are considered to be of lesser importance than men, for even their testimony is considered only half as valuable as a man's in court. This inequality, the authors assert, is also found in laws regarding marriage and divorce, but this repression of women draws barely any protest on some occasions. For instance, as they explain, a passage in the Qur'an that allows for wife beating under certain circumstances has led not only to a higher incidence of such abuse but also to an acceptance of these acts by their victims.

Madeleine Bunting offers a far different view of the role religion plays in the lives of Muslim women in her article "Can Islam Liberate Women?" Indeed, the six women Bunting interviews say they find Islam sexually and spiritually liberating and "don't need western feminism, which, they argue, developed as a reaction against the particular expression of western patriarchy." These women, like many others in Islam, find spiritual and intellectual resonance in those passages in the Qur'an that express the equality of the sexes in the eyes of God, or the genderless and nonracial qualities of God. Other women explain what they see as the benefits to wearing the hijab, which covers their heads and bodies. However, Bunting also reports that many Muslim women question the prophet Muhammad's relations to women, which included polygamy and marrying a girl when she was nine—a life deemed perfect by so many Muslim believers.

"American by Birth, Muslim by Choice" by Katherine Millett examines Muslim women from a different perspective—that of women who choose to convert to Islam in the United States. Millett asks why someone with the freedom she has in America would "convert to Islam, a religion that appears to treat women as inferior to men. . . . Why would they choose to limit their choices in dress and marriage, never again to socialize with men, run on the beach and drink a beer?" Among the reasons given to Millett is the importance of family in Islam, the way it stresses ethical behavior, and the way in which it gives women a greater ability to make a point with their minds rather with their appearance.

The Women of Islam[1]

By Lisa Beyer et al.
TIME, December 3, 2001

For his day, the Prophet Muhammad was a feminist. The doctrine he laid out as the revealed word of God considerably improved the status of women in 7th century Arabia. In local pagan society, it was the custom to bury alive unwanted female newborns; Islam prohibited the practice. Women had been treated as possessions of their husbands; Islamic law made the education of girls a sacred duty and gave women the right to own and inherit property. Muhammad even decreed that sexual satisfaction was a woman's entitlement. He was a liberal at home as well as in the pulpit. The Prophet darned his own garments and among his wives and concubines had a trader, a warrior, a leather worker and an imam.

Of course, ancient advances do not mean that much to women 14 centuries later if reform is, rather than a process, a historical blip subject to reversal. While it is impossible, given their diversity, to paint one picture of women living under Islam today, it is clear that the religion has been used in most Muslim countries not to liberate but to entrench inequality. The Taliban, with its fanatical subjugation of the female sex, occupies an extreme, but it nevertheless belongs on a continuum that includes, not so far down the line, Saudi Arabia, Kuwait, Pakistan and the relatively moderate states of Egypt and Jordan. Where Muslims have afforded women the greatest degree of equality—in Turkey—they have done so by overthrowing Islamic precepts in favor of secular rule. As Riffat Hassan, professor of religious studies at the University of Louisville, puts it, "The way Islam has been practiced in most Muslim societies for centuries has left millions of Muslim women with battered bodies, minds and souls."

Part of the problem dates to Muhammad. Even as he proclaimed new rights for women, he enshrined their inequality in immutable law, passed down as God's commandments and eventually recorded in scripture. The Koran allots daughters half the inheritance of sons. It decrees that a woman's testimony in court, at least in financial matters, is worth half that of a man's. Under Shari'a, or Muslim law, compensation for the murder of a woman is half the going rate for men. In many Muslim countries, these directives are

---

1. © 2001 TIME Inc. reprinted by permission.

incorporated into contemporary law. For a woman to prove rape in Pakistan, for example, four adult males of "impeccable" character must witness the penetration, in accordance with Shari'a.

Family law in Islamic countries generally follows the prescriptions of scripture. This is so even in a country like Egypt, where much of the legal code has been secularized. In Islam, women can have only one spouse, while men are permitted four. The legal age for girls to marry tends to be very young. Muhammad's favorite wife, A'isha, according to her biographer, was six when they wed, nine when the marriage was consummated. In Iran the legal age for marriage is nine for girls, 14 for boys. The law has occasionally been exploited by pedophiles, who marry poor young girls from the provinces, use and then abandon them. In 2000 the Iranian Parliament voted to raise the minimum age for girls to 14, but this year, a legislative oversight body dominated by traditional clerics vetoed the move. An attempt by conservatives to abolish Yemen's legal minimum age of 15 for girls failed, but local experts say it is rarely enforced anyway. (The onset of puberty is considered an appropriate time for a marriage to be consummated.)

Wives in Islamic societies face great difficulty in suing for divorce, but husbands can be released from their vows virtually on demand, in some places merely by saying "I divorce you" three times. Though in most Muslim states, divorces are entitled to alimony, in Pakistan it lasts only three months, long enough to ensure the woman isn't pregnant. The same three-month rule applies even to the Muslim minority in India. There, a national law provides for long-term alimony, but to appease Islamic conservatives, authorities exempted Muslims.

Fear of poverty keeps many Muslim women locked in bad marriages, as does the prospect of losing their children. Typically, fathers win custody of boys over the age of six and girls after the onset of puberty. Maryam, an Iranian woman, says she has stayed married for 20 years to a philandering opium addict she does not love because she fears losing guardianship of her teenage daughter. "Islam supposedly gives me the right to divorce," she says. "But what about my rights afterward?"

Women's rights are compromised further by a section in the Koran, sura 4:34, that has been interpreted to say that men have "pre-eminence" over women or that they are "overseers" of women. The verse goes on to say that the husband of an insubordinate wife should first admonish her, then leave her to sleep alone and finally beat her. Wife beating is so prevalent in the Muslim world that social workers who assist battered women in Egypt, for example, spend much of their time trying to convince victims that their husbands' violent acts are unacceptable.

Beatings are not the worst of female suffering. Each year hundreds of Muslim women die in "honor killings"—murders by husbands or male relatives of women suspected of disobedience, usually a sexual indiscretion or marriage against the family's wishes. Typically, the killers are punished lightly, if at all. In Jordan a man who slays his wife or a close relative after catching her in the act of adultery is exempt from punishment. If the situation only suggests illicit sex, he gets a reduced sentence. The Jordanian royal family has made the rare move of condemning honor killings, but the government, fearful of offending conservatives, has not put its

> *Sexual anxiety lies at the heart of many Islamic strictures on women.*

weight behind a proposal to repeal laws that grant leniency for killers. Jordan's Islamic Action Front, a powerful political party, has issued a fatwa, or religious ruling, saying the proposal would "destroy our Islamic, social and family values by stripping men of their humanity when they surprise their wives or female relatives committing adultery."

Honor killings are an example of a practice that is commonly associated with Islam but actually has broader roots. It is based in medieval tribal culture, in which a family's authority, and ultimately its survival, was tightly linked to its honor. Arab Christians have been known to carry out honor killings. However, Muslim perpetrators often claim their crimes are justified by harsh Islamic penalties, including death for adultery. And so religious and cultural customs become confused.

Female circumcision, also called female genital mutilation, is another case in point. It involves removing part or all of a girl's clitoris and labia in an effort to reduce female sexual desire and thereby preserve chastity. FGM is widespread in sub-Saharan Africa and in Egypt, with scattered cases in Asia and other parts of the Middle East. The World Health Organization estimates that up to 140 million girls and women have undergone the procedure. Some Muslims believe it is mandated by Islam, but the practice predates Muhammad and is also common among some Christian communities.

Sexual anxiety lies at the heart of many Islamic strictures on women. They are required to cover their bodies—in varying degrees in different places—for fear they might arouse the lust of men other than their husbands. The Koran instructs women to "guard their modesty," not to "display their beauty and ornaments" and to "draw their veils." Saudi women typically don a billowy black cloak called an abaya, along with a black scarf and veil over the face; morality police enforce the dress code by striking errant women with sticks. The women of Iran and Sudan can expose the face but must cover the hair and the neck.

In most Islamic countries, coverings are technically optional. Some women, including some feminists, wear them because they like them. They find that the veil liberates them from unwanted gazes and hassles from men. But many Muslim women feel cultural and family pressure to cover themselves. Recently a Muslim fundamentalist group in the Indian province of Kashmir demanded that women start wearing veils. When the call was ignored, hooligans threw acid in the faces of uncovered women.

Limits placed on the movement of Muslim women, the jobs they can hold and their interactions with men are also rooted in fears of unchaste behavior. The Taliban took these controls to an extreme, but the Saudis are also harsh, imposing on women some of the tightest restrictions on personal and civil freedoms anywhere in the world. Saudi women are not allowed to drive. They are effectively forbidden education in fields such as engineering and law. They can teach and provide medical care to other women but are denied almost all other government jobs. Thousands have entered private business, but they must work segregated from men and in practice are barred from advancement.

Muslim women are starting to score political victories, including election to office.

Though Iran is remembered in the West mostly for its repressive ayatullahs, women there enjoy a relatively high degree of liberty. Iranian women drive cars, buy and sell property, run their own businesses, vote and hold public office. In most Muslim countries tradition keeps ordinary women at home and off the street, but Iran's avenues are crowded with women day and night. They make up 25% of the work force, a third of all government employees and 54% of college students. Still, Iranian women are—like women in much of the Arab world—forbidden to travel overseas without the permission of their husband or father, though the rule is rarely enforced in Iran.

Gender reforms are slow and hard-fought. In 1999 the Emir of Kuwait, Sheik Jaber al-Ahmed al-Sabah, issued a decree for the first time giving women the right to vote in and stand for election to the Kuwaiti parliament, the only lively Arab legislature in the Persian Gulf. Conservatives in parliament, however, blocked its implementation. In addition, the legislature has voted to segregate the sexes at Kuwait University. Morocco's government has proposed giving women more marriage and property rights and a primary role in developmental efforts, but fundamentalists are resisting the measures.

Muslim women are starting to score political victories, including election to office. In Syria 26 of the 250 members of parliament are female. In Iraq the numbers are 19 out of 250. Four Muslim countries have been or are currently led by women. In Pakistan, Bangladesh and Indonesia, they rose to prominence on the coattails of deceased fathers or husbands. But Turkey's Tansu Ciller, Prime Minister from 1993 to 1995, won entirely on her own.

Turkey is an exception to many rules. Women in Turkey are the most liberated in the Muslim world, though Malaysia and Indonesia come close, having hosted relatively progressive cultures before Islam came to Southeast Asia in the 9th century. In Turkish professional life women enjoy a level of importance that is impressive not only by the standards of other Islamic countries but also by European lights. Turkey's liberalism is a legacy of the republic's founder, Mustafa Kemal Ataturk, an aggressive secularist who gave women rights unprecedented in the Muslim world (even if he found it hard to accept women as equals in his own life). Last week the Turkish parliament went a step further by reforming family law. Previously, a man was the head of the household, able to make unilateral decisions concerning children. No more. The law also establishes community property in marriages and raises the marriageable age of girls from 15 to 18.

Around the Islamic world, women are scoring other victories, small and large. Iran's parliament recently compromised with conservative clerics to allow a single young woman to study abroad, albeit with her father's permission. Bangladesh passed legislation increasing the punishments for crimes against women, including rape, kidnapping and acid attacks. Egypt has banned female circumcision and made it easier for women to sue for divorce. In Qatar women have the right to participate in municipal elections and are promised the same rights in first-ever parliamentary balloting scheduled to take place by 2003. Bahrain has assured women voters and candidates that they will be included in new elections for its suspended parliament.

Saudi Arabia, the chief holdout, has at least pledged to start issuing ID cards to women. Today the only legal evidence of a Saudi woman's existence is the appearance of her name on her husband's card. If she gets divorced, her name goes on her father's card; if he's dead, her brother's; and if she has no brother, the card of her closest male relative, even if she scarcely knows him. Manar, 35, a Riyadh translator, thinks ID cards for women will make a real difference. "As long as you are a follower, you cannot have a separate opinion, you cannot be outspoken," she says. "Once you have a separate identity, then other things will come." For most Muslim women, there are many things left to come.

Can Islam Liberate Women?[2]

BY MADELEINE BUNTING
THE GUARDIAN, DECEMBER 8, 2001

We're sitting in a stylish club, ArRum, in Clerkenwell, central London. Firelight is flickering on the leather sofas, there is contemporary art on the walls and delicious "fusion" food on the table, but what distinguishes this club from its many neighbours is that it is Muslim, there is no alcohol on the menu and downstairs there's a prayer room. The stylish place conveys a complex ethos—modern, yet true to its Muslim identity.

A suitable setting, then, chosen by the six Muslim women who agreed to meet me to discuss Islam and the position of women. All university graduates, all in their mid-twenties in careers ranging from journalism to teaching, all have chosen in the past few years to wear the hijab (a scarf wrapped tightly around their heads to conceal every wisp of hair). Most strikingly, however, all of these women fluently and cogently articulate how they believe Islam has liberated and empowered them. The Islam they describe is a million miles away from that of the Taliban, let alone the Islam practised in many Muslim countries from Pakistan to Saudi Arabia, but they insist—and back up their points with Koranic references—that the Islam they first discovered when they were teenagers is true to the Prophet's teachings. They don't need western feminism, which, they argue, developed as a reaction against the particular expression of western patriarchy. Within the Koranic tradition and the life of the Prophet lie the rights and inspiration a woman needs to achieve her full potential—the challenge ahead is to educate Muslim girls and women so that they have that knowledge. They justify wearing the hijab, either as a public statement of their own spiritual quest, or of their political identity in a world where Islam perceives itself as under threat, or both.

Shagufta, the 25-year-old editor of the Muslim magazine *Q News*, was brought up in London, in a traditional Pakistani home where the emphasis was on cultural conservatism rather than piety. A marriage to a cousin from Pakistan was arranged for her when she was about 10. Her parents had no wish for her to continue her education, and her adoption of the hijab was her rebellion against this traditional cultural background. "When I first put on hijab, my parents were shocked," she says. They would have been happier for her to wear the Pakistani shalwar kameez and a loose headscarf. "But I found liberation in Islam. It gave me the confidence to insist on a good education and reject the arranged marriage. Islam made sense to me, and I could understand it, as opposed to what I had grown up with. Plus, it was compatible with being British—being a British Muslim, rather than Pakistani."

Shagufta was influenced by her friend Soraya's decision to put on hijab. Soraya's French Catholic/Muslim liberal background could not have been more different but, like Shagufta, she found in the Koran an affirmation of herself as a woman: "The Koran says that men and women are equal in the eyes of God, and that we are like a garment for each other to protect one another."

Again and again, the women emphasize these two themes, evoked in richly poetic Koranic metaphor: first, the equality of the sexes in the eyes of God (the most meaningful equality of all, they argue), and second, the complementarity of the sexes. As the Koran puts it, "I created you from one soul, and from that soul I created its mate so that you may live in harmony and love."

It is true that there is plenty of material in the Koran that is more egalitarian than the western Christian tradition, which was heavily influenced by the misogyny of Greek thought. Perhaps the most fundamental is that the Islamic God does not have a gender. Arabic may refer to him by use of the male pronoun, but he is never described as "father" or "lord" as he is in the Judaeo-Christian tradition. Indeed, the Islamic God has characteristics that are expressly feminine; one of his most important "names" is al-Rahman (the All-Compassionate) from the Arabic *rahma*, which comes from the word *rahim*, meaning womb. In Islamic mysticism, the divinely beloved is female, unlike in Christian mysticism—for example, Bernini's famous statue in Rome of St Teresa of Avila is in love with the male Christ. As one Muslim women, Sartaz Aziz, writes, "I am deeply grateful that my first ideas of God were formed by Islam, because I was able to think of the Highest Power as one without sex or race and thus completely unpatriarchal."

> *There is plenty of material in the Koran that is more egalitarian than the western Christian tradition.*

Jasmin also escaped from an arranged marriage by discovering Islam. Her transition to full religious observance came after university, when she was working for a television company. "I went to Agadir on holiday, returned with a fantastic tan, but went back to work in a hijab. One week in a skimpy swimsuit, the next in a hijab. One of my colleagues couldn't understand. She was crying as she said to me, "One moment you were a sex kitten, the next you're all wrapped up. She thought I was repressing myself; I felt I had achieved liberation.

"The attention I got from the other sex changed. Instead of a sexual approach, they had to take an interest in what was in my head and in my personality, rather than my body. Sometimes, when I flick through a fashion magazine, I think of taking off the hijab, but it passes quickly. Too many women exert power through their sexuality, and that's degrading to women. It's a form of enslavement."

The importance of each of these women's decisions to wear the hijab leads quickly to a heated discussion about where and how and why one expresses one's sexuality. All the women agree that this is one of the biggest sources of misunderstanding between western feminists and Muslim women. They do not wish to express their sexuality in public, and believe that its proper place is in the privacy of an intimate relationship. Sexuality is not to be used to assert power but to express love, they add. What they hotly deny is that veiling, and modesty in public, is a form of repression. It is not about shame of the female body, as western feminists sometimes insist, but about claiming privacy over their bodies. The Moroccan writer, Fatima Mernissi, ponders on how, in the west, women reclaiming their bodies has led to the public expression of their sexuality, whereas in Islam it is about modesty. The associations with shame and repression stem from the influence of the Christian tradition's hostility to sexuality and hence women, and the legacy of confusion and guilt that has bequeathed western society. Islam, on the other hand, has a healthy honesty and acceptance of human sexuality, which is evident in a wealth of detail in Islamic jurisprudence, they argue.

Dr Tim Winter, a Muslim convert and Cambridge lecturer, probably one of the most respected Islamic scholars in Britain, corroborates the assertion that Islam does not accept the mythology of Eve seducing Adam, and thus triggering the Fall and the endless cycle of death and procreation. According to Christian thought, sex was the result of human beings' fallen state and was traditionally regarded with distaste; celibacy was promoted as a sublimation of sexual energies in pursuit of God, epitomised by Christ's celibate life.

Nothing provides a sharper contrast with that model of holiness than the life of the Prophet Muhammad, who took 12 wives after the death of his first wife, Khadija. His love for his wives and sexual relationships with them are referred to in the hadith (the sayings of the Prophet). One reference even extols the Prophet's virility, revealing how he could visit all of his wives in one night. This, says Dr. Winter, makes him a full, complete man, closer to models of holiness such as Krishna or a Jewish patriarch such as King Solomon with his many wives.

Indeed, one of the injunctions on a husband is that he must sexually satisfy his wife; the Prophet recommends foreplay, and a great Islamic scholar, Imam Ghazali, warned men not to come too quickly. As Mernissi points out in *Beyond the Veil*, Islam always understood that women's sexuality was active, while western Christianity socialised women into accepting sexual passivity— the "lie back and think of England" approach. The latter, argues Mernissi, was a way of internalising in women the control on female sexuality that men wanted; Muslim cultures used external controls of segregation and male authority.

Back at ArRum, the women say that, for them, the affirmation of women's sexuality in Islam renders pointless many of the battles fought by western feminists. They have no need of Madonna-style exhibitionism to assert the power of female sexuality. Indeed, one woman said that the one achievement of feminism that she admired was to break down the restrictive passivity of Victorian perceptions of female sexuality.

Aisha and Khadija come out as the two top Koranic role models for these women, and both are quoted as examples of the prominence of women in the development of Islam. Khadija, the Prophet's first wife, was old (40) by the standards of the day when she proposed to the 25-year-old Mohammed. His first believer, she was his sole wife and a close adviser until her death. It was only then that the Prophet took other wives; he married several older widows, but Aisha was much younger than the Prophet, highly intelligent and assertive. There are several stories of how jealous

---

All the women I interviewed roll off a long list of hadiths and Koranic verses to support women's rights.

---

she was of the Prophet's other wives and of how much he loved her. He died in her arms, and she became one of the first teachers of Islam after his death.

All the women I interviewed roll off a long list of hadiths and Koranic verses to support women's rights: the right to education; the right to work and their right to keep the money they earn, while men must use their earnings to look after their womenfolk; property rights; in one school of Islamic thought, women don't have to clean or cook for their husbands unless they are paid for it (wages for housework long before the 20th century thought it had invented it); the fact that the Prophet, according to Aisha, was something of a new man, and used to clean and sew when he wasn't praying; and then there is the praise lavished on the emotional qualities engendered by motherhood of nurturing and patience, with the Prophet's repeated injunctions to honour your mother.

But there are other parts of Koranic tradition that, to a western eye, seem deeply shocking. By some accounts, Aisha was only nine when her marriage to the Prophet (who was then in his fifties) was consummated. Or that, although the Koran insists that a man should treat all his wives equally, the Prophet admitted that he had a favourite, Aisha. Or the controversial incident when the Prophet glimpsed the wife of his adopted son and, after she had been divorced, he married her. Worst of all to a sceptical western eye, the Prophet often invoked God to explain such incidents.

This is very sensitive territory for devout Muslim women. For believers, the Prophet's life was perfect and according to God's plan. They haven't the freedom to develop the critical analytical tradition of western feminism, which has been so important in understanding how patriarchy has influenced religious, legal, moral and political systems. So, either they offer long explanations (such as that Aisha's age was due to the custom of the time and was probably not much different from the Virgin Mary's), or they acknowledge there are some things that they find very difficult. As one woman put it, "When I read about the Prophet's life, I feel it is unjust: he favoured one wife over another, and that makes me uneasy. I haven't found a scholar who can explain it, but I believe in a just God and the wisdom of the Prophet, so I take it on trust. That's faith. To have real knowledge of Islam is to study it for a long time; eventually, I might find an interpretation that satisfies me."

The fact remains that polygamy, though by no means the norm, is practised in all Muslim countries.

These are the sort of explanations that simply fail to convince a sceptical western mind. Perhaps one of the hardest things for a woman to accept in the Koranic tradition is polygamy and, indeed, many of the women I spoke to conceded some unease here. Although some were prepared to consider a polygamous marriage, they all confessed that it would be very difficult; one married woman had even included a prohibition on a second wife in her pre-nuptial contract (a Koranic invention that is mutually negotiated and can cover everything from housework to the frequency of sex). They had various explanations for why the Koran allows men to take four wives, such as the need to provide for war widows in a nomadic warrior culture. With the advent of the welfare state, such arguments are hard to sustain, as several of the women admitted.

Dr Rabia Malik, a psychotherapist, sometimes finds herself in the difficult position of having clients who want to take another wife: "Usually, the first wife doesn't satisfy them intellectually or sexually, and they start to think of taking a second wife, and I try to help them find solutions within their existing relationship."

Both Dr Malik and Humera Khan, founder of the women-run organisation An-Nisa, believe that the Koranic conditions on polygamy are so hard to meet that they virtually rule it out: only those men who can treat their wives equally are allowed more than one. But the fact remains that polygamy, though by no means the norm, is practised in all Muslim countries. Mernissi believes that this is an explicit humiliation of women, because it asserts that one woman can't satisfy a man; interestingly, Mernissi, a stout critic of certain aspects of Islam, is regarded with some suspicion by many of the women I spoke to.

Dr Winter takes a different tack, defending polygamy by arguing that it is widely practised in the west, from Bill Clinton to Prince Charles. It is, he says, simply more cruel in the west, because all the "wives" bar one are deprived of legal status and dignity. Controversially, he insists that "men are biologically designed to desire a plurality of women . . . and will always do so."

Such gender stereotypes (which are guaranteed to infuriate most western feminists) peppered all my interviews. The Muslim women I spoke to happily talked of women as being "more emotional" and men as "more rational." This was not the result of socialisation, but of nature, and western science was only finally catching up with Koranic insight into the profound differences and complementarity of the sexes. But they denied that this meant that women had to stay at home and men go out to work—they pointed out that many Muslim women work, both in the UK and abroad. The point was that equality did not mean the same in the two cultures, so that the preoccupation in western feminism to achieve and compete on equal terms in the public sphere was a response to the west's own history of seeing women as inferior. What the vast majority of women really want to do is to have and care for children, they said, and a genuinely equal society would be the one that honours that role and provides them with the financial resources to concentrate on it. After such responsibilities have been met (and, with the extended family, there are many to help with childcare), the woman is free to work. To Muslim women, equality means giving their femininity equal worth in the purpose of every human life—to know God. That's as possible in the domestic life of home and children as it is in the marketplace.

As Humera points out, Islam is a home-centred, family-oriented religion that, given the central role of women in both, explains the power of women in Muslim society. Part of the reason why westerners often don't grasp this, explains Dr Winter, is because this home life is private. Muslim cities don't have the grand civic spaces of European cities; they have little alleyways and the vibrant family life takes place behind high walls. The debate about the balance between the private and the public sphere has become much more acute, he says, with the development of industrialisation and the men leaving the home to work long hours. Dr Winter is sharply critical of the west's resolution of the balance between private family life and public life, arguing that the home has almost become a dormitory where the exhausted two-career couple meet briefly, rather than a setting in which children and the elderly can thrive, and where there is a range of familial relationships.

The way in which the traditional segregation is breaking down is one of the most problematic issues in current Islamic thinking. Dr. Winter believes that some form of segregation would benefit women in the way that single-sex schooling helps girls develop more confidence, and would help prevent the problems of marriage breakdown experienced in the west: "Segregation has proved a spur in Iran to employing more women, for example," he says. "They now have quotas in the universities so women can be taught by women." But he goes on to acknowledge that "the practice of early Islam did not mean strict segregation, and the historic record is of a more relaxed and open society."

Many Muslims argue that the Prophet's injunction that no one address his wives except through a veil is the model for relations between the sexes. Strict segregation with women confined to the private sphere has been the rule in most Muslim cultures, though rarely as extreme as under the Taliban in Afghanistan. Dr Winter admits that total segregation in the workplace is not practicable, so that leaves devout Muslims with a dilemma of balancing the woman's right to work and be educated with the need to keep to Koranic tradition. The women I met at ArRum all live with their families or relatives, yet they work in mixed environments and travel to attend study courses (they claim they are allowed to travel more than 50 miles from home without a male companion if they are studying Islam). They say they naturally prefer a degree of segrega-

---

> *Many Muslims argue that the Prophet's injunction that no one address his wives except through a veil is the model for relations between the sexes.*

---

tion, enjoying deeper female friendships, rather than the confusing ambiguities of friendships with men. But the result is intense pressure on the women themselves.

All the women I spoke to, without a moment's hesitation, dismiss the restrictions in the many Islamic countries that oppress women as unIslamic "cultural practices," for example women not being allowed to drive or travel alone in Saudi Arabia. Blaming Islam for practices such as female circumcision, they claim, is the equivalent of blaming feminism for domestic violence—it is linking totally unrelated phenomena. Again, the absence of a critical analysis of the tradition is striking, and there is no answer to the question of why, if Islam offers women a bill of rights, it has not liberated more women. The point, they reply, is that male chauvinism and its bid to control women exists the world over; it simply takes different forms, and when women are educated and know what Islam really means, they can fight back.

They refuse to accept that some of the provisions of Sharia law seem to institutionalise inequality, such as the rule that a woman's evidence must be backed up by another woman. Shagufta admitted that she could see how an outsider might find the idea of stoning adulterers to death, the punishment prescribed in Sharia, as horrific, but, as her friends quickly pointed out, it requires four witnesses to the act of sexual penetration to convict an adulterer—a standard of proof so exacting, they claim, that it would be virtually impossible to achieve.

What women such as Shagufta, Maha, Soraya, Fareena and Jasmin want is to return to the freedoms that Islam brought women in the 7th century and beyond, when women became prominent Islamic scholars, poets and thinkers. "We need a reformation in this global community," said Fareena. "We need to go back to the Islam of the golden age from the 7th to the 13th century." Soraya recognises that this desire to return to the 7th century is paradoxically close to the avowed aims of the Taliban and other fundamentalist groups, but the struggle is over interpretations of what is the true Islam, and British Muslim women are all too well aware of how fragile their position is, defending themselves against criticism from all sides—both from the westerners who accuse them of being oppressed and from the traditional Muslim cultures shocked by their independence and "westernisation."

The biggest danger is of a backlash in which the position of women is politicised as it was under the Taliban, where women were not allowed to work or be educated. In such a context, Dr Winter says, women are repressed to salve the sense of Islamic pride wounded by western hegemony and the savage poverty of many Muslim countries. Women are the traditional symbol of honour, and find themselves subjected to restrictions to safeguard their (and the next generation's) contamination from western culture.

So there is a striking bravery in these British Muslim women in their struggle to understand what they see as timeless truths and apply them to 21st-century life. They assiduously attend home-study circles, travel to California and the Middle East for special courses, take up correspondence courses with Islamic scholars and read to deepen their knowledge of Islam, and they believe they are pioneering a spiritual renewal and a rediscovery of their faith that empowers women.

American by Birth, Muslim by Choice[3]

BY KATHERINE MILLETT
CHICAGO TRIBUNE, DECEMBER 2, 2001

In the aftermath of September 11, struggling to understand mysteries of Muslim culture that had suddenly become frightening and dark, I picked up the phone and called Seema Imam, an American woman who had converted to Islam. She had made a strong impression on me two years earlier, when I listened to her tell a civil rights conference about the discrimination she felt after she left her family farm in central Illinois, became a Muslim and married a man from Pakistan. She wears hijab, the head scarf and robe that cover all but the face and hands. People who see her in the street sometimes yell, "Go back home." The day after the terrorist attacks, a man spat at her in her neighborhood. Recently, she has been pinning an American flag on her clothes.

She agreed to explain to me why a woman born in America, free to choose the way she wants to live, would convert to Islam, a religion that appears to treat women as inferior to men. Even if Muslim women in America lead less oppressive lives than they could in Afghanistan or Saudi Arabia, where a woman may be thrashed for letting her veil slip in public, or for walking to the drugstore at night without a male escort, they live by a far more strict set of rules than most of their neighbors. Why would they choose to limit their choices in dress and marriage, never again to socialize with men, run on the beach or drink a beer? Imam's surprising answer, echoed by Elizabeth Martin, a convert who grew up Catholic in the Beverly neighborhood, is that Islam is a religion that makes sense to her and a social system that actually "liberates" her from what she experienced as sexism in mainstream culture.

"Family and religion are very strong in Islam," says Imam, 48. "Women are valued for who they are, for what they contribute, not just their physical attributes. I look at American women's clothes, and the advertising that exploits them, and I think mainstream culture is very hard on women."

Adds Martin: "Western women don't realize how deep misogyny goes in their culture. The whole dating system needs a revolution. Men here have it made. They get fun and games, and if a woman gets pregnant, they tell her to get an abortion or raise the baby her-

---

self. As a Muslim woman, I have dignity and freedom. The Koran says very clearly that men and women are spiritually equal, and that they fulfill each other as partners."

Imam and Martin, 39, are among a growing number of women converts to Islam, according to the Institute of Islamic Information and Education in Chicago. Mary Ali, the institute's co-director and herself a convert who grew up in Iowa, says she does not know exact numbers for the Chicago area, but estimates that between 50,000 and 60,000 of local Muslim converts are African-American, and that Caucasians and Hispanics are converting at an increasing rate. The institute says there are about 350,000 to 400,000 Muslims in the Chicago area.

Imam began life as Martha Crandall, one of five children in a family that raised soybeans in Cerro Gordo, a farming town of about 1,500 people east of Decatur. When I saw her two years ago addressing the civil rights conference about anti-Muslim sentiment in the U.S., her appearance struck me as incongruous. Her healthy, farm-girl face, round and friendly, seemed constrained by the scarf wrapped tightly around her head and fastened under her chin with a silver pin. She wore glasses and a long, somber dress, decorated with a little embroidery. It loosely covered her, all the way to her ankles and wrists.

Yet wearing hijab could not disguise her obvious intelligence or her confident personality—two resources that she drew on heavily the morning of September 11. At 10 A.M., she had to walk into a classroom at National-Louis University in Wheaton, face the three professors on her doctoral committee, and present the topic she had been studying for three years to earn her Ph.D. in education: discrimination against Muslims in American society and public schools.

She later described the experience as "surreal." Hijacked airplanes had just crashed into the World Trade Center and the Pentagon, and media reports were naming Muslim militants as suspects. As the towers collapsed and the Pentagon burned, Imam stuck to her thesis—that negative attitudes among teachers are fed by a "terrorist icon" in American culture, and that it unfairly brands all Muslims as terrorists. Teachers should respect the cultural and religious differences of their Muslim students, she said. They should help Muslim girls feel comfortable wearing hijab in the classroom, and should tell their classes about the Islamic fast of Ramadan and the winter holiday of Eid, just as they teach about Christmas and Hanukkah.

"We didn't talk about what was happening until we finished discussing the dissertation," says Imam, who recently was granted her degree. "It was so horrible. While I was at home, getting ready to leave for my meeting, I saw the second plane crash, live on television. First I thought of all those innocent people dying, and their families. Then I thought of what this would do to us as Muslims. I knew we'd be blamed, just as we were at first for the Oklahoma City bombing."

For several days after the September 11 attacks, many of the Muslim women she knows stayed inside, afraid to be seen in public. Far more easily recognized as Muslims than men, they feared insults and violence and did not want to risk exposure by standing at bus stops or taking public transportation. When they finally left their houses, they traveled in pairs.

Near the mosque Imam attends on West 93rd Street in Bridgeview, which serves a predominantly Arab population of Muslim families in the southwest suburbs, hundreds of non-Muslim demonstrators had gathered several nights in a row to stage demonstrations she describes as "ominous, with squealing tires and lots of commotion."

About a week later, Imam invited me to visit her at home in Hickory Hills, to talk about what she calls "the joys of being free and

---

"I make a daily choice to wear hijab, and really, I have never regretted it. I think many Muslim women feel as I do, that a woman's power is in her modesty."—Seema Imam, a **Muslim convert**

Islamic," and to introduce me to Elizabeth Martin, who also attends the Bridgeview mosque.

American flags waved conspicuously from three out of every four front porches in her neighborhood of split-level houses and trim lawns. She greeted me at the door and smiled tactfully when I walked in and stepped on her prayer rug. She quietly rolled it up and moved it to a safer place, then showed me into her comfortable living room where framed verses of the Koran, rendered in elegant calligraphy, hung on the walls.

As we sat down, I asked her whether she ever took off her hijab, either to fend off negative reactions after the attacks or simply to relax in her old way of life.

"No! No way!" she said adamantly. "I make a daily choice to wear hijab, and really, I have never regretted it. I think many Muslim women feel as I do, that a woman's power is in her modesty."

Yet she acknowledges that looking different from virtually all the people she works and transacts business with can be painful. She considers the challenge especially great for young women, who feel pressures to fit in socially at school. "It's hard on anyone, unless your faith is strong."

When Imam first encountered Islam, 30 years ago, "it attracted me like a magnet," she says. She had started college at Eastern Illinois University in Charleston, and for the first time in her life, she met people from the larger world. In Cerro Gordo, she had never known African-Americans, Jews or even Catholics, let alone Muslims. She had been brought up devoutly in the Methodist Church. She played the organ on Sundays and went to Sunday school and vacation Bible school. But when she got to college and met students from foreign countries, especially Muslim students, everything changed.

"It was Ramadan, and I saw how disciplined and structured the religion was. The Muslim students were fasting every day, so the international student club met after dark, when they could all eat together. That impressed me." For the first five months of her freshman year, she studied the Koran on her own. At the end of the year, she converted to Islam.

The next year, she married a Muslim man, who she says was concerned about breaking custom by not marrying a woman chosen by his parents. Muslims often marry without ever having talked to each other, although both partners must agree to the arrangement. Imam's first marriage ended in divorce after her husband returned to Pakistan due to illness, and she has since remarried.

Attracted to the theology of Islam, she also welcomed its discipline as an antidote to some of the things that had disillusioned her as a teenager in Cerro Gordo. "This was the same God I had grown up with in the cornfields of Illinois, but in Islam it was much more than a Sunday God. I liked the daily practice of prayer.

"I also liked the dedication Muslims have to their religion as a way of life. In the town where I grew up, the grownups told us we should respect other people, but if a black person came to town, they would not let him stay overnight."

Imam also recalls her shock when she saw one of her teachers, a man Imam particularly admired, snuggling at a shopping mall food court with a girl less than half his age. "I knew his wife and kids, and I knew what he was doing was wrong."

She practiced the religion privately for several years and continued to appear in public as a typical college student and young wife. Inwardly, she says, she felt tremendous relief, a sense of having escaped the self-conscious turmoil of her high school years. She had hated her timid forays into the dating scene.

"There is a certain 'petiteness' that is required," she says, her blue eyes laughing behind her wire-rimmed glasses, "that is very hard on a lot of girls. They have to be thin, they have to dress in such a way that they can give themselves—to whom, for what? One of the things I felt when I converted was relief that I would never again have to shop for a strapless dress or a swimsuit.

"Besides," she adds, "I haven't had a bad hair day since I started wearing hijab."

Though it may have certain advantages, the veiling of women is one of the things about Islam that non-Muslim American women generally find hardest to accept, according to Jane Crosthwaite, head of the department of religion at Mt. Holyoke College."Requiring women to be veiled is a way of erasing them from the landscape," says Crosthwaite. "The idea behind it seems to be that since men can't control themselves, they veil the thing they most desire."

Muslims observe a strict division between the sexes in the mosque, at school and in social settings. One of Muhammad's most-quoted sayings is, "When a man and woman are alone together, Satan is their third."

Islam is not the only religion that trembles at the power of sex, Crosthwaite notes. "All religious traditions organize gender relations. The American Shakers may have chosen the most extreme model by vowing to remain celibate, but many religions, including Judaism and Christianity, have separated the sexes for worship."

The veiling of women is one of the things about Islam that non-Muslim American women generally find hardest to accept.

Dating is generally prohibited for all Muslim young people, even in the U.S. "We have marriage first, love later," explains Abdul Hadeem Dogar, director of the Islamic Foundation in Villa Park. "Marriage is an obligation in Islam for men and women. It is more important than in Christianity, perhaps because Jesus did not marry." Muhammad, whose life is considered exemplary, had nine wives at various times during his 62 years.

Once married, Dogar says, a Muslim woman generally is expected to have children, take care of them and not work outside the home. Exceptions are made for women to become doctors and teachers so they can attend to other women, though these exceptions appear to be aimed at serving the community—and perpetuating gender segregation—more than at fulfilling the desire of any particular woman to develop herself professionally.

Western women who convert to Islam often consider this closely structured way of life more appealing than the kind of freedom they find in mainstream society, says Crosthwaite. "Some people get tired of having to negotiate for everything in life, for their space, their financial security and their sexual identity. Having these things settled for them by religious beliefs may free them to do other things with their energies. But they should be aware that there are opportunities as well as dangers they are veiling. They are still part of the real world, with all its ambivalence."

Imam has directed her energies both inside and outside the home. She and her second husband, Syed Shahab Imam, have raised seven children. He works for the Illinois Department of Transportation;

she teaches teachers at National-Louis University, supervises her student teachers in several public school systems, advocates for civil rights as a founding member of a local non-profit organization, Muslim Americans for Civil Rights and Legal Defense, and somehow finds time to home-school her youngest son, Ibrahim, a polite, energetic 2nd grader.

She readily concedes that Muslim women in America can do things—get an education, work outside the home, travel freely—prohibited for women in Afghanistan or Saudi Arabia, a point emphasized by others familiar with how Islam is practiced around the world.

"It is important to recognize that American converts live a particular expression of Islam," says Crosthwaite. "They may want to purify themselves from aspects of our society that bother them, but they still have the advantages of living in this society."

Imam interrupted our interview at noon and summoned Ibrahim to drive to the mosque for Friday prayer. Because of the recent attacks, Chicago police officers were directing traffic around the brick building, which is flanked by two Muslim schools. Imam was the first principal for Universal School, where girls and boys are educated together only until 4th grade; thereafter, classrooms are segregated.

At the front of the mosque, we waved goodbye to Ibrahim. He ran up a flight of concrete steps and disappeared into the main sanctuary, the men's prayer room. I followed Imam around a corner and down some stairs to the women's prayer room in the basement. It is a former school classroom with an orange carpet, fluorescent lights and lines of tape on the floor to orient the rows of women east toward Mecca.

There were dozens of women inside. I was the only one with an uncovered head. A few of the women greeted Imam and ignored me. Others smiled warmly at me but seemed surprised when I tried to shake hands. Their grasp felt timid, or at least unaccustomed. I later learned that Muslim women are permitted to shake hands with other women, but they seldom do. They are strictly forbidden to shake hands with men.

The Bridgeview congregation has grown rapidly, and between 400 and 600 women pray together on an average Friday. The noon prayer has been split into two services, which the women follow by responding, unheard, to the image of their male leader on a television monitor. He is upstairs, leading the men.

Imam is untroubled by the segregation of the sexes, and says she often prefers it in social situations. When families entertain, the women and men get together in different parts of the house. Imam says the privacy of this arrangement makes women more open and confident than they feel in the company of men. "It's not that different from the way men and women split up for Monday night football," she says. Families often buy two-flats or rent adjoining apartments so that men and women can spend their days separately.

Her decision to convert has not been without cost. She was estranged from her parents as well as her four brothers and sisters for 14 years after she made her pilgrimage to Mecca in 1978 and started wearing hijab. Now she is reconciled with her family, but she knows that her decision hurt them initially, which was painful for her as well.

"It was something I needed to do," she says.

Upon meeting Elizabeth Martin, a vivacious and amusing woman who lives in Oak Lawn, I immediately feel old. She asks me if I remember the ERA, the Equal Rights Amendment that almost became part of the U.S. Constitution in the 1970s and would have guaranteed equal rights for women.

When families entertain, the women and men get together in different parts of the house.

"Well, I used to wear an ERA bracelet," she says, moving the sleeve of her long dress to reveal her wrist. "I was a feminist, and I still am." Martin, who kept her name when she married Amer Haleem, in accordance with Saudi Arabian custom, schools their eight children at home. Martin does not work outside the home, but she regularly encounters Muslim and non-Muslim men in the course of community work and business transactions.

"Dealing with men while wearing hijab is a real kick," she says. "I encourage all women to try it. When you're talking with a man and you give him, up front and in his face, the message that you are a modest and serious person, then he must deal with your thoughts, and not the wonders of his macho-ness.

"As for the 'liberated' American woman, do you mean some chick in a two-inch skirt, spine-deforming spike heels, a masked face and a coifed head that cost her oodles in money and more in precious time? If she wants to tell me I'm dressing for men—well, I would humbly disagree with the choices she has made.

"Let's face it," says Martin, "if a woman in mainstream society is not willing to sleep around with a series of guys—men who are obligated to demonstrate little, if any, concern for her self and her future—then she will have a hard time finding a husband. Islam really forces men to be responsible for and committed to the women in their lives. This is something some feminists may scoff at, but for me personally, it's been a great blessing."

She acknowledges that a Muslim man can divorce his wife merely by saying, "I divorce you" three times, and he is virtually guaranteed legal custody of the children because he is financially responsible for them under Islamic law. Martin cites this as a major problem for women, although she points out that because of the rule, Muslim men probably are less likely than others to shirk their duty to their children after divorce.

Islamic law also requires men to pay dowries to their wives. The first payment may take the form of a wedding gift—a valuable piece of jewelry, for example—but if the couple divorces, a second payment, agreed upon before the marriage, serves as "insurance" for the wife. Dowries of $100,000 are not uncommon among local professionals, says Martin, and $20,000 would be a typical dowry for a working-class couple.

Martin grew up Catholic in the Beverly neighborhood of Chicago, graduating from Mother McAuley Liberal Arts High School. Martin's identity had always been tied to her parish and to the larger Catholic communities of Beverly and the Christian faithful worldwide. Yet within a few months of starting college, she left both Beverly and Rome. At Richard J. Daley Community College she fell under the spell of an evangelical Protestant group, the Campus Crusade for Christ.

"I knew that I wanted to be a worshiper," she says, "and what appealed to me was the personal commitment to God that I saw in these students. They had very immediate relationships with God. Catholicism seemed rigid and ritualistic in comparison. Pretty soon, I wanted to save everybody."

Martin became especially concerned about saving the soul of Amer Haleem, a Saudi man and an older student who had recently been discharged from the Navy. They met in a philosophy course. "We were talking about existentialism, and he and I were the two that ended up arguing for a religious point of view," Martin says. "Religion was extremely important to both of us, but he was Muslim and I was Christian. So I asked him if he had ever read the Bible, and he said, 'Have you ever read the Koran?' " She is now married to Haleem, with whom she has raised eight children.

Martin says she was drawn to Islam for several reasons. Its "rock-solid" theology made more sense to her than some Christian teachings. She says she "never really understood the Trinity" and wanted to worship one God. In addition, she was attracted to Islam's concept of individual accountability, which calls on Muslims to earn entrance to heaven by submitting to God's will on Earth. She contrasts this with the Christian idea that "Jesus died for your sins," which to her implies salvation through the act of another. Moreover, she notes that the Koran was written after the Bible, and thinks that to believe only the Bible is to ignore the final scriptural revelation from God.

Martin's theological reasons for converting to Islam are fairly typical of people coming from Christian backgrounds, according to Karen Armstrong, a former nun who has written extensively about Islam, Christianity and Judaism. As Armstrong noted in "The History of God," the divinity of Jesus is a problematic concept for many people, in part because it tends to encapsulate the "word of God" in his life and preclude the validity of the later Koran as scripture.

After she converted, Martin spent six painful years out of communication with her family in Beverly. "My sisters thought I was ruining my life when I converted," she says, "but now they think I made the right choice. They wonder how I managed to raise my kids the way I did. They say my children are polite and respectful, and I guess that isn't so common anymore."

Martin acknowledges, somewhat reluctantly, that Muslim family life is not perfect. For example, domestic violence is a major problem among Muslims here as well as abroad, she says.

"Muslims almost never completely live up to Islam," she says. "It runs the full gamut, from people who are dedicated to the religion to those who abuse its privileges. I see racism too. Muslims suffer from all the same diseases as the rest of society."

But Martin has no regrets about her decision to convert, and does not feel that being a Muslim woman is depriving her of a satisfying social life. She recently gave a party for her oldest child, a girl of 18,

---

"My sisters thought I was ruining my life when I converted, . . . but now they think I made the right choice."—**Elizabeth Martin, a Muslim convert**

---

who was moving away from home. "I had a big group, about 60 women and girls. A lot of them wore elegant clothes, makeup and styled their hair. As long as men will not be present, we don't have to wear hijab.

"I can't tell you how pleased all the non-Muslim women in my family were. They said they had never had so much fun at a party. I can't say we miss anything by not partying with the guys. Frankly, I like not having the burden of making conversation with my husband's friends. Men tend to dominate social groups, and women act so differently when they're not around."

Islam and Gender Roles

Rules for living an Islamic life come from two sources: the Koran and the Sharia.

The Koran is believed to be the literal word of God, recited to the prophet Muhammad, recorded in a book about the length of the New Testament of the Bible. Many Muslims commit the Koran to memory. Sharia is the "common law" of Islam based on religious principles that derive from the life of Muhammad, the last messenger of God and a mortal filled with divine knowledge and an exemplary sense of morality. His words and actions were recorded by various people in a text known as the hadith. Some sources of hadith are considered more reliable than others.

Sharia interprets both the Koran and hadith. A kind of "common law," it fills shelves of books with a code of rules, analysis and commentary. Different governments may find support for their laws and policies in different provisions of sharia.

The Sharia includes these rules governing gender roles:

- Muslim women should stay home as much as practicable, depending on their economic circumstances and the norms of their surrounding society.

- The husband is the head of the household. He may consult his wife, but final decisions rest with him alone.

- A husband must support his wife financially, even if she is a millionaire, in return for which she obeys him.

- Men are obligated to support the unmarried women in their families.

- To avoid tempting men beyond the limits of their self-control, which Islam sets at a lower threshold than mainstream American culture, women cover themselves in public. From the age of 10 or 12, they wear loose clothing and head scarves except when they are at home, in the exclusive company of immediate family.

- Men and women do not mix in social or educational settings after age 10. They pray in different parts of the mosque and gather in different parts of private residences.

- A Muslim man may marry a non-Muslim woman, but a Muslim woman cannot marry outside the faith.

- Marriages can be quickly performed in the presence of witnesses. The man and woman need only declare publicly that they are husband and wife.

- A man has the right to divorce his wife by saying, three times, not in anger, "I divorce you."

- A woman can separate herself from her husband, but she must have the assistance of men in official positions to dissolve her marriage.

- A woman receives a dowry from her husband when she marries, and she can keep it even if the marriage dissolves.

IV. Islam and Democracy

Editor's Introduction

Most Muslim nations are led by military dictators and absolute monarchs, rather than a democratic system of government. Any attempt to change social or political attitudes in the Muslim world thus requires democratic reform. The implementation of democratic systems of government in Muslim nations across the Middle East and Africa could have a serious impact on the advancement of women's rights, the process of law, foreign policy, and the understanding of Islam itself throughout the world. A major transition such as this would require a repudiation of the views of such rulers as King Fahd of Saudi Arabia, who says Islam does not permit democracy while using vague passages in the Qur'an to justify his position. Moreover, the question is made thorny by the popularity of Islamism—the belief in an Islamic state—among many Muslims. Should Arab countries in the Middle East attempt to implement a democratic form of government, there is the danger of a rise in the number of fundamentalist, Islamist groups attaining power.

In David Lamb's article "Arab World Sees a Resurgence of Islamic Politics" the author analyzes the close relationship that the religion of Islam has with the politics of the Muslim world. He points out that the recent surge of Islamism can be partially tied to U.S. foreign policy and the Israel-Palestinian conflict. As Muslims increasingly feel their culture is being threatened, Lamb indicates, the number of people who identify with a narrow Islamic viewpoint has also risen. Lamb notes that many scholars believe the only way for many of these nations to combat chaos and Islamism is through the introduction of democracy.

In John L. Esposito and John O. Voll's article "Islam and Democracy," the authors examine the question of whether or not Islam itself is at the root of democracy's inability to take hold in Muslim countries. The authors note that some Muslim intellectuals are opposed to the very idea of a popularly elected government on the grounds that such a system would replace the notion of a sovereign God with a form of idolatry. This view, Esposito and Voll write, has been fostered by the establishment of secular military regimes in such places as Iraq. On the opposite side of the argument are those who assert that democracy allows Muslims to participate fully in their religion in the modern world. These individuals believe that having to live under a single tyrant is more harmful to the notion of a united humanity praising one god than a democracy is.

"Faith-Based Initiatives" by Ray Takeyh focuses on the call from within for change in Middle Eastern politics, as exemplified in Iran and Tunisia's new generation of political thinkers. It reiterates the complications that could arise if Islamists took power by popular vote, such as the continued application of aspects of shariah that deny women the same rights as men. However, as a large degree of Islamist support does come from women, Takeyh suspects the government would have to compromise in certain areas. He also notes that moderate Islamists might approach relations with the West with a cautious but greater openness, believing that, while civilizations have the right to their own cultural and political independence, they should be open to dialogue and better relations with each other.

Mark R. Woodward's article "Indonesia, Islam, and the Prospect for Democracy" relates the political situation in what is the world's most populous Muslim country. It is also a nation in which democracy is still new and, as Woodward states, fragile. In Indonesia, he explains, Islamic scholarship has in fact led to the overthrow of an authoritarian regime and the implementation of a democracy. However, a vigorous debate has followed over the role of Islam in the government and in state law, a dispute that would no doubt be mirrored in the Middle East if there were a shift toward democracy there. This debate involves several diverse groups, including anti-Western Islamists and those who follow an indigenized Islam and believe in the coming of a divinely ordained leader. Woodward predicts a more centrist position will prevail, but, whatever political form Islam takes in Indonesia, it will lead many to speculate on the future of democracy in the Muslim world.

Arab World Sees a Resurgence of Islamic Politics[1]

By David Lamb
Los Angeles Times, November 2, 2002

Gripped by frustration and a sense of powerlessness, particularly in the aftermath of the Sept. 11 terrorist attacks, multitudes of Arabs are embracing a more conservative interpretation of Islam to define their identity and reclaim some faith in the future.

The growing influence of Islamism, Arab scholars and Western analysts generally agree, has turned religion into the leading political force in the region. It is, they say, the most significant political movement since Pan-Arabism, preached by Egyptian President Gamal Abdel Nasser in the 1950s and '60s, and a source of concern to Arab regimes that allow little democracy or freedom of expression.

In Morocco's September election, a moderate Islamist party was the third-largest vote-getter.

In Egypt, Islamists, who by government order had to run as independents, won at least one-quarter of the National Assembly seats in 2000. Preachers such as Amr Khaled in Cairo have been elevated to celebrity status with sermons that are conservative but not inflammatory. And across much of the Arab world, women of all classes are putting on the *hijab*, the head scarf their grandmothers fought to take off half a century ago as a symbol of women's oppression. "My neighbor had been going to religion classes for several years and tried to convince me to go, but I wasn't ready," said Omniya Mahmoud, 27, a Cairo teacher. "I used to be the type who really took care of what I wore, dyed my hair, put on makeup. But when I started the classes, I found lots of other women my age. I realized this was the right thing to do. It is what God wants.

"I veiled about a year ago," she said. "Being veiled doesn't mean I'm a fanatic, despite what they think abroad. It just means I'm doing what God wants me to do as a good Muslim."

In Cairo's sidewalk coffee shops, where men sip coffee and puff on water pipes, the topic that is endlessly debated is not Arab unity, Iraq or the fate of the Palestinians. It is what actions and beliefs fit into an Islamic context. Saudi Arabia and Iran also are debating the meaning of being Muslim.

---

1. Article by David Lamb from *Los Angeles Times* November 2, 2002. Copyright © *Los Angeles Times*. Reprint with permission.

Scholars are divided over whether this searching represents reform or is a discussion somehow manipulated by regimes sensitive to Islam's image and Western misperceptions that Islam condones violence and condemns modernity.

> *"'Moderate Muslim' doesn't mean what many people think."*—Frank Vogel, Harvard University

"The moderate Muslim is looking for a Muslim ideology he can identify with, one that doesn't put him on a collision course with world powers and doesn't lead to catastrophic killings or psychotic acts like we've seen," said Frank Vogel, an Islamic scholar at Harvard University. "What he doesn't want is some kind of new Western or global order imposed on him willy-nilly that has nothing to do with his Islamic identity or authenticity.

"But 'moderate Muslim' doesn't mean what many people think. A mainstream Muslim often does believe in things like religion having a role in politics and in state law. At first blush those beliefs seem fundamentalist. But if we mistranslate them as extremist, we'll misjudge what's going on in the Middle East and we'll fail to play a positive role in the emergence there of moderate and successful political systems."

The roots of Islamic revival go back to 1967, when Arabs believed that their defeat in the Six-Day War against Israel was an expression of God's anger for drifting too far from their religion. The mosques started filling and the veils reappearing.

Many attribute the latest wave of Islamism, at least in part, to signals and language emanating from the United States: the Bush administration's disengagement from the Israeli-Palestinian conflict, the war in Afghanistan and the possibility of another in Iraq, President Bush's remark in April that Prime Minister Ariel Sharon was "a man of peace" as Israel was reoccupying the West Bank, and the Rev. Jerry Falwell's comment that the prophet Muhammad was "a terrorist."

"What we're seeing now isn't about Islam; it's about frustration and finding an identity for yourself," said Manal Kahmhawy, a 54-year-old homemaker. "I think also that since Sept. 11 more people are considering themselves Muslims because Islam is threatened now. It's an enemy of the West, so people cling to it. It's a matter of pride, not religion. We're on the defensive."

The frustrations are understandable, given the fact that Arabs were once on the cutting edge of progress and knowledge. Fifteen centuries ago, while Attila the Hun was raiding Gaul and Italy, Arab tribes were gathering annually for weeklong poetry festivals. Arabs believed that the world was round when Europeans thought that it was flat. Arabs devised algebra, invented the universal astrolabe—forerunner of the sextant—and discovered and named chemical substances such as alkaline.

Later, after the birth of Islam in the 7th century, the great Arab cities—Cairo, Damascus, Baghdad and Cordoba in Spain—were the intellectual centers of the world.

Egyptians recorded their history in a written language while nomadic tribes were still roaming Europe and sleeping in mud huts. Egyptians invented surveying, produced the first paper, made the first beer from grain (which they put in glass jars sealed with mud tops), developed astrology and established the 365-day calendar, with each day divided into 24 hours. Men shaved, cut their hair, wore wigs. Women used perfume and cosmetics.

"There's a feeling today we didn't really participate in the postindustrial era, that we haven't achieved anything to add to the modern progress of the world," said Hala Mustafa, an Egyptian social and political commentator. "This lack of accomplishment creates a gap between the Arab and Western worlds."

A United Nations report, prepared by Arab scholars and published this year, offers confirmation of social and economic stagnation in the 22 members of the Arab League. Their access to the Internet and use of computers are lower than that in sub-Saharan Africa. Their 1999 gross domestic product of $531 billion was less than that of Spain. Their 15% unemployment is among the highest in the developing world. About 10 million children between the ages of 6 and 15 don't go to school. Half of the women are illiterate. One out of every five people in the Arab world lives on less than $2 a day.

Just as disturbing, the wave of democracy that swept over Latin America, Asia, Eastern Europe and parts of Africa in the 1980s and '90s hardly touched the lives of the 280 million Arabs. Using indicators such as the political process, civil liberties, political rights and independence of the media, the U.N.'s *Arab Human Development Report 2002* said the Arab world has the lowest "freedom score" of the globe's seven regions.

"When so much has failed, it's natural for people to say: 'Let's try Islam. Maybe that will give us some of the happiness the world holds,'" said Ali Darwish, an Egyptian poet.

There is no word in classical Arabic for fundamentalism, so linguists have had to invent one: usuliyya, which translates roughly as "basic principles."

If the debate over Islam in the cafes of Cairo and other places indeed represents a reform movement, it is not clear what triumphs: tradition or modernity, extremism or tolerance, secularism or sectarianism.

The answer, many believe, depends on whether regimes are willing to give people more civil liberties and open the safety valve of free expression in a region where democracy has never been part of culture and collectivism has always been valued more than individualism.

"All regimes in the region became concerned with the implications of a lack of social and economic development after 9/11," said Hafez abu Saada, secretary-general of the Egyptian Human Rights Organization. "It's late in the game, but their future, and Egypt's, depends on taking steps toward democracy. The alternative is chaos or Islamism."

Islam and Democracy[2]

BY JOHN L. ESPOSITO AND JOHN O. VOLL
HUMANITIES, NOVEMBER/DECEMBER 2001

The Relationship between Islam and democracy in the contemporary world is complex. The Muslim world is not ideologically monolithic. It presents a broad spectrum of perspectives ranging from the extremes of those who deny a connection between Islam and democracy to those who argue that Islam requires a democratic system. In between the extremes, in a number of countries where Muslims are a majority, many Muslims believe that Islam is a support for democracy even though their particular political system is not explicitly defined as Islamic.

Throughout the Muslim world in the twentieth century, many groups that identify themselves explicitly as Islamic attempted to participate directly in the democratic processes as regimes were overthrown in Eastern Europe, Africa, and elsewhere. In Iran such groups controlled and defined the system as a whole; in other areas, the explicitly Islamic groups were participating in systems that were more secular in structure. The participation of self-entified Islamically oriented groups in elections, and in democratic processes in general, aroused considerable controversy. People who believe that secular approaches and a separation of religion and politics are an essential part of democracy argue that Islamist groups only advocate democracy as a tactic to gain political power. They say Islamist groups support "one man, one vote, one time." In Algeria and Turkey, following electoral successes by parties thought to be religiously threatening to the existing political regimes, the Islamic political parties were restricted legally or suppressed.

The relationship between Islam and democracy is strongly debated among the people who identify with the Islamic resurgence in the late twentieth century and the beginning of the twenty-first. Some of these Islamists believe that "democracy" is a foreign concept that has been imposed by Westernizers and secular reformers upon Muslim societies. They often argue that the concept of popular sovereignty denies the fundamental Islamic affirmation of the sovereignty of God and is, therefore, a form of idolatry. People holding these views are less likely to be the ones participating in elections. Many limit themselves to participating in intellectual debates in the media, and others hold themselves aloof from the political dynamics of their societies, hoping that

---

2. Article by John L. Esposito and John O. Voll from *Humanities* November/December 2001.

their own isolated community will in some way be an inspiration to the broader Muslim community. Many prominent Islamic intellectuals and groups, however, argue that Islam and democracy are compatible. Some extend the argument to affirm that under the conditions of the contemporary world, democracy can be considered a requirement of Islam. In these discussions, Muslim scholars bring historically important concepts from within the Islamic tradition together with the basic concepts of democracy as understood in the modern world.

The process in the Muslim world is similar to that which has taken place within other major religious traditions. All of the great world faith traditions represent major bodies of ideas, visions, and concepts fundamental to understanding human life and destiny.

> *Many prominent Islamic intellectuals and groups . . . argue that Islam and democracy are compatible.*

Many of these significant concepts have been used in different ways in different periods of history. The Christian tradition, for example, in premodern times provided a conceptual foundation for divine right monarchy; in contemporary times, it fosters the concept that Christianity and democracy are truly compatible. In all traditions, there are intellectual and ideological resources that can provide the justification for absolute monarchy or for democracy. The controversies arise regarding how basic concepts are to be understood and implemented.

A relatively neutral starting point for Muslims is presented in a 1992 interview in the *London Observer* with the Tunisian Islamist leader and political exile, Rashid Ghanoushi: "If by democracy is meant the liberal model of government prevailing in the West, a system under which the people freely choose their representatives and leaders, in which there is an alternation of power, as well as all freedoms and human rights for the public, then Muslims will find nothing in their religion to oppose democracy, and it is not in their interests to do so." Many Muslims, including Ghanoushi himself, go beyond this and view democracy as an appropriate way to fulfill certain obligations of the faith in the contemporary world.

The Islamic tradition contains a number of key concepts that are presented by Muslims as the key to "Islamic democracy." Most would agree that it is important for Muslims not simply to copy what non-Muslims have done in creating democratic systems, emphasizing that there are different forms that legitimate democracy can take. Iran's President Mohammad Khatami, in a television interview in June before that country's presidential elections, noted that "the existing democracies do not necessarily follow one formula or aspect. It is possible that a democracy may lead to a liberal system. It is possible that democracy may lead to a socialist system. Or it may be a democracy with the inclusion of religious norms in the government. We have accepted the third option." Khatami presents a view common among the advocates of Islamic democracy that "today world democracies are suffering from a major vacuum, which is the vacuum of spirituality," and that Islam can provide the framework for combining democracy with spirituality and religious government.

The synthesis of spirituality and government builds on a fundamental affirmation at the heart of Islam: the proclamation that "There is no divinity but The God" and the affirmation of the "oneness" of God. This concept, called *tawhid*, provides the foundation for the idea that one cannot separate different aspects of life into separate compartments. Ali Shariati, who made important contributions to the ideological development of the Islamic revolution in Iran, wrote in *On the Sociology of Islam*, that tawhid "in the sense of oneness of God is of course accepted by all monotheists. But tauhid as a world view . . . means regarding the whole universe as a unity, instead of dividing it into this world and the hereafter . . . spirit and body." In this worldview, the separation of religion from politics creates a spiritual vacuum in the public arena and opens the way for political systems that have no sense of moral values. From such a perspective, a secular state opens the way for the abuse of power. The experiences of Muslim societies with military regimes that are secularist in ideological origin, such as the Baath Arab Socialist regime of Saddam Hussein in Iraq, reinforce this mistrust of separating religious values from politics.

Advocates of Islamic democracy argue that the Oneness of God requires some form of democratic system; conservatives contend that the idea of the sovereignty of the people contradicts the sovereignty of God; often the alternative then becomes some form of a monarchical system. The response to this is an affirmation of tawhid, as expressed by a Sudanese intellectual, Abdelwahab El-Affendi, in the October 2000 edition of *Islam 21*: "No Muslim questions the sovereignty of God or the rule of Shari'ah [the Islamic legal path]. However, most Muslims do (and did) have misgivings about any claims by one person that he is sovereign. The sovereignty of one man contradicts the sovereignty of God, for all men are equal in front of God. . . . Blind obedience to one-man rule is contrary to Islam." In this way, it is argued that the doctrine of tawhid virtually requires a democratic system because humans are all created equal and any system that denies that equality is not Islamic.

There are a number of specific concepts that Muslims cite when they explain the relationship between Islam and democracy. In the Qur'an, the righteous are described as those people who, among other things, manage their affairs through "mutual consultation" or shura (42:38 Qur'an). This is expanded through traditions of the Prophet and the sayings and actions of the early leaders of the Muslim community to mean that it is obligatory for Muslims in managing their political affairs to engage in mutual consultation. Contemporary Muslim thinkers ranging from relatively conservative Islamists to more liberal modernists to Shi'ite activists emphasize the importance of consultation. There would be little disagreement with the view of Ayatollah Baqir al-Sadr, the Iraqi Shi'ite leader who was executed by Saddam Hussein in 1980, who said in *Islamic Political System*, that the people "have a general right to dispose of their affairs on the basis of the principle of consultation." What this meant for the constitutional system of the Islamic Republic of Iran, which was influenced by al-Sadr's thought, was affirmed by President Khatami in last June's interview: the "people play a fundamental role in bringing a government to power, in supervising the government and possibly the replacement of the government without any tension and problems."

Another basic concept in the development of Islamic democracy is "caliph." In contemporary discussions, traditional political usage of the term caliph has been redefined. Historically the term caliph was used as the title of the monarchs who ruled the medieval Muslim

---

> **By the late twentieth century, Muslim intellectuals began to see the importance of the concept of all humans as "caliphs" or God's stewards.**

---

empire. When medieval Muslim political philosophers spoke of the institutions of caliphal rule, the caliphate, they were analyzing the political institution of the successors to the Prophet Muhammad as the leader of the Muslim community. However, this concept of the caliphate was something that developed after the death of the Prophet.

In the Qur'an, the Arabic words for caliph (*khalifah*) and caliphate (*khilafah*) have a different meaning. These terms in the Qur'an have the more general meaning of steward and stewardship or trustee and trusteeship. In this way, Adam, as the first human, is identified as God's caliph or steward on earth (2:30). Muhammad is instructed to remind humans that God made them the caliphs (stewards or trustees) of the earth (6:165). In this way, in the Qur'an, the term caliphate refers to the broad responsibilities of humans to be the stewards of God's creation.

By the late twentieth century, long after the last vestiges of the political caliphate had been abolished by the reforms of Ataturk in Turkey in 1924, Muslim intellectuals began to see the importance of the concept of all humans as "caliphs" or God's stewards. As the intellectual dimensions of the late twentieth-century Islamic resurgence became more clearly defined, Ismail al-Faruqi, a scholar of Palestinian origins, outlined an ambitious project in a small book, *Islamization of Knowledge*. The concept of the caliphate involved responsibilities for all humans, in all dimensions of life, but especially the political: "Rightly, Muslims understand khilafah as directly political. . . . Islam requires that every Muslim be politicized (i.e., awakened, organized, and mobilized)."

The implications of this reassertion of a more explicitly Qur'anic meaning of human stewardship for Islamic democracy were spelled out by the South Asian Islamist leader, Abu al-Ala Mawdudi in *The Islamic Way of Life*: "The authority of the caliphate is bestowed on the entire group of people, the community as a whole. . . . Such a society carries the responsibility of the caliphate as a whole and each one of its individual[s] shares the Divine Caliphate. This is the point where democracy begins in Islam. Every person in an Islamic society enjoys the rights and powers of the caliphate of God and in this respect all individuals are equal."

In theory and concept, Islamic democracy is, at the beginning of the twenty-first century, quite well developed and persuasive. In actual practice the results have been less encouraging. Authoritarian rulers such as Ja'far Numayri in Sudan and Zia al-Haqq in Pakistan initiated formal programs of Islamization of the law and political system in the 1980s with results that were not encouraging for democracy. A military coup brought a combination of military and civilian Islamists to rule in Sudan in 1989 and despite the proclaimed goal of creating an Islamic democracy, the regime's human rights record in terms of treatment of non-Muslim minorities and Muslim opposition groups is deplorable.

International human rights groups have also been critical of the treatment of non-Muslim minorities in Iran, where the Shah was overthrown in 1979. During its first decade, the Islamic Republic set narrow limitations on political participation. However, the end of the nineties saw the unprecedented presidential election victory of Mohammad Khatami, who had not been favored by the conservative religious establishment. He was reelected by an overwhelming majority again in 2001. Although there are continuing grounds for criticizing Iran in terms of its repression of opposition and minorities, increasing numbers of women and youth are voting in elections. Instead of "one man, one vote, one time," the "one man" is being joined by "one woman" as a voting force.

Beyond the formally proclaimed Islamic political systems, there has also been an increasing role for democracy with an Islamic tone. In many countries, Muslims who are not activist Islamists have participated in electoral processes and brought a growing sense of the need for morality and Islamic awareness in the political arena. In an era when politics in many countries is becoming "desecularized," leaders of Islamic organizations play important roles in electoral political systems that are not explicitly identified as Islamic. When the military regime of Suharto in Indonesia was brought to an end, the person who became president in 1999 as a result of the first open elections was Abd al-Rahman Wahid, the leader of Nahdat ul-Ulama, perhaps the largest Islamic organization in the world. He did not campaign on a platform of Islamizing the political system, even though he participated in the democratic system as a clearly identifiable Islamic leader. When he was removed as president this year, it was by a process of orderly replacement, and neither his followers nor his opponents engaged in religious warfare.

Similarly, Islamically oriented political parties have operated successfully in the secular electoral politics of Turkey, with the leader of one such party, Necmettin Erbakan, serving as prime minister briefly in 1996–1997. Although in succession, the Islamically oriented Turkish parties have been suppressed and many of their leaders jailed, the response of the people in the parties has simply been to form new parties and try again within the political system rather than withdrawing into a violent underground opposition.

The Turkish experience reflects the fact that many Muslims, whether living in formally secular or formally Islamic states, see democracy as their main hope and vehicle of effective political participation. One important dimension of this participation is that despite conservative Muslim opposition to the idea of rule by a woman, the three largest Muslim states in the world—Indonesia, Bangladesh, and Pakistan—have had or now have elected women as their heads of government. None of these women was explicitly Islamist and one was directly opposed by an Islamist party.

In this complex context, it is clear that Islam is not inherently incompatible with democracy. "Political Islam" is sometimes a program for religious democracy and not primarily an agenda for holy war or terrorism.

Faith-Based Initiatives[3]

BY RAY TAKEYH
FOREIGN POLICY, NOVEMBER/DECEMBER 2001

The televised footage of an airliner crashing into the World Trade Center is now the prevailing image of Islam. Media pundits decry anti-Muslim bigotry and hasten to remind the public that Islam is a religion of peace and tolerance, notwithstanding the actions of an extremist minority. But in the same breath many of those pundits warn of a clash of civilizations—a war that pits the secular, modernized West against a region mired in ancient hatreds and fundamentalist rage.

This simplistic choice between "Islam" and "modernity" ignores a third option that is emerging throughout the Middle East. Lost amidst the din of cultural saber-rattling are the voices calling for an Islamic reformation: A new generation of theological thinkers, led by figures such as Iranian President Muhammad Khatami and Tunisian activist Rached Ghannouchi, is reconsidering the orthodoxies of Islamic politics. In the process, such leaders are demonstrating that the region may be capable of generating a genuinely democratic order, one based on indigenous values. For the Middle East today, moderate Islam may be democracy's last hope. For the West, it might represent one of the best long-term solutions to "winning" the war against Middle East terrorism.

Militant Islam continues to tempt those on the margins of society (and guides anachronistic forces such as Afghanistan's Taliban and Palestine's Islamic Jihad), but its moment has passed. In Iran, the Grand Ayatollah's autocratic order degenerated into corruption and economic stagnation. Elsewhere, the Islamic radicals' campaign of terror—such as Gamma al-Islamiyya in Egypt and Hezbollah in Lebanon—failed to produce any political change, as their violence could not overcome the brutality of the states they encountered. The militants' incendiary rhetoric and terrorism only triggered public revulsion, not revolutions and mass uprisings. Indeed, the Arab populace may have returned to religion over the last two decades, but they turned to a religion that was tolerant and progressive, not one that called for a violent displacement of the existing order with utopias.

Political Islam as a viable reform movement might have petered out were it not for one minor detail: The rest of the world was changing. The collapse of the Soviet Union and the emergence of democratic regimes in Eastern Europe, Latin America, and East

Asia electrified the Arab populace. Their demands were simple but profound. As one Egyptian university student explained in 1993, "I want what they have in Poland, Czechoslovakia. Freedom of thought and freedom of speech." In lecture halls, street cafes, and mosques, long dormant ideas of representation, identity, authenticity, and pluralism began to arise.

The task of addressing the population's demand for a pluralistic society consistent with traditional values was left to a new generation of Islamist thinkers, who have sought to legitimize democratic concepts through the reinterpretation of Islamic texts and traditions. Tunisia's Ghannouchi captures this spirit of innovation by stressing, "Islam did not come with a specific program concerning life. It is our duty to formulate this program through interaction between Islamic precepts and modernity." Under these progressive readings, the well-delineated Islamic concept of *shura* (consultation) compels a ruler to consider popular opinion and establishes the

> *The new generation of Islamists has quickly embraced the benefits wrought by modernization and globalization in order to forge links between Islamist groups and thinkers in the various states of the Middle East.*

foundation for an accountable government. In a modern context, such consultation can be implemented through the standard tools of democracy: elections, plebiscites, and referendums. The Islamic notion of *ijma* (consensus) has been similarly accommodated to serve as a theological basis for majoritarian rule. For Muslim reformers, Prophet Mohammed's injunction that "differences of opinion within my community is a sign of God's mercy" denotes prophetic approbation of diversity of thought and freedom of speech.

The new generation of Islamists has quickly embraced the benefits wrought by modernization and globalization in order to forge links between Islamist groups and thinkers in the various states of the Middle East. Through mosques, Islamists easily distribute pamphlets, tracts, and cassettes of Islamic thinkers and writers. In today's Middle East, one can easily find the Egyptian Brotherhood's magazine *Al-Dawa* in bookstores in the Persian Gulf while the Jordanian Islamist daily *Al-Sabil* enjoys wide circulation throughout the Levant. The advent of the Internet has intensified such cross-pollination, as most Islamist journals, lectures, and conference proceedings are posted on the Web. The writings of Iranian philosopher Abdol Karim Soroush today appear in Islamic curricula across the region, and Egypt's Islamist liberal Hassan Hanafi commands an important audience in Iran's seminaries.

In the future, such Islamists will likely vie to succeed the region's discredited military rulers and lifetime presidents. But what will a prospective Islamic democracy look like? Undoubtedly, Islamic democracy will differ in important ways from the model that evolved in post-Reformation Europe. Western systems elevated the primacy of the individual above the community and thus changed the role of religion from that of the public conveyor of community values to a private guide for individual conscience. In contrast, an Islamic democracy's attempt to balance its emphasis on reverence with the popular desire for self-expression will impose certain limits on individual choice. An Islamic polity will support fundamental tenets of democracy—namely, regular elections, separation of powers, an independent judiciary, and institutional opposition— but it is unlikely to be a libertarian paradise.

The question of gender rights is an excellent example of the strengths—and limits—of an Islamic democracy. The Islamists who rely on women's votes, grass-roots activism, and participation

---

Moderate Islamists are likely to be most liberal in the realm of economic policy.

---

in labor markets cannot remain deaf to women's demands for equality. Increasingly, Islamic reformers suggest the cause of women's failure to achieve equality is not religion but custom. The idea of black-clad women passively accepting the dictates of superior males is the province of Western caricatures. Iran's parliament, cabinet, and universities are populated with women, as are the candidate lists for Islamic opposition parties in Egypt and Turkey. But while an Islamic democracy will not impede women's integration into public affairs, it will impose restrictions on them, particularly in the realm of family law and dress codes. In such an order, women can make significant progress, yet in important ways they may still lag behind their Western counterparts.

Moderate Islamists are likely to be most liberal in the realm of economic policy. The failure of command economies in the Middle East and the centrality of global markets to the region's economic rehabilitation have made minimal government intervention appealing to Islamist theoreticians. Moreover, a privatized economy is consistent with classical Islamic economic theory and its well-established protection of market and commerce. The Islamist parties have been among the most persistent critics of state restrictions on trade and measures that obstruct opportunities for middle-class entrepreneurs.

The international implications of the emergence of Islamic democracies are also momentous. While revolutionary Islam could not easily coexist with the international system, moderate Islam can serve as a bridge between civilizations. The coming to power of moderate Islamists throughout the Middle East might lead to a lessening of tensions both within the region and between it and other parts of the world. Today, security experts talk of the need to "drain the swamps" and deprive terrorists of the state sponsorship that provides the protection and funding to carry out their war against the West. Within a more open and democratic system, dictatorial regimes would enjoy less freedom to support terrorism or engage in military buildups without any regard for economic consequences.

Ultimately, however, the integration of an Islamic democracy into global democratic society would depend on the willingness of the West to accept an Islamic variant on liberal democracy. Islamist moderates, while conceding that there are in fact certain "universal" democratic values, maintain that different civilizations must be able to express these values in a context that is acceptable and appropriate to their particular region. Moderate Islamists, therefore, will continue to struggle against any form of U.S. hegemony, whether in political or cultural terms, and are much more comfortable with a multipolar, multi-"civilizational" international system. Khatami's call for a "dialogue of civilizations" presupposes that there is no single universal standard judging the effectiveness of democracy and human rights.

Certainly, the West should resist totalitarian states who use the rhetoric of democracy while rejecting its essence through false claims of cultural authenticity. But even though an Islamic democracy will resist certain elements of post-Enlightenment liberalism, it will still be a system that features regular elections, accepts dissent and opposition parties, and condones a free press and division of power between branches of state. As such, any fair reading of Islamic democracy will reveal that it is a genuine effort to conceive a system of government responsive to popular will. And this effort is worthy of Western acclaim.

Indonesia, Islam, and the Prospect for Democracy[4]

BY MARK R. WOODWARD
SAIS REVIEW, SUMMER/FALL 2001

Indonesia is the world's most populous Muslim country and among the world's newest and most fragile democracies. Democratic transitions are difficult in part because they require changes in political culture as well as in political institutions. In societies where concepts of authority and leadership are rooted in deeply-held religious beliefs, transforming political culture requires serious theological reflection. Islam, like Judaism and unlike Christianity, is a religion of law. In principle, Islamic law is a comprehensive guide to all aspects of religious and social life. The ways in which Islamic law is understood and interpreted have profound implications for political development in Muslim countries. Indonesia is no exception.

For nearly four decades, ex-President Suharto's authoritarian "New Order" regime sought to de-politicize and domesticate Indonesian Islam. Scholarship and personal piety were encouraged, but explicitly Islamic political discourse was severely restricted. Ironically, the expansion of Muslim education and reflection on the role of Islam in the modern, secular world system contributed significantly to the growth of the democracy movement that emerged as a major political force following the economic crisis of 1997. There is a new generation of Muslim scholars, Nurcholish Madjid being the most prolific and best known, who have strong theological as well as political commitments to democracy and religious and cultural pluralism.

In the days after the fall of Suharto there was great enthusiasm for democracy. Many Indonesians embraced the view that democracy and elections would provide a quick fix for the nation's shattered economy. Most portentous for Islam was the end of press censorship (and self censorship) and of the restrictions on political parties. It soon became clear that Indonesian Islam was not as apolitical and domesticated as had seemed in the late new order period. Debate over the role of Islam in public life is a lasting element of Indonesia's civic discourse.

---

4. Woodward, Mark R. "Indonesia, Islam, and the Prospect for Democracy." *SAIS Review* 21:2 (2001), 29–37. © The Johns Hopkins University Press. Reprinted with permission of The Johns Hopkins University Press.

There is widespread concern that the emerging party system may lead to the type of "identity politics" that contributed to the collapse of Indonesia's first experiment with parliamentary democracy in the 1950s. Many observers have noted similarities between the alignment of parties contesting the 1955 and 1999 elections. In both cases party affiliation tends to reflect "primordial loyalties": class, ethnicity, and religion. The major fault lines lie between the Javanese and other ethnic groups and between orthodox (*santri*) and local (*abangan*) forms of Islam in Java.[1] The orthodox Muslim community is rent in turn by theological disputes between modernists and traditionalists and between advocates of a secular, democratic state and those who would see Indonesia become an Islamic republic. Indonesians worry that democracy may prove to be just a venue for power struggles among the leadership of these communal groups.

Anderson has suggested that the emergence of an Indonesian mid-

---

A distinction is often made between parties that are "Islamist" and those that are just based in the Muslim community or established by Muslim leaders.

---

dle class may have laid the foundations for a democratic order in which primordial loyalties are less pronounced.[2] Despite the expansion of the middle class and modern education under Suharto, such loyalties predominated in the 1999 election. Of forty-eight parties, fifteen are Islamic in some sense. There is, however, heated debate about what constitutes a Muslim party. A distinction is often made between parties that are "Islamist" and those that are just based in the Muslim community or established by Muslim leaders.[3] The Islamist faction only accepts parties that explicitly describe themselves as Islamic. Prior to the election, a representative of *Dewan Dakwah* (the Association for the Propagation of Islam, an Islamist think tank, missionary organization, and publishing house) explained that all Muslims were obligated to choose a Muslim party (in the strict sense) and that those who did not would have "left the path of Islam." This is identity politics in its purest form. It identifies Islam, as a religion, with a small group of Islamist political parties and defines millions who consider themselves devout Muslims as non-believers.

There are five basic religious orientations within the Indonesian Muslim community. (1) Indigenized Islams, in which religion is a thoroughly integrated component of a larger cultural system, are common throughout the country, particularly in east and central Java. (2) The traditional Sunni Islam of *Nahdlatul Ulama* is rooted in the study of the classic legal, theological, and mystical texts. It is most prevalent in east Java. (3) The Islamic modernism of *Muhammadiyah* rejects mysticism and extols modern education and social services. Modernists are usually found in urban areas. (4) Islamist groups espouse a highly politicized and anti-Western interpretation of Islam. They are most common on university campuses and in large urban centers. (5) Finally, neo-modernism seeks to find Islamic foundations for many features of modernity, including democracy and religious and cultural pluralism.

Indigenized Islam

East and central Java are strongholds of indigenized Islam.[4] The conflation of ritual and religious belief is often referred to as *Islam Jawa* (Javanese Islam) or Javanism. Javanists think of themselves as Muslims but generally skirt the ritual behavior required by Islamic law. Their religious practices include many elements of popular or folk Sufism (Islamic mysticism), including pilgrimages to sacred graves and the veneration of saints. Javanist Islam is closely related to the imperial Islam of the central Javanese palaces, according to which Javanese kings are Muslim saints who speak and act with divine authority. Javanists rely on more observant and learned Muslims to conduct major rituals like weddings and funerals but are often highly suspicious of what they consider to be the "Arabism" of orthodox Muslims. Javanist Islam has a tradition of political authority according to which leaders are chosen by God and endowed with great spiritual power. Many times in Java's history, this belief has inspired both extreme loyalty and messianic rebellions based on the assumption that a *ratu adil* (just king) will restore order and prosperity to the realm.

Javanists are the core supporters of Megawati Sukarnoputri and her Democratic Party of Struggle. Many believe that she has inherited the spiritual powers of her father Sukarno, Indonesia's first president, and that if she becomes president such power will enable her to solve the nation's problems. In the Yogyakarta region of central Java, many Javanists have similar feelings about their sultan, Hamengkubuwana X. Many Javanists see elections as one means of bringing a divinely ordained leader to power. Yogyakarta, for example, was one of the centers of the democracy movement, yet the provincial legislature refused even to vote on Hamengkubuwana X's nomination for governor, arguing that he was entitled to the office because he was the sultan.

The Traditional Islam of Nahdulatul Ulama

Nahdlatul Ulama (NU), or Renaissance of the Ulama, is Indonesia's largest Muslim organization—indeed it is the largest in the world, with over thirty million members. It represents the traditional *ulama* (Islamic scholars) and their disciples. It is also the political base of President Abdurrahman Wahid. NU was founded in 1921 in response to the Wahabi conquest of Mecca and the spread of Islamic fundamentalism in the Netherlands Indies. The group's original purpose was to promote and defend Sunni Muslim traditionalism, which combines adherence to the teachings of the four classical legal traditions with Sufi devotional practice and mysticism. It had six stated goals: to promote solidarity among traditional Islamic scholars, to distribute Islamic texts to educational institutions, to promote orthodox legal scholarship, to expand the network of Islamic religious schools; to build mosques, and to provide assistance to orphans and the poor.

NU is closely associated with a vast network of Islamic schools (*pesantren*). Some pesantren teach only religious subjects. Others add vocational or secular academic subjects to the curriculum. Many graduates pursue further studies in religious and secular universities overseas. The next generation of NU leaders will include many with doctorates from prestigious Western universities.

Despite its essentially religious orientation, NU has always been a potent force in Indonesian politics. Its leaders participated actively in the independence movement. In 1945, they declared the Indonesian revolution a *jihad*. In the early days of the republic, NU was affiliated with the pan-Islamic political party *Masyumi*, though it became an independent political party in 1952. Following the abortive coup of 1965 the NU youth organization, known as *Ansor* (the helpers), helped massacre Communist Party members and their supporters.

After the 1971 parliamentary elections the Suharto regime required all Muslim political parties to "fuse" into the nominally secular United Development Party. In 1984, at then-Chairman Wahid's urging, NU abandoned active participation in politics, declaring itself to be a religious and social organization. Following the fall of Suharto, Wahid and other NU leaders established the National Resurrection Party, described as "the party of the NU community." While technically a secular party, its support comes almost exclusively from NU loyalists, most of whom are peasant farmers or urban laborers.

NU is an extremely hierarchical organization based on a complicated system of student-teacher relationships. Wahid and other prominent NU leaders are considered to be living saints who speak with divine authority. One of the central religious doctrines of traditionalist Islam is taklid, or absolute obedience. Because Wahid and other NU leaders are committed to democratic reform, NU's masses feel bound to follow their lead. At the same time, they are willing and able to use non-democratic means to respond to any challenge to Wahid's authority.

Islamic Modernism

Islamic modernism emerged in Indonesia at the turn of the twentieth century. From the beginning, it has combined theological and social agendas. Theologically, Indonesian modernism accepts the validity of none but the primary texts of the Islamic tradition (the

Qur'an and the *Hadith*, the traditions of the Prophet Mohammed). Modernists think that mysticism and the ritual practices associated with it, especially pilgrimage to holy graves, are non-Islamic and that those who practice them are not Muslims. The feud between modernist and traditional Muslims is extremely bitter. For much of this century it has prevented the two factions from working on common social or political agendas.

Since the colonial period modernist organizations, especially Muhammadiyah, have maintained a network of schools and universities that provides modern education in an Islamic context. With approximately twenty million members, Muhammadiyah is the largest modernist Muslim movement in Indonesia. Muhammadiyah also supports an extensive system of clinics and hospitals. As an organization, Muhammadiyah has refrained from direct involvement in politics, though many of its members are active in Islamic parties.

The emergence of Islamist rhetoric and self-proclaimed jihads are the most troubling developments in the new Indonesia.

Other modernist organizations have more explicitly political programs. Most of these trace their theological and political roots to the thought of Mohammed Natsir (1908–1993). Natsir was one of the leading figures in *Persatuan Islam* (the Unity of Islam), which shares most of Muhammadiyah's theological agenda but places much greater emphasis on political struggle and on establishing an explicitly Islamic state. A number of contemporary political parties, including *Partai Bulan Bintang* (the Star and Moon Party) and *Partai Keadilan* (the Justice Party), share this view. So do many religious foundations, of which Dewan Dakwah is the most influential. Despite the fact that his own political party, *Partai Amanat Nasional* (National Mandate Party), is nominally secular and open to non-Muslims, Amein Rais, the former general chairman of Muhammadiyah, shares much of this agenda.

As a whole, Indonesia's Islamic modernists are committed to working within the established political system. While many advocate a more explicitly Islamic political and social system, they seek to attain this goal through participation in the democratic process.

Islamism

The emergence of Islamist rhetoric and self-proclaimed jihads are the most troubling developments in the new Indonesia. Indonesian Islamists participate in a global Muslim discourse centered on jihad and *shariah* law. Like Islamists elsewhere, they have a conspiratorial view of global politics. Discussions of Western attempts to destroy Islam can be found in mosques, in print, and increasingly on the Internet. This discourse demonizes the Christian and Jewish West as the source of conflict and economic stagnation. The establishment of nation-states based on shariah law and global Islamic cooperation is understood as the only solution to the problems of Muslim societies. This discourse provides a coherent, if highly inaccurate, explanation of global and local events.

Indonesian Islamists argue that the ethnic and religious violence in eastern Indonesia is the product of a complex conspiracy: Christian forces, supposedly supported and financed by the Netherlands, the United States, Israel, Australia, and the Vatican are attempting to destroy Muslim communities in the region. This conspiracy also explains events in East Timor. The United States has supposedly established Australia as the "Deputy Sheriff" of Southeast Asia and has given the entire region to the "country of the kangaroos." Humanitarian aid programs and the activities of human rights organizations are dismissed as fig leaves for covert operations.

The Indonesian Islamist movement touts the establishment of shariah law as the basis of social, political, and economic life as the solution to these problems. One of the more important components of this diverse movement is *Laksar Jihad Ahlus Sunnah wal Jammah* (Holy War Brigade of the People of the Muslim Community and Tradition). Al-Ustaz Ja'far Umar Tholib, the commander of Laksar Jihad, is a veteran of the Afghan war who later studied "Islamic Education" in Pakistan. His organization claims to have sent over 3,000 *mujahedin* to eastern Indonesia, and to have suffered an undetermined number of casualties. Laksar Jihad is virulently anti-Western and rejects democracy and the secular state as un-Islamic. Those who support these concepts are accused of apostasy, for which the strict interpretation of Islamic law advocated by Laksar Jihad requires the death penalty.

Neo-Modernism

As the name suggests, neo-modernism is a new development. Neo-modernist thinkers and NGOs differ fundamentally from both Islamists and modernists. They do not accept the view that economic and social progress depends on the establishment of Islamic institutions. They are concerned more with Muslim values and ethics than with law. Indonesian neo-modernists come from both modernist and traditionalist backgrounds. They consider Islamic law to be an open-ended tradition that must adapt to changing historical and cultural contexts. Many neo-modernists explicitly reject the restrictions on women that are included in Islamic codes and classical criminal law. Abdurrahman Wahid has gone so far as to describe punishments mandated by classical shariah as barbaric. In this sense Wahid is more "modern" than many modernists. At the same time, he takes care to root his own opinions in the classical tradition of Islamic jurisprudence. He argues from within rather than in opposition to the classical tradition of Islamic legal scholarship.

The view that Islam does not mandate a particular form of government is shared by many neo-modernists, most of whom reject the notion that there is or can be an "Islamic state." Instead, they argue that Islam mandates pious and ethical behavior that can establish justice in a variety of political systems. Neo-modernists often argue that the concept of the nation-state is foreign to Islam, but that it is a socio-political system within which Islam can be put into practice. Egyptian philosopher Hassan Hanafi, pro-democracy Muslim scholar Nurcholish Madjid, and Indonesia's theologian-president are among the best-known proponents of neo-modernism.

Neo-modernism also emphasizes religious tolerance and pluralism. Hanafi indicates that his own views of struggle in the world are closely related to those of Christian liberation theologians. He writes that liberation theology is the most viable paradigm for dialogue between religions, at least in the developing world. He describes Christian and Muslim variants of liberation theology as being "part of the struggle in which the wretched of the earth are engaged," and that religions and ideologies are tools for the betterment of humankind. What is distinctively Muslim in his thought is the idea that commanding the good and prohibiting the evil is the "highest implementation of faith."[5]

Wahid holds similar views. He has described Islam as a "transformative force" for the betterment of the human condition. In part because of the presence of substantial Christian minorities in Indonesia, he has also emphasized pluralism and religious tolerance, going so far as to teach at Catholic seminaries. He describes the relationship between the "first" and "third" worlds as potentially "win-win" and interprets "commanding the good and prohibiting the evil" in economic as well as moral terms.

Wahid became president of Indonesia at a time of great political, economic, and moral crisis. His opponents include Islamists, secularists, militarists, and a privileged class that remains loyal to the oppressive policies of the old regime. His presidency is of more than local importance. It is a test of the ability of neo-modernist theologians to translate theory into practice.

Islam is and will remain one of the most important elements of Indonesian political discourse and practice. But there is not one Islam. There are many Islams, with varying commitments to Islamic law, to democracy, and to pluralism. Some of Indonesia's Islams are apolitical. Others range from Megawati Sukarnoputri's charismatic Javanism, to *Partai Cinta Damai* (the Peace and Love Party), which advocates prayer as the solution to all of the nation's problems, to the pragmatism and pluralism of the Wahid government, to hybrids like Dewan Dakwah, which advocates using democratic strategies to establish an Islamic state, to the radicalism of Laksar Jihad. It seems unlikely that either the mystics of Partai Cinta Damai or the warriors of Laksar Jihad will come to power.

Given the complex, splintered nature of Indonesian politics and the enormous problems the country faces, it is impossible to predict which of the more centrist positions will prevail. What is clear is that whatever path Indonesia may follow in decades to come, it will be one rooted in Islamic theology and discourse.

Notes

1. On this distinction see Mark R. Woodward, *Islam in Java: Normative Piety and Mysticism in the Sultanate of Yogyakarta* (Tucson: University of Arizona Press, 1989).
2. Benedict Anderson, *The Spectre of Comparisons: Nationalism, Southeast Asia, and the World* (London: Verso, 1998), pp. 282–83.
3. *Hidayatuallah*, 15 March 1999.
4. For detailed studies of this variant of Indonesian Islam see Clifford Geertz, *The Religion of Java* (Glenco: The Free Press, 1960); Woodward, op. cit.
5. Commanding the good and prohibiting the evil is a Quranic injunction and the most basic principle of Islamic law.

V. Islam and the Other Abrahamic Traditions

Editor's Introduction

Ever since the rise of Islamic militancy in the 1970s, and particularly since the terrorist attacks on New York City and Washington, D.C., on September 11, 2001, many in the United States and other Western nations have questioned whether or not there is something particular to Islam that encourages violence and intolerance. While the behavior of suicide bombers in Israel and the militant insurgents into Indian-controlled Kashmir continue to prompt this question, religious scholars point out that in the Qur'an God's mercy and forgiveness are mentioned over ten times more frequently than His vengefulness. They also note several passages that approve of good relations with "people of the book," which refers explicitly to Jews, Christians, and Sabians (now commonly called Mandeans). In fact, they add, the amount of violence condoned in the Old Testament is comparable to that in the Qur'an. Yet as long as militant Muslims quote from other passages in the Qur'an that they construe as indicating God's approval of holy war against any who do not follow Islam or adhere to their interpretation of it, the question will remain at the heart of many discussions on the religion.

Kenneth L. Woodward examines the similarities and differences between the Qur'an and Jewish and Christian scripture and discusses the notion of violence within them in his article "In the Beginning, There Were the Holy Books." He notes that, while Muslims consider the Qur'an to be God's eternal word, most Jews and Christians view the divinely sanctioned violence in early biblical texts as simply a historical experience. Woodward also points to the life of Muhammad as something that can be used as a rationale for modern-day violence, since the Prophet commanded an army himself. In looking at the differences among the holy texts, Woodward considers the significance of Muslims' having to pray in Arabic (the language in which the Qur'an was originally set down) as well as the appearance in the Qur'an of prophets and figures from both Jewish and Christian scripture. Woodward concludes that it is not so much what is in the Qur'an that is causing such difficulty today as it is the way it is being interpreted.

In his article "Pluralism, Intolerance, and the Qur'an," Ali S. Asani looks at Qur'anic issues of intolerance through the eyes of a practicing Muslim scholar. Asani, like Woodward, asserts that the Qur'an is essentially a tolerant scripture that "has been subjected to anti-pluralist, or exclusivist, interpretations in order to advance hegemonic goals, both political and religious." For proof that Islam has at its heart a universal message that allows for plural manifestation, he points to the Qur'anic passages that state that God's message has been revealed to all people and to all cultures. Asani believes that the growing belief in exclusivity—that it is only to Muslims that the truth has been given—has caused most of the antagonism toward Muslims.

Intolerance by Muslims toward those of other faiths has also risen over land issues, particularly the creation of the state of Israel and the displacement of the Palestinians. Throughout Muslim nations, this particular event has led to profound anti-Semitic feeling that has been fanned by such fundamentalists as Osama bin Laden. Susan Sachs's article "Anti-Semitism Is Deepening Among Muslims" addresses this problem and reports just how prevalent anti-Semitic imagery has become in the Muslim world, appearing not only in sermons in mosques but also in the press and academic journals. Sachs points out that anti-Semitism is nothing new to the Islamic world and had been present in popular culture prior to the creation of Israel, probably originating in the days of the Qur'an's first appearance, when many Jews would not accept Muhammad's prophecy.

The relationship between Christianity and Islam has been problematic in recent years. Muslims in the Middle East are often angered by Christian efforts to convert them, while many Christians in the West view Islam as a religion of extremists. Nonetheless, both religions revere Jesus, who Muslims believe is the Messiah who will come and a prophet surpassed in importance only by Muhammad. Jesus is mentioned often in the Qur'an, where stories are related about his life that are not found in the Christian Bible. Other non-Qur'anic stories have been collected and translated by Tarif Khalidi in his book *The Muslim Jesus: Sayings and Stories in Islamic Literature*. In her article "The Islamic Jesus," Sara Miller claims this work "offers a likely map of the paths by which Christian legend, including the Apocrypha, made its way into another, younger religion and evolved as testimony to the latter's veracity. It reveals . . . the deep theological insights of Islam and the brilliance of its scholars, spiritual writers, and men of letters." Miller suggests that this connection between the two religions could potentially form new groundwork for discussion and friendship.

In the Beginning, There Were the Holy Books[1]

BY KENNETH L. WOODWARD
NEWSWEEK, FEBRUARY 11, 2002

He was a pious family man, a trader from Mecca who regularly retreated into the hills above the city to fast and pray. In his 40th year, while he was praying in a cave on Mount Hira, the angel Gabriel spoke to him, saying, "Muhammad, you are the Messenger of God," and commanded him to "Recite!" Muhammad protested that he could not—after all, he was not gifted like the traditional tribal bards of Arabia. Then, according to this tradition, the angel squeezed him so violently that Muhammad thought he'd die. Again Gabriel ordered him to recite, and from his lips came the first verses of what eventually became the Qur'an, regarded as the eternal words of God himself by some 1.3 billion Muslims around the world.

Until that moment, 13 centuries ago, the Arabs were mostly polytheists, worshiping tribal deities. They had no sacred history linking them to one universal god, like other Middle Eastern peoples. They had no sacred text to live by, like the Bible; no sacred language, as Hebrew is to Jews and Sanskrit is to Hindus. Above all, they had no prophet sent to them by God, as Jews and Christians could boast.

Muhammad and the words that he recited until his death in 632 provided all this and more. Like the Bible, the Qur'an is a book of divine revelation. Between them, these two books define the will of God for more than half the world's population. Over centuries, the Bible fashioned the Hebrew tribes into a nation: Israel. But in just a hundred years, the Qur'an created an entire civilization that at its height stretched from northern Africa and southern Europe in the West to the borders of modern India and China in the East. Even today, in streets as distant from each other as those of Tashkent, Khartoum, Qom and Kuala Lumpur, one can hear from dawn to dusk the constant murmur and chant of the Qur'an in melodious Arabic. Indeed, if there were a gospel according to Muhammad, it would begin with these words: in the beginning was the Book.

But since the events of September 11, the Qur'an and the religion it inspired have been on trial. Is Islam an inherently intolerant faith? Does the Qur'an oblige Muslims to wage jihad—holy war—on those who do not share their beliefs? And who are these "infidels" that the Muslim Scriptures find so odious? After all, Jews and Christians are monotheists, too, and most of their own prophets—Abraham, Moses and Jesus especially—are revered by Muslims through their holy book. Listening to the rants of Osama bin Laden and other radical Islamists, Jews and Christians wonder who really speaks for Islam in these perilous times. What common ground—if any—joins these three "Peoples of the Book," as Muslims call their fellow monotheists? What seeds of reconciliation lie within the Qur'an and the Bible and the traditions that they represent? Does the battle of the books, which has endured for centuries between Mulsims and believers in the West, ensure a perpetual clash of civilizations?

The Qur'an does contain sporadic calls to violence, sprinkled throughout the text. Islam implies "peace," as Muslims repeatedly

> ### *Listening to the rants of Osama bin Laden and other radical Islamists, Jews and Christians wonder who really speaks for Islam in these perilous times.*

insist. Yet the peace promised by Allah to individuals and societies is possible only to those who follow the "straight path" as outlined in the Qur'an. When Muslims run into opposition, especially of the armed variety, the Qur'an counsels bellicose response. "Fight them [nonbelievers] so that Allah may punish them at your hands, and put them to shame," one Qur'anic verse admonishes. Though few in number, these aggressive verses have fired Muslim zealots in every age.

The Bible, too, has its stories of violence in the name of the Lord. The God of the early Biblical books is fierce indeed in his support of the Israelite warriors, drowning enemies in the sea. But these stories do not have the force of divine commands. Nor are they considered God's own eternal words, as Muslims believe Qur'anic verses to be. Moreover, Israeli commandos do not cite the Hebrew prophet Joshua as they go into battle, but Muslim insurgents can readily invoke the example of their Prophet, Muhammad, who was a military commander himself. And while the Crusaders may have fought with the cross on their shields, they did not—could not—cite words from Jesus to justify their slaughters. Even so, compared with the few and much quoted verses that call for jihad against the infidels, the Qur'an places far more emphasis on acts of justice, mercy and compassion.

Indeed, the Qur'an is better appreciated as comprehensive guide for those who would know and do the will of God. Like the Bible, the Qur'an defines rules for prayer and religious rituals. It establishes norms governing marriage and divorce, relations between men and

Bin Laden's Twisted Mission*

By Christopher Dickey
Newsweek, February 11, 2002

When Osama bin Laden proclaimed his "Jihad against Crusaders and Jews" in 1998, he knew he was on shaky religious ground. This was his declaration of "holy war" to justify bombing U.S. embassies in Africa a few months later and, eventually, the attacks of September 11. It was his theological license "to kill the Americans and plunder their money wherever and whenever they are found." And it was based on a lie: that Islam itself was under attack by the United States, that "crimes and sins committed by the Americans are a clear declaration of war on God, his messenger and Muslims." The fact that Americans defended Muslims against the likes of Saddam Hussein and Slobodan Milosevic was ignored because, for bin Laden's bloody-minded purposes, it had to be.

Without that lie about American aggression, none of the many verses of the Qur'an that bin Laden cites would justify violence, much less the unholy slaughter of civilians. There are many interpretations of jihad—which means, literally, "effort." Often it describes the personal struggle merely to be a better, more pious Muslim. The empire builders of Islam waged military offensives in the name of jihad as late as the 17th century, and not a few turned their righteous doctrines on each other. But according to Gilles Kepel, author of the forthcoming book *Jihad: The Trail of Political Islam*, the defensive holy war that bin Laden claims to fight is the most potent and most dangerous form of all. It is seen by many Muslims, if it is justified, as a personal obligation that supersedes all others, and may ultimately challenge all authority. "It's a two-edged sword," says Kepel. "Once you open the gate of defensive jihad, it's very difficult to close it again."

"To those against whom war is made, permission is given to fight," says the 22d chapter of the Qur'an—especially "those who have been expelled from their homes. . . for no cause except that they say,' 'Our Lord is Allah'." Thus in Muslim theology defensive holy war was justified against European Crusaders and conquerors who attacked Muslims in the name of Christ and imposed the Inquisition, with all its horrors. Thus, in more recent times, Afghans could wage their war against the atheistic Soviets with plenty of religious backing. Few if any Muslim scholars will speak out against jihad by Palestinians fighting Israeli occupying troops. But bin Laden, a Saudi, was never persecuted for his faith. The goals he fought for initially were political and personal: to overthrow the Muslim rulers of his own country. And the jihad he declared against the United States, in the eyes of most religious scholars, was never a holy war, it was a blatant fraud.

women and the way to raise righteous children. More important, both books trace a common lineage back to Abraham, who was neither Jew nor Christian, and beyond that to Adam himself. Theologically, both books profess faith in a single God (Allah means "The God") who creates and sustains the world. Both call humankind to repentance, obedience and purity of life. Both warn of God's punishment and final judgment of the world. Both imagine a hell and a paradise in the hereafter.

Divine Authority

As sacred texts, however, the Bible and the Qur'an could not be more different. To read the Qur'an is like entering a stream. At almost any point one may come upon a command of God, a burst of prayer, a theological pronouncement, the story of an earlier prophet or a description of the final judgment. Because Muhammad's revelations were heard, recited and memorized by his converts, the Qur'an is full of repetitions. None of its 114 suras, or chapters, focuses on a single theme. Each sura takes its title from a single word—The Cow, for example, names the longest—which appears only in that chapter. When Muhammad's recitations were finally written down (on palm leaves, shoulders of animals, shards of anything that would substitute for paper) and collected after his death, they were organized roughly from the longest to the shortest. Thus there is no chronological organization—this is God speaking, after all, and his words are timeless.

Nonetheless, scholars recognize that the shortest suras were received first, in Muhammad's Meccan period, and the longest in Medina, where he later became a political and military leader of the

The Qur'an's fluid structure can be confusing, even to Muslims.

emerging community of Muslims. As a result, the longer texts take up matters of behavior and organization which are absent in the shorter, more "prophetic" suras that announce the need to submit. ("Muslim" means "submission" to God.) The Qur'an's fluid structure can be confusing, even to Muslims. "That's why one finds in Muslim bookstores such books as 'What the Qur'an says about women' or 'What the Qur'an says about a just society'," observes Jane McAuliffe of Georgetown University, editor of the new Encyclopaedia of the Qur'an.

Like the Bible, the Qur'an asserts its own divine authority. But whereas Jews and Christians regard the Biblical text as the words of divinely inspired human authors, Muslims regard the Qur'an, which means "The Recitation," as the eternal words of Allah himself. Thus, Muhammad is the conduit for God's words, not their composer. Moreover, since Muhammad heard God in Arabic, translations of the Qur'an are considered mere "interpretations" of the language of God's original revelation. "In this very important sense," says Roy Mottahedeh, professor of Middle Eastern history at Harvard, "the Qur'an is *not* the Bible of the Muslims." Rather, he says, it is like the oral Torah first revealed to Moses that was later written down. In gospel terminology, the Qur'an corresponds to Christ himself, as the *logos*, or eternal word of the Father. In short, if Christ is the word made flesh, the Qur'an is the word made book.

The implications of this doctrine are vast—and help to explain the deepest divisions between Muslims and other monotheisms. For Muslims, God is one, indivisible and absolutely transcendent. Because of this, no edition of the Qur'an carries illustrations—even of the Prophet—lest they encourage idolatry (*shirk*), the worst sin a Muslim can commit. Muslims in the former Persian Empire, however, developed a rich tradition of extra-Qur'anic art depicting episodes in the life of Muhammad, from which the illustrations for this story are taken. But for every Muslim, the presence of Allah can be experienced here and now through the very sounds and syllables of the Arabic Qur'an. Thus, only the original Arabic is used in prayer—even though the vast majority of Muslims do not understand the language. It doesn't matter: the Qur'an was revealed through the Prophet's ears, not his eyes. To hear those same words recited, to take them into yourself through prayer, says Father Patrick Gaffney, an anthropologist specializing in Islam at the University of Notre Dame, "is to experience the presence of God

---

Readers of the Bible will find in the Qur'an familiar figures such as Abraham, Moses, David, John the Baptist, Jesus and even the Virgin Mary.

---

with the same kind of intimacy as Catholics feel when they receive Christ as consecrated bread and wine at mass."

"People of the Book"

Why then, does the Qur'an acknowledge Jews and Christians as fellow "People of the Book," and as such, distinguish them from nonbelievers? Contrary to popular belief, "the Book" in question is not the Bible; it refers to a heavenly text, written by God, of which the Qur'an is the only perfect copy. According to the Qur'an, God mercifully revealed the contents of that book from time to time through the words of previous Biblical prophets and messengers— and also to other obscure figures not mentioned in the Bible. But in every case those who received his revelations—particularly the Jews and Christians—either consciously or inadvertently corrupted the original text, or seriously misinterpreted it. On this view, the Qur'an is not a new version of what is contained in the Bible, but what Jane McAuliffe calls a "re-revelation" that corrects the errors of the Hebrew and Christian Scriptures. Readers of the Bible will find in the Qur'an familiar figures such as Abraham, Moses, David, John the Baptist, Jesus and even the Virgin Mary, who appears much more often than she does in the New Testament, and is the only woman mentioned in the Qur'an by name. But their stories differ radically from those found in the Bible. In the Qur'an all the previous prophets are Muslims.

Abraham (Ibrahim), for example, is recognized as the first Muslim because he chose to surrender to Allah rather than accept the religion of his father, who is not mentioned in the Bible. Neither is the Qur'anic story of how Abraham built the Kaaba in Mecca, Islam's holiest shrine. Abraham's importance in the Qur'an is central: just as the Hebrews trace their lineage to Abraham through Isaac, his son by Sarah, the Qur'an traces Arab genealogy—and Muhammad's prophethood—back through Ishmael, a son Abraham had by Hagar.

The Qur'anic Moses (Musa) looks much like his Biblical counterpart. He confronts the pharaoh, works miracles and in the desert ascends the mountain to receive God's commandments. But in the Qur'an there is no mention of the Passover rituals, and among the commandments one of the most important for Jews—keeping the Sabbath—is absent. Obedience to parents is stressed repeatedly, but as in the Qur'anic story of Abraham, disobedience is required when parents are polytheists.

As a prophet rejected by his own people, the Qur'anic Jesus (Isa) looks a lot like Muhammad, who was at first rejected by the people of Mecca. He preaches the word of God, works miracles, is persecuted and—what is new, foretells his successor: Muhammad. But the Qur'an rejects the Christian claim that he is the son of God as blasphemous and dismisses the doctrine of the Trinity as polytheistic. The Crucifixion is mentioned in passing, but according to the Qur'an Jesus mysteriously does not die. Instead, Allah rescues him to heaven from where he will descend in the last days and, like other prophets, be a witness for his community of believers at the Final Judgment.

What Muhammad may have known about the Bible and its prophets and where he got his information is a purely scholarly debate. The Qur'an itself says that Muhammad met a Jewish clan in Medina. He even had his followers bow to Jerusalem when praying until the Jews rejected him as prophet. Some scholars claim that Muhammad had in-laws who were Christian, and they believe he learned his fasting and other ascetic practices from observing desert monks. But Muslims reject any scholarly efforts to link the contents of the Qur'an to the Prophet's human interactions. They cherish the tradition that Muhammad could not read or write as proof that the Qur'an is pure revelation. It is enough for them that Islam is the perfect religion and the Qur'an the perfect text.

That belief has not prevented Muslim tradition from transforming the Qur'an's many obscure passages into powerful myths. By far the most significant is the story developed from one short verse: "Glory be to Him who carried His servant at night from the Holy Mosque to the Further Mosque, the precincts of which we have blessed, that we might show him some of our signs" (sura 17:1). From this Muslims have elaborated the story of Muhammad's mystical nighttime journey from Mecca to Jerusalem, where he addresses an assembly of all previous prophets from Adam to Jesus. Yet another version of this story tells of his subsequent Ascension (*mi'raj*) from Jerusalem to the throne of Allah, receiving honors along the way from the prophets whom he has superseded. For Sufi mystics, Muhammad's ascension is the paradigmatic story of the soul's flight to God. For many Muslim traditionalists, however, the journey was a physical one. Either way, its geopolitical significance cannot be ignored because the spot where the ascension began is Islam's third holiest shrine: the Dome of the Rock on Jerusalem's Temple Mount.

In Islam's current political conflicts with the West, the major problem is not the Muslims' sacred book but how it is interpreted. Muslims everywhere are plagued by a crippling crisis of authority. The Qur'an envisioned a single Muslim community (the *umma*), but as subsequent history shows, Muslims have never resolved the tension between religious authority and Islamic governments. When Islam was a great medieval civilization, jurists learned in the Qur'an decided how to apply God's words to changed historical circumstances. Their *fatwas* (opinions) settled disputes. But in today's Islamic states, authoritative religious voices do not command widespread respect. Like freewheeling fundamentalists of every religious stripe, any Muslim with an agenda now feels free to cite the Qur'an in his support. Osama bin Laden is only the most dangerous and obvious example.

Deciphering Meanings

But the Qur'an has its moderate interpreters as well. Since September 11, brave voices scattered across the Middle East have condemned the terrorist acts of killing civilians and judged suicide bombing contrary to the teaching of the Qur'an. Returning to the text itself, other scholars have found verses showing that Allah created diverse peoples and cultures for a purpose and therefore intended that the world remain pluralistic in religion as well. "The Qur'an," argues Muslim philosopher Jawat Said of the Al-Azhar Institute in Cairo, "gives support and encouragement to sustain the messengers of reform who face difficult obstacles."

America, too, has a core of immigrant and second-generation Muslim scholars who have experienced firsthand the benefits of democracy, free speech and the Bill of Rights. They think the Qur'an is open to interpretations that can embrace these ideals for Islamic states as well. Islam even has feminists like Azizah Y. al-Hibri of the University of Richmond Law School, who are laying the legal groundwork for women's rights through a careful reconsideration of the Qur'an and its classic commentators.

It is precisely here that the Bible and the Qur'an find their real kinship. As divine revelation, each book says much more than what a literal reading can possibly capture. To say that God is one, as both the Qur'an and the Bible insist, is also to say that God's wisdom is unfathomable. As the Prophet himself insisted, God reveals himself through signs whose meanings need to be deciphered. Here, it would seem, lie the promising seeds of religious reconciliation. Humility, not bravado, is the universal posture of anyone who dares to plumb the mind of God and seek to do his will.

Pluralism, Intolerance, and the Qur'an[2]

By ALI S. ASANI
THE AMERICAN SCHOLAR, WINTER 2002

> Infuse your heart with mercy, love and kindness for your subjects . . . either they are your brothers in religion or your equals in creation.
>
> —from a letter written by the Muslim Caliph Ali ibn Abi Talib (d. 661) to Malik al-Ashtar on the latter's appointment as governor of Egypt

As a Muslim involved in teaching and scholarship on the Islamic tradition, I have received many invitations over the past several weeks to speak about the role that religion and religious ideas may or may not have played in the horrific events of September 11, 2001. Non-Muslim audiences have wanted to know how Islam, a religion whose very name signifies peace for many Muslims, could be used to promote violence and hatred for America and the West? Why, many in these audiences wonder, are some Muslims and some governments in Muslim nations anti-American, antagonistic to America and the West, and willing to condone or even applaud the loss of innocent American lives? For their part, Muslims I have spoken to have similar concerns. Why, many of them wonder, are some Americans and Europeans and some American and Western policies anti-Islamic, antagonistic to Muslim interests, and heedless to the loss of innocent Muslim lives? In an atmosphere rampant with stereotypes about the "other," I have been engaged in providing audiences with historical and religious perspectives on the complex factors that have created such deep and profound misunderstandings among Muslims and non-Muslims alike. While I have participated in many public forums, this has also been a time of reflection for me personally as, indeed, for many Muslims who are bewildered by the bizarre and repugnant behavior of individuals who committed these acts allegedly in the name of God.

The paradox of a religious tradition being used to promote harmony and tolerance on the one hand, and to justify war and intolerance on the other, is not unique to Islam. History shows us that all religions, particularly their scriptures, have been interpreted by believers to justify a wide range of contradictory political, social, and cultural goals. The Qur'an, the scripture believed by Muslims to have been revealed by God to Muhammad, Prophet of Islam, is no exception. With regard to the issue of peace and violence, my

2. Reprinted from *The American Scholar*, Volume 71, No. 1, Winter 2002. Copyright © 2002 by the author.

contention is that the Qur'an essentially espouses a pluralist world-view, one that promotes harmony among nations and peoples. Through the centuries, however, it has been subjected to anti-pluralist, or exclusivist, interpretations in order to advance hegemonic goals, both political and religious. It is within the framework of this dichotomy between a pluralist Qur'an and anti-pluralist interpretations that we can best understand the conflicting and contradictory uses of Qur'anic texts. (I should add that my understanding of the conflict between pluralist and exclusivist strands within the Islamic tradition has been greatly influenced by Abdulaziz Sachedina's pioneering study, *The Islamic Roots of Democratic Pluralism*. I am also indebted to my colleague Roy Mottahedeh, whose article "Towards an Islamic Theology of Toleration," *Islamic Law Reform and Human Rights*, ed. T. Lindholm and K. Vogt, I've found helpful.)

First, I would like to provide some sense of how I became aware of the Qur'an's teachings on pluralism. I was born and raised in Kenya, East Africa, in a devout Muslim family of South Asian ancestry. My ancestors had migrated to Africa from India more than two hundred years before. The society in which I grew up was a colonial one, under British rule. It was marked by racial and religious diversity, but also by strict racial segregation. The idiom of British imperialism in this part of Africa was racial, dividing society into three distinct classes: the European, or "white" ruling class; the Asian, or trading and clerical class (in Kenya, the term "Asian" denotes a person of South Asian ancestry); and the African, or "black" class, which mostly provided labor. Thus I grew up in an environment deeply conscious of racial differences as well as of tensions between classes. I was also keenly aware of religious diversity. Among the Asians, I knew that not all followed the same religion: there were Hindus, Sikhs, Jains, Muslims—all of whom were further divided into subgroups, such as the Arya Samaj, the Visha Oshwal, the Shia, and the Sunni. Among the Africans, there were many different tribes that spoke different languages and that were on occasion antagonistic to one another. I was also aware that some Africans were Muslims, others were Christians of various persuasions, and still others practiced what were termed "traditional African religions." About the Europeans I knew very little, since they kept mostly to themselves and I had no occasion to interact with them.

When I was nine or ten years old and wondering about racial and religious diversity, I asked my father, a devout Muslim, "Why didn't Allah make human beings all the same? Why did Allah make us all different?" In response, my father quoted a verse from the Qur'an: "O humankind, We [God] have created you male and female, and made you into communities and tribes, so that you may know one another. Surely the noblest amongst you in the sight of God is the most godfearing of you. God is All-knowing and All-Aware" (Qur'an 49:13). This verse from the Qur'an formed the first teaching I received as a child on the subject of pluralism. Now, many years later, as I reflect on it and its meaning, I believe it is clear that from the perspective of the Qur'an, which forms the core of Islamic tradition, the divine purpose underlying human diversity is to foster knowledge and understanding, to promote harmony and cooperation among peoples. God did not create diversity as a source of tensions, divisions, and polarization in society. Indeed, whether we recognize it or not, our diversity is a sign of divine genius. The Qur'anic verse also envisages a world in which people, regardless of their differences, are united by their devotion to God. These sentiments are, in fact, echoed in another verse, in which God addresses humankind and affirms the principle of unity in diversity: "Surely this community of yours is one community, and I am your Lord; so worship me" (Qur'an 21:92). The emphasis on the universality of God's message is reflected in the Qur'an's fundamental teaching that God has revealed it to *all* peoples and to *all* cultures; not a single people or nation has been forgotten (Qur'an 35:24). Although humans may have misinterpreted that message to suit their needs in creating conflicting traditions, all religions, at their core, have sprung from the same divine source and inspiration.

The Qur'anic verse ... envisages a world in which people, regardless of their differences, are united by their devotion to God.

The idea that God's message is universal, but its manifestations are plural, provides the basic underpinning of the manner in which the Qur'an relates itself and the faith it preaches to the religious traditions that preceded it in the Middle East, namely Judaism and Christianity. Far from denying the validity of these predecessor traditions, the Qur'an repeatedly affirms their essential truth, acknowledging that their message comes from one and the same God, and that the Qur'an is only the latest of God's revelations to affirm and confirm those that preceded it. Characteristic of this affirmative and pluralistic stance is this command to believers: "Say: we believe in God and what has been revealed to us and what was revealed to Abraham, Ismail, Isaac, Jacob, and the tribes, and in what was given to Moses, Jesus, and the prophets from their Lord. We make no distinction between one and another among them and to Him [God] do we submit" (Qur'an 3:84).

Qur'anic beliefs in the truth of the Judaic and Christian traditions are also encapsulated in another term: the *ahl al-kitab*, or People of the Book. This is the umbrella term in the Qur'an to refer to communities, or peoples, who have received revelation in the form of scripture. It is commonly used to refer to Jews, Christians, and Muslims. The pluralistic nature of this term is evident in the use of the noun *Book* in the singular rather than the plural, to emphasize that Jews, Christians, and Muslims follow one and the same Book, not various conflicting scriptures. The Old and New Testaments and the Qur'an are seen as being plural, earthly manifestations of the one heavenly Scripture in which God has inscribed the Divine word. Significantly, the Qur'an does not claim that it abrogates the scriptures revealed before it. On the contrary, it affirms their validity. In one verse addressed to the prophet Muhammad, God advises him, "And if you [Muhammad] are in doubt concerning that which We reveal to you, then question those who read the scripture [that was revealed] before you" (Qur'an 10:94). Another verse addressed to the Muslim faithful says, "And argue not with the People of the Book unless it be in a way that is better, save with such of them as do wrong; and say we believe in that which has been revealed to us and to you; our God and your God is one and unto Him we submit" (Qur'an 29:46).

While the concept of the People of the Book was originally coined to refer to the major monotheistic traditions in the Arabian milieu, there were attempts to expand the term theologically to include other groups, such as the Zoroastrians in Iran and Hindus and Buddhists in India, as the Islamic tradition spread outside the Middle East and Muslims encountered other religious traditions. In seventeenth-century India, Dara Shikoh, a prince from the ruling Mughal dynasty who was strongly influenced by the pluralistic teachings

---

The Qur'an does not deny the salvific value of the Judaic or the Christian traditions.

---

within Islamic traditions of mysticism, considered the Hindu scriptures, the Upanishads, to be the "storehouse of monotheism" and claimed that they were the *kitab maknun*, or "hidden scripture," referred to in the Qur'an (56:77–80). He personally translated these Sanskrit texts into Persian and held that it was the duty of every faithful Muslim to read them. Admittedly, not all Muslims were comfortable with the broadening of the term "People of the Book" to include religious scriptures and traditions not mentioned specifically by name in the Qur'an, but the fact remains that these types of interpretation were made possible by the pluralistic nature of the Qur'anic worldview.

With such a universalist perspective, it goes without saying that the Qur'an does not deny the salvific value of the Judaic or the Christian traditions. Salvation, according to the Qur'an, will be granted to anyone who is a submitter to Divine Will (the literal meaning of the word muslim). Indeed, Islamic scripture regards Abraham, the patriarch, and all the other prophets of the Judaeo-Christian tradition, including Moses and Jesus, as being *muslim* in the true sense of the word. Typically, the third chapter of the Qur'an contains the following verses: "Some of the People of the Book are a nation upstanding: they recite the Signs of God all night long, and they prostrate themselves in adoration. They believe in God and the Last Day; they enjoin what is right and forbid what is wrong and they hasten to do good works. They are in the ranks of the righteous" (Qur'an 3:113–114). Repeatedly, the Qur'an declares that on the Day of Judgment all human beings will be judged on their moral performance, irrespective of their formal religious affiliation.

The Qur'an's endorsement of religiously and culturally plural societies and the recognition of the salvific value of other monotheistic religions greatly affected the treatment of religious minorities in Muslim lands throughout history. While there have been instances when religious minorities were grudgingly tolerated in Muslim societies, rather than being respected in the true spirit of pluralism, the Qu'ranic endorsement of a pluralistic ethos explains why the violent forms of anti-Semitism generated by exclusivist Christian theology in medieval and modern Europe, and the associated harsh treatment of Jewish populations that eventually culminated in the Holocaust, never occurred in regions under Muslim rule.

From the earliest periods of Muslim history, we have examples of respect for the rights of non-Muslims under Muslim rule. For

---

> ### *From the earliest periods of Muslim history, we have examples of respect for the rights of non-Muslims under Muslim rule.*

---

instance, the fourth Caliph, Ali ibn Abi Talib (d. 661), instructed his governor in Egypt to show mercy, love, and kindness to all subjects under his rule, including non-Muslims, whom he declared to be "your equals in creation." Such tolerance is later reflected in the policies of the Arab dynasties of Spain, the Fatimids in North Africa, and the Turkish Ottomans in the Middle East, granting maximum individual and group autonomy to those adhering to a non-Islamic religious tradition. We can also cite the example of the Mughal emperor Akbar (d. 1605), who—much to the dismay of the religious right wing of his time—promoted tolerance among the various traditions that composed the Indian religious landscape.

How can a scripture that celebrates pluralism be the source of the intolerance and hatred that a few contemporary Muslim groups show toward the West? How can a scripture that declares "Let there be no compulsion in religion" be invoked by those who would forcibly impose their religious views on others, Muslim and non-Muslim alike? How can a scripture that instructs Muslims to regard the People of the Book as among the righteous be used to declare that Christians and Jews are infidels? The answers to these questions can be traced to the emergence of an unfortunate mode of Qur'anic interpretation that is exclusivist in nature.

A complex and intricately connected set of factors has given rise to this exclusivist discourse. Here I would briefly mention two: the doctrine of supersession and the religious legitimation of political hegemony. Supersession is the idea that Islam, as the latest of the monotheistic revelations, supersedes all revelations that preceded it. It postulates that since Islam is the successor to the Judaic and Christian traditions, it is the latest and most complete form of revelation. Moreover, since Muhammad was the last of approximately 124,000 prophets sent to humanity by God, he was therefore the bearer of God's revelation in its most perfect form. According to this doctrine, the Qur'anic revelation abrogated all preceding scriptures. As God's last revelation, the Qur'an alone had validity until the end of time. Thus the possibility of attaining salvation through religions other than Islam, if admitted at all, was at best limited.

Such exclusivist conceptions were helpful in fostering a sense of identity among adherents of a new religious community, eventually becoming an important means of forging solidarity among various Arab tribes that had previously been engaged in petty rivalries and wars. In the eighth and ninth centuries, this social and political solidarity became the backbone of the early Arab Muslim empire, for it provided an effective basis for aggression against those who did not share this solidarity with the community of believers. It is within this context that political concepts such as *dar al-islam* (territories under Muslim suzerainty) and *dar al-harb* (territories under non-Muslim control) became prominent, although they have no real basis in the Qur'an. In the same vein, the notion of jihad was reinterpreted to justify imperial goals. In the Arabic language, this term, which is fraught with definitional ambiguities, literally means "struggle." It was initially interpreted, at the time of the prophet Muhammad, to connote an ethical and moral struggle against an individual's base instincts, or as a defensive struggle by the early Muslims against religious persecution: "Leave is given to those who fight because they are wronged—surely God is able to help them—who were expelled from their habitations without right, except that they say 'Our Lord is God'" (Qur'an 22:39–40). "And fight [struggle] in the way of God with those who fight with you, but aggress not: God loves not the aggressors" (Qur'an 2:190). Under the influence of the political realities of later centuries that witnessed an expansion of Arab rule, what was clearly a reference in the Qur'an to a moral struggle, or an armed struggle in the face of provocation and aggression, came to be interpreted as a general military offensive against nonbelievers and as a means of legitimizing political dominion. (For more about the theological debates on the term *jihad* in early Islam, see R. Mottahedeh and R. Al-Sayyid, "The Idea of *Jihad* in Islam before the Crusades," *The Crusades from the Perspective of Byzantium and the Muslim World*, ed. A. Laiou and R. Mottahedeh [Dumbarton Oaks Center Studies, 2001].)

To be sure, the religious justification for promoting imperialist interests had to be sought in the Qur'an, the very text that forbade compulsion in religious matters and contained verses of an ecumenical nature recognizing not only the authenticity of other monotheistic traditions, but the essential equality of all prophets sent by God.

For this purpose, as Abdulaziz Sachedina has so ably demonstrated, several Muslim exegetes devised terminological and methodological strategies to mold the exegesis of the sacred text in order to provide a convincing prop for absolutist ends. The principal means by which the exclusivists were able to promote their view was by declaring that the many verses calling for pluralism, commanding Muslims to build bridges of understanding with non-Muslims, had been overridden by other verses that called for fighting the infidel. The verses in question were revealed after war broke out in the seventh century between the small, beleaguered Muslim community and its powerful pagan Arab, Christian, and Jewish adversaries. Typical of these verses is the following: "Then when the sacred months are drawn away, slay the idolators wherever you find them, and take them, and confine them, and lie in wait for them at every place of ambush. But if they repent and perform the prayer and pay *zakat* [the alms tax], let them go their way. Surely God is forgiving and merciful" (Qur'an 9:5). Another verse, revealed when certain Jewish and Christian groups betrayed the Muslim cause and joined in the military assault by the pagan Arabs against the prophet Muhammad and the Muslim community, cautioned against taking Jews and Christians as close political allies (Qur'an 5:51). It is only by completely disregarding the original historical contexts of revelation of such verses and using them to engage in a large-scale abrogation of contradictory verses that the exclusivist Muslim exegetes have been able to counteract the pluralist ethos that so thoroughly pervades the Qur'an.

Exclusivist interpretations of the Qur'an have . . . been used to justify dominion over other Muslims.

Historically, exclusivist interpretations of the Qur'an have also been used to justify dominion over other Muslims, specifically those whose interpretation of the faith and religious practices were perceived as deviating from the norms espoused by exclusivists. During the seventeenth and eighteenth centuries, for instance, several areas of the Muslim world witnessed the rise of movements that, in response to what was perceived as a general moral decline, attempted to "purify" Islam. The leaders of those movements targeted a range of practices and beliefs among fellow Muslims that, in their eyes, constituted evidence of religious backsliding. In particular, Sufi forms of Islam were attacked as not deriving from "authentic" Islam. In certain cases, the attacks took on a military character, and *jihads* were launched against fellow Muslims with the intention of forcibly imposing upon them those interpretations favored by the exclusivists.

The most dramatic and influential of these movements was the so-called Wahhabi movement in Arabia. Named after the reformer Abd al-Wahhab, who died in 1791, this puritanical movement acquired an explosive energy after its founder allied himself with a petty Arab chieftain, Muhammad Ibn Saud. Abd al-Wahhab was influenced in his thought by the writings of a controversial four-teenth-century thinker, Ibn Taiymiyyah, whose exclusivist and lit-eralist interpretations of the Qur'an led him to declare that the descendants of the Mongols were infidels, notwithstanding their public profession of belief in Islam. To propagate their particular brand of Islam, the Wahhabis attacked fellow Muslims, whose prac-tices they considered "un-Islamic." Targeting in particular popular expressions of Sufi practice as well as Shii Muslims, the Wahhabis steadily expanded their power over central and western Arabia until they were able to effect the political unification of the penin-sula into the kingdom of Saudi Arabia. Once established, the Wah-habi authorities instituted a religious police force, which, among its other functions, compels Muslims to perform ritual prayer at appro-priate times of the day, in direct contradiction of the Qur'an's com-mandment, "Let there be no compulsion in religion." Not surprisingly, this movement considered Jews and Christians to be infidels. To this day, Saudi Arabia's state version of Islam is founded on an exclusivist interpretation of the Qur'an, intolerant of both interreligious and intrareligious plurality. Bankrolled by mil-lions of petrodollars, the Saudis' exclusivist interpretation of Islam has been exported all over the Muslim world, much to the dismay of the pluralists.

In recent times, exclusivist views have also been heavily promoted by so-called fundamentalist groups in the Muslim world. (Though I recognize that the term *fundamentalist* is not an academically accu-rate term to describe these groups, I use it here because of its broad acceptance in popular discourse.) The reasons for the rise of such groups are complex. Broadly speaking, these movements are a reac-tion against modernity, Westernization, economic deprivation, glo-bal domination by Western powers (particularly the United States), and support by such powers for repressive regimes in predomi-nantly Muslim lands. The failure of borrowed ideologies, such as capitalism, communism, or socialism, to deliver economic and social justice in many Muslim countries has created exclusivist groups seeking a "pure" and "authentic" language in which to criticize the failed modern Muslim state, a state that has marginalized, or dis-placed, traditional religious authorities in a bid to maximize politi-cal power. The search for a solution to the myriad political, social, and economic problems confronting Muslims has led these exclusiv-ist groups to use Islam as a political ideology for the state: "Islam is the solution." The commitment of such groups to understand Islam in a "pure" monolithic form, to engage in revisionist history, and to read religious texts in an exclusivist manner that denies any plural-ity of interpretations, has unleashed a struggle in the Muslim world between the members of such movements and those who uphold the pluralist teachings of the Qur'an. An important dimension of the struggle between the exclusivists and the pluralists is the debate over the role and status of women in Muslim societies, for exclusivists tend to be anti-egalitarian in their interpretations of gender roles.

For Muslims to participate in the multireligious and multicultural world of the twenty-first century, it is essential that they fully embrace Qur'anic teachings on pluralism. Exclusivist interpretations of the Qur'an that are premised on the hegemony of Islam over non-Islam and that employ a rhetoric of hate and violence to attain such goals are outdated in a global society in which relations between different peoples are best fostered on the basis of equality and mutual respect—a basic principle underlying the Qur'anic worldview. Since in several key Muslim nations the exclusivist message has been propagated by *madrasas*, or religious schools, sponsored by exclusivist groups or by the state itself, a key to the outcome of the struggle between pluralism and exclusivism in the Islamic tradition lies in the re-education of Muslim peoples about the pluralism that lies at the heart of the Qur'an. Without this pluralist education, they will continue to rely on the monolithic interpretations of scholars and demagogues to access the Qur'an. Only by raising levels of religious literacy in the Islamic world will Muslims become aware of the centrality of Qur'anic teachings concerning religious and cultural pluralism as a divinely ordained principle of coexistence among human societies.

As a pluralist Muslim who is American, I am struck by the resonance between the pluralism espoused in the Qur'an and that in the constitution and civic culture of the United States. Contrary to what some may claim, one can be fully American and fully Muslim simultaneously. Although it is true that there are certain American foreign policies relating to Muslim peoples and nations—including partisanship for illiberal Israeli policies and support for an intolerant Saudi state, as well as for exclusivist Muslim groups—that I believe call for critical inquiry and reappraisal, I also believe that my questioning of these U.S. policies must be coupled with my challenging of intolerant and textually dubious exclusivist interpretations within my religious tradition. In the end, a struggle against the flaws of the "other"—whether that other is "the West" or "Islam"—is worthwhile only if it is joined with a struggle (*jihad*) against the flaws within one's own traditions. In the necessary work of struggling against such errors, one should not lose sight of how much there is to be proud of in those traditions. As one who is proud both of Islam and of my adopted country, and is inspired by the consonance of their pluralism, I close with words from the Qur'an that also resonate in the American collective consciousness: "In God We Trust" (Qur'an 7:89).

Anti-Semitism Is Deepening Among Muslims[3]

By Susan Sachs
The New York Times, April 27, 2002

Stay in a five-star hotel anywhere from Jordan to Iran, and you can buy the infamous forgery *Protocols of the Elders of Zion*. Pick up a newspaper in any part of the Arab world and you regularly see a swastika superimposed on the Israeli flag.

Such anti-Semitic imagery is now embedded in the mainstream discourse concerning Jews in much of the Islamic world, in the popular press and in academic journals. The depictions are not limited to countries that are at war with Israel but can be found in general-interest publications in Egypt and Jordan, the two countries that have signed peace agreements with Israel, as well as in independent religious schools in Pakistan and Southeast Asia.

Arab leaders, for their part, have long rejected the accusation that their state-controlled press, universities and television stations promulgate anti-Semitic views. Islamic history, they say, contains nothing like the anti-Semitic horrors that occurred in Christian Europe, and Islam as a religion accepts many of the revelations embodied in Judaism.

The use of Nazi imagery, the newspaper caricatures of Jews with fangs and exaggerated hook noses, even the Arab textbooks with their descriptions of Jews as evil world conspirators—all of that, Arab leaders often insist, reflect a dislike for Israelis and Zionism but not for Jews and Judaism.

Yet in many Muslim countries the hatred of Jews as Jews, and not only as citizens of Israel, has been nurtured through popular culture for generations.

Take for instance an official Jordanian government textbook for high school students. It describes Jews as innately deceitful and corrupt. "Up to the present," it states, "they are the masters of usury and leaders of sexual exhibitionism and prostitution."

In the view of many scholars of Islam, such texts are a sign that the Arab-Israeli conflict has been transformed in Muslim culture from a political, nationalist and territorial battle into a cosmic war between religions and, indeed, between good and evil.

The length of the Middle East conflict has contributed to this shift.

"You see a certain level of anti-Semitism that you look at and think, how can smart people really believe this?" said John L. Esposito, a professor of religion and international affairs at Georgetown University. "Part of the explanation is that they grew up with this, but part is also that they grew up in a confrontational situation. You make the world into 'us and them,' and therefore you buy into every possible caricature of the other."

Both Jews and Muslims engage in hatemongering based on skewed readings of their holy books, said Professor Esposito, author of the recent book *Unholy War: Terror in the Name of Islam*.

Islamic fundamentalists frequently refer to Jews as either the sons or the grandsons of apes and monkeys. These sorts of descriptions can sometimes be heard in sermons at mosques in the Palestinian territories as well as from some Saudi religious leaders.

The reference is drawn from a verse in the Koran that, taken in context, refers to Jews and Christians who break the Sabbath and who mock the early Muslims for their beliefs. The Koran says that

---

Both Jews and Muslims engage in hate-mongering based on skewed readings of their holy books.

God made those people as despicable as monkeys, pigs and idol worshipers.

"In all faiths, more exclusivist or militant verses are taken out of context by some and amplified in popular culture," Professor Esposito said. The Koran also contains complimentary verses about law-abiding Jews, at one point saying that the "believers and the Jews" who do right will be rewarded by God.

Islamic doctrine concerning Christians has also been reinterpreted in recent decades in an effort to forge a bond between Muslims and Christians against the Jews.

Literal Islam recognizes Jesus as a prophet but does not believe that he was crucified. The Koran says that Jews tried to crucify him, but that God rescued Jesus and that the Jews instead killed only a likeness of Jesus.

Yet a common charge from Muslims these days is that the Jews did indeed kill Jesus. When Pope John Paul II visited Damascus last year, President Bashar al-Assad greeted him with a speech accusing Jews of just that. Mr. Assad's minister of religion affairs, Muhammad Ziyadah, later embellished the remarks, saying, "We must be fully aware of what the enemies of God and malicious Zionism conspire to commit against Christianity and Islam."

The pope did not respond directly but called for reconciliation and peace.

That Jews would be demonized by some Arabs, and Arabs demonized by some Jews may not be surprising after nearly a century of conflict over Palestine. Even in less enduring wars, nations have engaged in vicious and sometimes racist wartime propaganda against the enemy. And since Israel was founded as a Jewish nation, the issue of religion has always been an element in its relations, or lack of relations, with its Arab neighbors.

Still, the breadth and viciousness of the anti-Semitism is striking.

Recent attacks on Jewish centers in France and an ancient synagogue in Tunisia have been attributed to Arabs or Muslim fundamentalists.

Last month the Saudi daily Al Riyadh published an article that accused Jews of consuming the blood of Christian and Muslim children during the holiday of Purim. The author, a lecturer at King Faisal University in Dammam, Saudi Arabia, called this medieval fiction a "well-established fact."

After the article was translated from the Arabic and publicized by an Israel-based group called the Middle East Media Research Institute, the editor of the newspaper repudiated the article, saying it was nonsense and should not have been published.

The recycling of such stories has become a fixture of Muslim discourse, said Bernard Lewis, a historian of Islam and the Middle East, who has called this trend the "Islamization of anti-Semitism."

Its literature, he has written, includes classic European anti-Semitic writings like *Protocols*, introduced to the Middle East in the late 1800's and now easily available in Arabic throughout the region and in English. In recent decades this material has been supplemented by a home-grown body of work, ascribed to Islamic teachings, that describes what it calls the innate wickedness of the Jewish people throughout the ages.

Yet Jews were minor players in Islamic theological writing for centuries, Professor Lewis wrote in *Semites and Anti-Semites*.

They figure in the Koran, which Muslims call the final and perfect revelation of God, as obstinate antagonists to the prophet Muhammad's efforts to bring Islam to the people of the Arabian Peninsula. Of the tribes he encountered, the Jews were the most hostile to his message. But in the end, the Jewish tribes were defeated, and the Koran refers to them as a people whose rebelliousness had always been punished by God.

In more modern Islamic teachings, which can be found in Arab textbooks and mainstream newspaper articles, the Koran's description of the Jews' opposition to Muhammad takes on monumental importance. The Jews corrupted the word of God from the start, the more recent interpretations say, and their scheming against the prophet was an expression of their innate wickedness.

"Some people confuse certain verses of the Koran attacking the Jews of that day, as an attack on Judaism," said Seyyed Hossein Nasr, a professor of Islamic studies at George Washington University. "It's not innocent confusion. It's deliberate confusion, and it happens on both sides."

This is a modern development, less theological than emotional, and leaves as its casualty a long tradition of amity between Islam and Judaism, he added.

"If religious authorities in both religions put the demands of God above nationalistic and ethnic feelings," Professor Nasr said, "then maybe something can be done."

The Islamic Jesus

A Wandering Prophet[4]

BY SARA MILLER
THE CHRISTIAN CENTURY, JANUARY 2–9, 2002

> *The Muslim Jesus: Sayings and Stories in Islamic Literature.*
> Edited and translated by Tarif Khalidi. Harvard University
> Press, $22.95

There are many Jesuses, despite the fact that there was only one. Permutations began appearing as early as the first century and have not abated, making efforts to uncover the historical Jesus, the real man from Nazareth, notoriously fraught and conflicting endeavors—as Christians who have tried can attest. The written record is incomplete and contradictory; archaeology can only assist and often merely confounds; scholars must detect and filter the "errors" of early accounts while keeping their own biases at bay. It is probably easier to meet Jesus in one's heart than to find him in the past—a venerable Christian theme, perhaps the most venerable.

More than a decade has passed since the Jesus Seminar published its study of the Gospels purporting to identify the authentic sayings of Jesus from the accumulated inventions of the evangelists. About a third of Jesus' teachings and deeds made the cut, consigning much of what Christians have been believing for 2,000 years to the dustbin of the dubious and the false. What remained of the man Jesus appeared, to some eyes, a little thin. The effect of this effort on the community of biblical scholars was predictable: conniptions, followed by factions. Among the statements declared inauthentic was this telling one: "Who do you say that I am?"

It may be possible to come at the problem from the opposite side—call it the fat Jesus. A study of the permutations themselves won't bring us closer to the historical figure, but what they tell us of our own longings and intentions could be invaluable.

Enter Islam, admittedly an unlikely place to look for answers to the conundrums of Christian history. In the Christian view, however, unlikelihood is the whole point; one dismisses it at one's peril. The portrait of Jesus that comes to us from Islamic literature ought not be dismissed either by traditionalists or by revisionists, despite the fact that this Jesus was himself no Christian at all. He was a Muslim prophet, a wandering ascetic, an exemplary spiritual guide and master—not a god but a man, like Muhammad, bearing God's

---

word—appropriated from Christian history and reinvented for Islamic eternity. One can meet this remarkable Muslim in the 300 or so known citations of his teachings and deeds found outside the Qur'an. These have been newly collected, translated and annotated by Cambridge University Arabist Tarif Khalidi.

This work, at first glance a tiny scholarly tributary, provides three large services. It offers a likely map of the paths by which Christian legend, including the Apocrypha, made its way into another, younger religion and evolved as testimony to the latter's veracity. It reveals, almost by the way, the deep theological insights of Islam and the brilliance of its scholars, spiritual writers and men of letters, who put their own faith's wisest words on Jesus' lips. And it introduces a Jesus of startling dimension and complexity, at once likable, pitiable, fallible and alarmingly recognizable not as God but as us.

Islam, born some 600 years after Christianity (Muhammad died in 632 C.E.), found its genesis in a world overflowing with Christian lore and wisdom. Much else was percolating in the Near East at

---

As a Muslim, Jesus speaks God's word in accord with various attitudes in Islamic belief.

---

that time as well: Judaism, Zoroastrianism, Samaritanism. The stories and testimonies of early Christians seeped into the traditional Arabic literature beginning around the eighth century and were still being added and redacted in the 18th. There are many references to Jesus in the Qur'an, where he is venerated but made to conform rather woodenly to Islamic doctrine (the adoption of Jesus, but not of Christian beliefs about him, was itself a muscular theological feat which Khalidi addresses in his introduction). And it is well known by Muslims that the prophet Muhammad esteemed the prophet Jesus in singular fashion. But it is from the extraneous religious texts—the Hadith, or early Islamic wisdom literature; the biographies of prophets and saints; the devotional works; the Adab, or belles lettres; and various guides to ethics and conduct—that the more intriguing and delightful portrait of Jesus emerges. This is the Jesus of what Khalidi has named the "Muslim gospel."

The contours of this Jesus distinguish him from the New Testament Jesus in predictable but also novel ways. Khalidi reminds us that in the Islamic version of history Jesus was not crucified, nor did he die for humanity's sins. In this he resembles the Jesus of the Gospel of Thomas and other apocryphal Christian scripts which accented the mystery Jesus came to reveal rather than his messiahship. Muslims aver that he was absorbed into heaven, but not resurrected. The Virgin Birth is accepted, and Jesus' mother is celebrated in Islamic art and appears in a few of the sayings. As a Muslim, Jesus speaks God's word in accord with various attitudes in Islamic belief, among them asceticism (early Islam), mysticism or spirituality of the heart (Sufism), and alternating sectarian views regarding law, sin, predestination and teaching authority.

As in the New Testament, Jesus speaks both masterfully and humbly. The Islamic sayings are, by any account, surpassingly beautiful. Khalidi alerts us to this in his introduction, but there is no way to quite prepare for it. Their rhetorical elegance ranges from the elliptical ("Be in the middle but walk to the side"), to the terse ("Fine clothes, proud hearts"), to the witty ("Piety is nine-tenths silence, and one-tenth fleeing from people"), to the paradoxical ("You shall not attain what you desire except by suffering what you do not desire"; "One should not marvel at how they were damned, those who were damned, but rather at how they were saved, those who were saved!") to the poignant ("Console me, for my heart is soft and I hold myself in low esteem") to the tender and merciful:

> It is related that on one of his journeys Jesus passed by a man asleep, wrapped in his cloak. Jesus woke him up and said, "Sleeper, get up and mention God Almighty." "What do you want from me?" said the sleeper, "I have abandoned this world to its people." Jesus said, "Sleep on, my beloved."

There are a number of intact sayings from the Gospels, but even the most familiar images—salt of the earth," "eye of a needle"—have been tailored to fit Islamic precepts or glossed with an "acceptable Muslim explanation." Many of the famous reversals of the New Testament, such as "the last shall be first" or the up-ended expectations of the parables, find their complement in such striking Muslim counterparts as: "If people appoint you as their heads, be like tails."

Or the incident in which Jesus met a man and asked him, "What are you doing?" "I am devoting myself to God," the man replied. Jesus asked, "Who is caring for you?" "My brother," replied the man. Jesus said, "Your brother is more devoted to God than you are."

Yet it is whom Jesus speaks to, and who answers, and what they say in the Muslim gospel that may most surprise students of Christian scripture. There is, for starters, his special sympathy with the creation (Khalidi terms him "an interrogator of nature"), evident in his discourses with skulls, stones, animals and the dead:

> A pig passed by Jesus. Jesus said, "Pass in peace." He was asked, "Spirit of God, how can you say this to a pig?" Jesus replied, "I hate to accustom my tongue to evil."

Khalidi explains that the Islamic import of this saying concerns purity (pigs being unclean) and slander, yet he also remarks that the saying could easily have been uttered by the Jesus of the Gospels.

While the caution against speaking ill does seem apt, students of scripture might argue that Jesus did not, even would not, address mere animals in this fashion, being concerned quite exclusively with the human estate. The Gospels do report that Jesus cast out demons from a herd of swine, but what this cure revealed was his command over evil spirits, and it was these he addressed. (There is, however, the Gospel incident in which Jesus speaks witheringly to a fig tree—a somewhat unsettling display of Christ's pique—yet here too the lesson is not in nature but beyond it.)

In his encounters with the dead and ruined, the Muslim Jesus again betrays an intimacy unparalleled in the New Testament:

> While on his travels, Jesus passed by a rotting skull. He commanded it to speak. The skull said, "Spirit of God, my name is Balwan ibn Hafs, king of Yemen. I lived a thousand years, begat a thousand sons, deflowered a thousand virgins, routed a thousand armies, killed a thousand tyrants, and conquered a thousand cities. Let him who hears my tale not be tempted by the world, for it was like nothing so much as the dream of a sleeper." Jesus wept.

Sorrow, Khalidi tells us, is the mark of the true Sufi, thus Jesus' tears signal his devotion in that quarter. But what is so startling in this incident is the casualness of the act of "resurrection" and the astounding fact that the skull is imparting wisdom to Jesus and not the other way around. The frequency and depth of the Islamic resurrection stories, which run seductively on in the manner of enchantments long before their theology is exposed, highlights this distinction marvelously. While not himself divine, the Muslim Jesus moves in and out of supernatural realms with extraordinary ease and zeal. The New Testament Jesus does so only deliberately, if not reluctantly. For him who is divine the adventure is on earth, in human hearts.

This pattern of Jesus as pilgrim and disciple, receiving wisdom even as he dispenses it, turns up in several charming exchanges with God, John the Baptist and Satan, in which Jesus is alternately chagrined, rebuked, justified and enlightened. There is this rather mortifying encounter with John:

> John the son of Zachariah met Jesus the son of Mary, John smiling of face and welcoming while Jesus was frowning and gloomy. Jesus said to John, "You smile as if you feel secure." John said to Jesus, "You frown as if you are in despair." God revealed, "What John does is dearer to us."

And this corrective from the Almighty:

> Jesus passed by a man making saddles who said as he prayed, "O God, if I knew where the ass You ride is, I would make him a saddle studded with jewels." Jesus shook him and said, "Woe to you! Does God Almighty have an ass?" God revealed to

Jesus, "Leave the man alone, for he has glorified me as best he can."

And this dialogue with the devil:

> It is related that Satan appeared to Jesus decked out in pendants of diverse colors and kinds. Jesus asked, "What are these pendants?" "These are the lusts of mankind," Satan replied. "Have I anything to do with any of them?" Jesus asked. "Perhaps you ate your fill and we made you too sluggish to pray or mention God," Satan replied. "Is there anything else?" asked Jesus. "No," said Satan. "I vow before God never to fill my belly with food," said Jesus. "And I vow before God never again to advise a Muslim," Satan replied.

Where the New Testament Jesus rejects worldliness and cautions against the evils of possessions, the Muslim Jesus harbors a much deeper disdain for both. In the early sayings he is fiercely ascetical, reflecting that current in Islam and perhaps, Khalidi speculates, in the Christian desert fathers as well. Yet even here, in the struggle to renounce every comfort save that of God, Jesus is himself a work in progress:

> Jesus owned nothing but a comb and a cup. He once saw a man combing his beard with his fingers, so Jesus threw away the comb. He saw another drinking from a river with his hands cupped, so Jesus threw away the cup.

If he makes no allowances for the world, however, toward the poor and his followers the Muslim Jesus is generous to the point of indulgence, a trait shared by Muhammad, Khalidi tells us, and by God:

> They asked Jesus, "Show us an act by which we may enter paradise." Jesus said, "Do not speak at all." They said, "We cannot do this." Jesus replied, "Then speak only good."

Although Khalidi does not refer to it, Christians may here recall the Gospel story of the rich young man who asked a similar question of Jesus and was told to sell all he owned and give the money to the poor, a sacrifice that apparently proved impossible as the young man "went away sad." It is a touching turn that the Muslim Jesus would relax a standard so that his followers could meet it, and it echoes the mercifulness of God who indulges those who glorify him "as best they can."

G. K. Chesterton once mused that the only thing Jesus hid from the world was his mirth. We could as easily say it was his vulnerability, for while we are told in the Gospels that Jesus weeps, suffers and mourns, we are rarely privy to his inner moods and moments, where helplessness really lives. One of the Muslim gospel's great themes is Jesus' human weakness. Where the agony in the garden reported by the Evangelists is compacted into the single terse aside to God, "Take from me this cup," the Muslim Jesus is more revealing:

> Jesus said to his disciples, "Pray God that He may make this agony—meaning death—easy for me, for I have come to fear death so much that my fear of death has made me acquainted with death."

Whether the New Testament Jesus shared these mortal shivers is, on closer inspection, arguable. Mark and Matthew tell us that he "began to feel terror and anguish," and Jesus himself confesses, "My soul is sorrowful to the point of death" (Mark 14:34; Matt. 26:38). In Luke his sweat falls "like great drops of blood" (Luke 22:44). But the confession of the Muslim Jesus is almost unbearably frank, his fear for himself so unselfconscious and plainly spoken that in this saying as much as in any other we see how masterfully Jesus' towering spirit was wedded to his mere humanity by the Muslim scribes. The idea, furthermore, that in mortality lies kinship is, it hardly needs to be said, a major testament of the New Testament.

There is no religion that is not measured according to the works and devotion of its followers. In Islamic literature, a giant of devotional practice and religious conduct was the great Sufi thinker Abu Hamid al-Ghazali. His masterpiece, *The Revival of Religious Sciences*, is worth a side trip for the many citations and thoughtful discussions of Jesus—unique in Islamic literature, Khalidi believes—and also for the poignant accounts of ascetic struggle in which all great Muslims, including Jesus, famously contended. In Ghazali we meet souls in solitude and souls who have denied themselves not only women and wine, but honey and bread. Yet these deprivations stunt neither their longings, nor the objects of their longings, nor their humanity. Quite the opposite. Ascetic discipline is an attempt to regain one's self, as any "recoverer" can attest. Westerners, who sometimes forget the wages of luxury until they have to pay them, should have no difficulty commiserating with these medieval Muslims. At the very least, in this age of addictions the travails of people wrestling with appetites are not to be mocked.

It might seem that this judicious book, published some four months previous to September 11, could not have appeared at a more inauspicious moment. Even before that date Western sympathies were parched by the fundamentalist mirage: Islam as a shallow pond rather than a fathomless well. Readers may find it impossible, at least temporarily, to resist the urge to glean dark meanings and sinister motives from the words of the Muslim Jesus, or to find in them the seeds of militancy. But people of faith and reason, when they collect themselves, will notice that the Muslim Jesus was recruited to rescue sinners, not dash them to eternal pieces. It is this Jesus, in fact, who resurrects tormented bones in the here and now. For Christians he is a redeemer; for Muslims, a reanimator.

Readers will also discover that the struggle described by today's analysts between an oppressive "medieval" Islam and a democratic and modern one may be the falsest jihad of all. The aforementioned religious reformer al-Ghazali, the physician and Aristotelian scholar Avicenna, the philosopher Averroës, the mathematician and poet Omar Khayyám—all worldly figures of enormous sophistication and learning—were medieval men. Osama bin Laden is a modern one. One could make the case that Islamic history, in particular the temperance, genius and wisdom of its golden age, is precisely what today's fundamentalists have discarded, not what they cling to.

Khalidi does not make such a case, but the classically disinterested way *The Muslim Jesus* traces Islam's complex intentions in its adoption of Jesus is especially felicitous in this regard. The book also gives a revealing overview of the development of Qur'anic exegesis, which turns out to be bedeviled by precisely the same controversies and polemics surrounding critical research about Christian scripture. Khalidi refrains from any attempt to authenticate the Islamic sayings, noting that the Muslim Jesus too is a composite, perhaps even a "fabrication." Religionists might find this tack a bit coy, yet Khalidi seems to appreciate that the proper way to handle someone else's God is delicately.

What the Muslim gospel does offer is Jesus as Islam wished him to be and so made him to appear—a remarkable compliment for one faith to have paid another. Christians, who in the name of Jesus took the entire Hebrew Bible as their own, are hardly in a position to object. And if and when our current lamentations subside, we may even find, in what is faddishly called "the other," our brother.

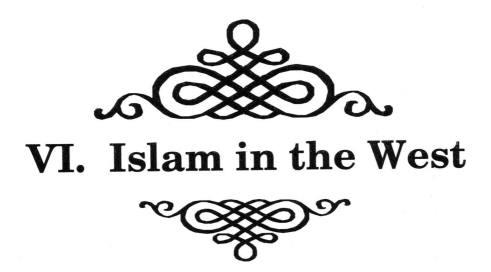

VI. Islam in the West

Editor's Introduction

The future shape of Islam in the West will likely alter not only Western relations with Muslim countries but also, to a degree, global Islamic thought. The freedom of speech inherent in most Western cultures that is absent in many Muslim nations has afforded Muslim immigrants to the West a new opportunity to seek a deeper understanding of their religion. Because this questioning of Islamic thought goes against the beliefs of the more strict Islamic sects, such as Wahhabism (the most prevalent form of Islam among imams [Islamic leaders and scholars] in the United States), Islam in the West will undergo many struggles and clashes while finding its identity. The cultural and religious diversity of Muslims in the United States, for example, has already created a dynamic new face for the religion, as traditional Muslim immigrants share mosques with African-American converts and the growing number of Westerners attracted to Sufism. The role of the Muslim in the Western world is complicated, however, by the rise in Islamic terrorism. Tensions between Muslims and non-Muslims have risen dramatically since the terrorist attacks of September 11, 2001, with a growing degree of mistrust and fear emerging between the two communities.

In "Defining Islamic Values in America," Jane Lampman discusses the difficulties Muslim immigrants have had reconciling their traditional culture with a secular one, a problem that existed prior to the events of September 11. Lampman looks at the growing debate among Muslims over what level of engagement with American society is appropriate. She also touches on the multicultural fabric of the Muslim population in the United States, which has risen from around 500,000 to over 6 million in the past thirty years. Hailing from across the globe and from all walks of life, this community of first-, second-, and third-generation immigrants is shaping American Islam as traditional values mix with new religious thought.

"Native Speakers" is Michelle Cottle's report on the role Islam has played in the lives of African-Americans, around 1 million (roughly one-sixth of the Muslim-American population) of whom are converts to the faith. Cottle notes that among the African-American Muslim community there is a great diversity of belief, and that, while many have found new peace in Islam, others have used the religion to express their rage at the United States government and Caucasians. Cottle also examines the difficult relationship African-American Muslims have had with Middle Eastern–born Muslims, who, she reports, often hold their opinions on Islam to be superior to those held by converts.

Islam's rising importance in world affairs and the greater interest paid to it by the West in recent years has led to the first major non-Muslim academic investigations into the Qur'an, a study that is often avoided for the amount of hostility it tends to provoke among many Muslims. As the Qur'an is recognized as the unaltered work of God given to the prophet Mohammed, any attempt to analyze it as a historically developing text influenced by other sources has been seen as an attack on Islam itself. In exploring these problems, Alexander Stille's article "Scholars Are Quietly Offering New Theories of the Koran" looks at the work of Christoph Luxenberg, who has been investigating whether several key passages of the Qur'an have been mistranslated for centuries. The article also explains why some scholars believe the text continued to evolve decades after Mohammed's death.

In "Islam in Russia" Aleksei Malashenko examines the uneasy role Muslims are playing in modern-day Russia. Because of terrorism connected to Islamic militant activity in the North Caucasus region, there has been a rise in prejudice against Muslims in Russia fostered by a consistently negative portrayal of Muslims in the Russian media. This negative coverage has made Russian citizens reluctant to grant Muslims the rights to build houses of worship and meeting halls. As he examines some of the roots of fundamentalism and Islamism, along with their propagation in the Chechnya region, Malashenko notes that it is difficult for Russians to detach themselves from the terrorism that has been linked to hundreds of deaths in their country. He proposes a dialogue between Muslims and non-Muslims as the first step toward overcoming fears and prejudices that exist on both sides.

Defining Islamic Values in America[1]

By Jane Lampman
The Christian Science Monitor, August 19, 1999

For these loving parents and dedicated Muslims, the little details of daily life pose perpetual challenges. The daughter who has chosen to wear the hijab in public school is called "rag head" by classmates or even has her scarf ripped from her head. A young son is given the role of "terrorist" by playmates in an updated version of "cops and robbers." A teenage son (brought up in a faith that eschews alcohol) becomes entranced by the Budweiser frog in a popular commercial.

As Egyptian Muslims who have chosen to make their life in the United States, Salma Al-Ashmawi and Hassan Ibrahim must be vigilant in negotiating their family's encounter with American culture.

Yet these young professionals (she has worked in the public schools in northern Virginia and he is a professor of accounting and business) clearly relish the life they lead. They send their four children to public rather than Islamic school so they "learn to swim" in U.S. society and understand that "being different is something to be proud of—everyone is different." And they are active in a vigorous faith community that, given families from many countries with varied Islamic practices, has to sort out what it means to be truly Muslim.

The most significant way in which America is affecting Islam, says Al-Ashmawi, is in "purifying it." In worshiping together, she says, Muslims from various cultures have "to pare it down to the essentials."

The couple's experience reflects a fast-growing facet of American life that remains little understood. The U.S. Muslim population has risen in 30 years from about 500,000 to more than 6 million. A recent report says their median income falls in the upper middle class. A large proportion are engineers, physicians, computer specialists, and professionals in business, finance, and academia.

And this most diverse Muslim community in the world is engaged in a lively discussion about how America may shape Islam and how Islam may shape America.

In a host of Muslim organizations, publications, and youth associations, "they are searching for the essence of Islam" and are deeply involved in "determining the nature and authenticity of an indige-

---

nous American Islam," says Jane Smith, professor of Islamic studies at Hartford Seminary in Connecticut, and co-director of its Center for the Study of Islam and Christian-Muslim Relations.

Dr. Smith opens a wide and enlightening window on this world in her new book, *Islam in America* (Columbia University Press). A survey of the evolving scene rather than the story of individual lives, it nevertheless reflects the voices of Muslims all along the spectrum.

A number of Muslims believe, Smith says in a recent interview, that "this American context provides the opportunity for fresh thinking without the sense that it may be objectionable to somebody." One of the main issues is that of authority—who has the right to decide what is the "good" or "true" Islamic way.

At the same time, a community made up of first-, second-, and third-generation immigrants from Asia, Africa, and the Middle

---

Muslims, proud of Islam's global reach and practice of equality, feel it has something to teach a society still rife with racism.

East, as well as African-Americans and other U.S. converts (Anglos, Latinos, native Americans) is bound to have a multitude of perspectives. They range from "isolationists"—who want no contact with non-Muslims—to "accommodationists"; from those accustomed to following strict authorities to those who see it as their own responsibility to determine what is proper practice.

There are non-practicing Muslims. And there are groups that call themselves Muslim although most Muslims say they do not follow a legitimate form of Islam, such as Louis Farrakhan's Nation of Islam.

One of the most intriguing and least publicized stories of American Islam is the remarkable shift of the vast majority of African-Americans in Elijah Muhammad's Nation of Islam away from his teachings on black separatism into Sunni Islam, under the leadership of Elijah's son, Warith Deen Muhammad.

Now recognized as one of the major Muslim leaders in the U.S., Imam Warith Deen was the first of his faith to open the U.S. Senate with a prayer and, Smith says, "is responsible for certifying all Muslim Americans who wish to undertake the hajj to Mecca."

Muslims, proud of Islam's global reach and practice of equality, feel it has something to teach a society still rife with racism. They put a high priority, Smith says, on bringing together the diverse groups in U.S. Islam. While many mosques cater to specific ethnic groups, "there are increasing efforts not only at communication but at mutual representation on *shura* [consensus councils]."

The internal debate ranges over a host of issues—equal rights and responsibilities for women and men, appropriate dress, youths' participation in social activities, public or private Islamic education, proper financial practices, engagement in politics. Smith's book highlights the issues and gives helpful context: the basic elements of Islamic faith and practice, roles of historical figures in Islam's development, how Islam took root in the U.S. and its various manifestations here, and how the demands of U.S. society are reshaping Muslim experience. For instance, imams, are having to take on multiple roles not played in Muslim societies similar to the demands made on Christian pastors.

Even as the U.S. serves as "a place both of experimentation and affirmation of traditional values," Muslims feel Islam has much to offer American society—whether it be liberation from addictions, a recapturing of fundamental moral values, or a deeper appreciation of communal responsibilities.

They talk a great deal about *da'wa*—the spreading of the faith. Perspectives on what that entails, Smith says, vary from simply being a good example to active propagation of Islam. For some, the goal is making the U.S. a Muslim country. For the most part, "what they are talking about is not a kind of actively taking over and propagating, but a slow process by which increasing numbers come to understand Islam and accept it."

What isn't often understood is that "freedom of conscience is a very important thing" in Islam, Smith adds. The Qur'an says, "There is no compulsion in religion." The restriction or persecution of other faiths in some Islamic countries is a tough issue, she admits: "How do you reconcile some very hard truths with the ideals? It's like trying to justify the Inquisition and ask, 'Was this a Christian thing?'. . . So much of what is happening that is extremist is disavowed by most Muslims."

Native Speakers

African American Muslims, and Why It's Hard to Be Both[2]

By Michelle Cottle
The New Republic, November 19, 2001

You didn't need to go trick-or-treating on Halloween to get a good scare. All you had to do was flip on C-SPAN2 any time between 7 and 11 o'clock and watch the "New Black Panther Party and Muslims for Truth and Justice Town Hall Meeting" at the National Press Club in Washington. Moderated by Panther Amir Muhammad, the event featured a parade of exceedingly angry imams, activists, and audience members melding black-power salutes and Koranic quotations with loud denunciations of the United States as "the Great Satan." Beefy Panthers in military-style garb formed a menacing backdrop for prayer leaders peddling conspiracy theories—in particular, the U.S. government and media's cover up of Israel's role in every terrorist episode from the 1998 American Embassy bombings to the September 11 hijackings. Uncle Sam, charged Amir Muhammad, "is the number-one oppressor in the history of the planet Earth, the number-one murderer on the planet Earth, and the number-one spreader of terror on the planet Earth."

Flash forward two days to Friday services at Masjid Muhammad in Northwest D.C. Inside the prayer hall, some 150 worshipers sit beneath whirring fans, listening to visiting Imam Abdul Malik Mohammed denounce the C-SPAN event. "Do you want me to believe that the environment that guarantees me protection to pray five times a day and that ordains itself, its credibility, under God's trust—you want me to suspect it? To feel bad about it?" he bellows. "Go to hell!" The imam not only defends the United States, he suggests it is the Middle East where something has gone badly wrong with Islam. "[W]hile the Muslim World has had the Koran and they have recited the Koran and the Koran has dwelled in their hearts . . . I contend that, in view of circumstances that we have witnessed for many years, Mohammed the Prophet is not known to them." Chiding listeners to stop deferring to foreign-born Muslims just because "they step before you and they're wearing robes and turbans and it makes you think they're back there with Mohammed the Prophet," he argues that Old World Muslims have been mere

---

"warm-up speakers" for African Americans. "God is correcting [misconceptions of] Islam in the world," he says, "and he is not correcting it in the East! He is correcting it in the West!"

In fact, during these troubled times, African American Muslims should be well positioned to do much "correcting" of American misperceptions about Islam, not to mention Muslim misperceptions of the United States. African American Muslims are, after all, living proof that Islam has deep roots on these shores. That it need not speak with a foreign accent. That it is no more alien, or hostile, than the streets of Harlem, Chicago, or East St. Louis, where it thrives.

But then, that is precisely the problem. The people who might best speak to the Muslim world about the United States are themselves often deeply conflicted Americans. For every imam like Abdul Malik Mohammed, who promotes a distinctly American Islam, free from the hatreds of the Middle East, there is an Amir Muhammed, whose Islam represents a direct rejection of American culture, a righteous banner under which African Americans must rally against their historical oppressors.

African American Muslims are . . . living proof that Islam has deep roots on these shores.

But if it's difficult for black Muslims to speak to the Islamic world as proud Americans, it's often just as difficult for them to speak to Americans about Islam. For most Americans, Muslim means Arab. And black leaders complain that, for too long, immigrant Muslims have set themselves up as the sole gatekeepers of the faith. As a result, instead of now serving as ambassadors for their religion or for their country, many African American Muslims feel trapped in the center of a storm, unable to make themselves heard, and unsure, perhaps, of even what they want to say.

It's no secret that "the black community has its own beef with the white community," notes Aminah McCloud, an associate professor of Religious Studies at DePaul University in Chicago. Indeed, the very roots of Islam among African Americans are tangled up in the fight against white racism. Though Islam first arrived here in the hull of slave ships, it didn't catch fire until the 1950s and 1960s, with the rise of the Nation of Islam under the late Elijah Mohammed and Malcolm X. Initially bearing little resemblance to orthodox Islam, the Nation peddled a black nationalist ideology that was more about toppling white power than serving Allah. Today, though most African American Muslims practice a more traditional Islam, traces of racial struggle remain, both in sermons and in the way con gregants interpret Islam's message.

All of which makes it hard for African American Muslims to tell their brethren overseas that the United States does not hate their faith. Nationwide, polls show that black Americans are more critical than whites of the U.S. war on terror, and in certain circles suspicion runs high that the government is using September 11 as an excuse to wage war on Islam. "We know, as only people who have lived subserviently among Caucasians can, that the white men who run the country . . . are lying," says McCloud's husband, Frederick Thaufeer al-Deen, formerly an imam with the federal prison system. This so-called war on terror is just the government's latest attempt to justify unjust foreign policy decisions ranging from the support of Palestinian oppression to the presence of U.S. troops in Saudi Arabia, he says. "We're trying to do something over there that is wrong."

In this worldview, Osama bin Laden is more scapegoat than villain. The always controversial Louis Farrakhan made waves recently with his demand for the United States to produce evidence of bin Laden's guilt—a call echoed more quietly by many in the black community. Ghayth Nur Kashif, imam of the Masjidush-Shura in Southeast Washington, does not say explicitly whether he believes bin Laden to be innocent, but compares the U.S. hunt for the Saudi exile to "the Klan-type activities" of the 1930s and 1940s. "Whenever something happened to a white girl or white woman," he recalls, "people would grab the first black man who was about the right height and age." Now he and others insist that bin Laden is being similarly targeted. "When [Bush] said he wanted [bin Laden] dead or alive," a local pastor told *The Washington Post*, "he was calling out the posse, and black people know the posse. They come by and get you in the middle of the night and kill you without due process." Some go even further. "For the record, I love Osama bin Laden," says al-Deen. "I don't excuse any tactic he had to use by being a guerrilla-warfare fighter, but I understand."

One voice notably absent from the public arena has been W. Deen Mohammed, son of the late Elijah Mohammed and head of the Muslim American Society, the nation's largest organization of African American Muslims. In 1975 it was W. Deen who rejected the racialist ideology of the Nation of Islam and led the group's members into orthodox Sunnism (opening a schism with black-power advocates like Farrakhan that has only begun to heal in the past year or so). W. Deen is arguably the most authoritative voice for black Muslims. But since issuing a brief condemnation of the September 11 attacks and a plea for Muslims to "stay calm and remain in our good sense," the imam has remained largely silent, leaving a chorus of others to fill the void. Which is a pity. Because if African Americans don't reject the loud voices spewing hate-filled messages, Imam Abdul Malik Mohammed (a devotee of W. Deen) warned the folks at Masjid Muhammad, the radicals will taint the entire community. "Persons will watch this and associate that kind of thinking with us," he said. Americans will see all of this "ugly ranting and raving, this irresponsible language," and think of all Muslims, "This is what they feel in their hearts."

But if many African American Muslims reject the role of American ambassadors to their coreligionists, they also face obstacles in serving as interpreters of Islam for a U.S. audience. "When folks want to know about Islam, they have always gone to the immigrant community," gripes McCloud. It's telling, she says, that after September 11, "who came to the White House to represent Islam? The immigrant community. The African American community felt very dismayed." Even Oprah Winfrey has been accused of bias: Kashif's wife, Hafeeza, says she was dismayed one afternoon to see "all these Muslims on—and not one was African American."

In part, this is because when most Americans think of American Muslims, they think of immigrants. But it's also because the immigrant community itself at times treats African Americans as second-class Muslims. "I used to be around a lot of Eastern Muslims," says Muhammad Abdul Rahman, a member of Masjidush-Shura. "They would come over here and treat us like we were babes in Islam. They thought they should be our leaders just because they could speak Arabic. They would come into [our] *masjids* and try to be our teachers." September 11, he says, "is bringing all this stuff back up."

The divide is partly cultural and economic. McCloud notes, "We have in the African American community a host of imams who are men who work full-time jobs. . . . They don't have the luxury of being paid to be just an imam." Al-Deen, expressing the views of many he counseled over the years, puts it more bluntly: "They have the money and we don't. It's a sour-grapes kind of thing." And, he says, Muslim immigrants have traditionally failed to reach out to African Americans: "They come over with their money and their degrees and with an insular view of Islam. . . . They hide in their jobs and their little communities."

For a people long considered second-class citizens within their own country, being treated like second-class citizens within their own religion is a sore point—particularly now, when Islam's role in America is a topic of unprecedented public debate. "Our role in America is critical," says Imam Kashif. "Immigrant Muslims to a great extent don't know the terrain. They don't understand the European mind—the American authorities' mind. We do." It's a nice thought. Until you realize that what many in Kashif's community "understand" about the American mind is that it insists on viewing Osama bin Laden as guilty, when in truth he's just another innocent victim.

Scholars Are Quietly Offering New Theories of the Koran[3]

By Alexander Stille
The New York Times, March 2, 2002

To Muslims the Koran is the very word of God, who spoke through the angel Gabriel to Muhammad: "This book is not to be doubted," the Koran declares unequivocally at its beginning. Scholars and writers in Islamic countries who have ignored that warning have sometimes found themselves the target of death threats and violence, sending a chill through universities around the world.

Yet despite the fear, a handful of experts have been quietly investigating the origins of the Koran, offering radically new theories about the text's meaning and the rise of Islam. Christoph Luxenberg, a scholar of ancient Semitic languages in Germany, argues that the Koran has been misread and mistranslated for centuries. His work, based on the earliest copies of the Koran, maintains that parts of Islam's holy book are derived from pre-existing Christian Aramaic texts that were misinterpreted by later Islamic scholars who prepared the editions of the Koran commonly read today.

So, for example, the virgins who are supposedly awaiting good Islamic martyrs as their reward in paradise are in reality "white raisins" of crystal clarity rather than fair maidens.

Christoph Luxenberg, however, is a pseudonym, and his scholarly tome "The Syro-Aramaic Reading of the Koran" had trouble finding a publisher, although it is considered a major new work by several leading scholars in the field. Verlag Das Arabische Buch in Berlin ultimately published the book.

The caution is not surprising. Salman Rushdie's *Satanic Verses* received a fatwa because it appeared to mock Muhammad. The Egyptian novelist Naguib Mahfouz was stabbed because one of his books was thought to be irreligious. And when the Arab scholar Suliman Bashear argued that Islam developed as a religion gradually rather than emerging fully formed from the mouth of the Prophet, he was injured after being thrown from a second-story window by his students at the University of Nablus in the West Bank. Even many broad-minded liberal Muslims become upset when the historical veracity and authenticity of the Koran is questioned.

The reverberations have affected non-Muslim scholars in Western countries. "Between fear and political correctness, it's not possible to say anything other than sugary nonsense about Islam," said one

3. Article by Alexander Stille from *The New York Times* March 2, 2002. Copyright © 2002 by The New York Times Co. Reprinted by Permission.

scholar at an American university who asked not to be named, referring to the threatened violence as well as the widespread reluctance on United States college campuses to criticize other cultures.

While scriptural interpretation may seem like a remote and innocuous activity, close textual study of Jewish and Christian scripture played no small role in loosening the Church's domination on the intellectual and cultural life of Europe, and paving the way for unfettered secular thought. "The Muslims have the benefit of hindsight of the European experience, and they know very well that once you start questioning the holy scriptures, you don't know where it will stop," the scholar explained.

The touchiness about questioning the Koran predates the latest rise of Islamic militancy. As long ago as 1977, John Wansbrough of the School of Oriental and African Studies in London wrote that subjecting the Koran to "analysis by the instruments and techniques of biblical criticism is virtually unknown."

Mr. Wansbrough insisted that the text of the Koran appeared to be a composite of different voices or texts compiled over dozens if

---

The touchiness about questioning the Koran predates the latest rise of Islamic militancy.

---

not hundreds of years. After all, scholars agree that there is no evidence of the Koran until 691—59 years after Muhammad's death—when the Dome of the Rock mosque in Jerusalem was built, carrying several Koranic inscriptions.

These inscriptions differ to some degree from the version of the Koran that has been handed down through the centuries, suggesting, scholars say, that the Koran may have still been evolving in the last decade of the seventh century. Moreover, much of what we know as Islam—the lives and sayings of the Prophet—is based on texts from between 130 and 300 years after Muhammad's death.

In 1977 two other scholars from the School for Oriental and African Studies at London University—Patricia Crone (a professor of history at the Institute for Advanced Study in Princeton) and Michael Cook (a professor of Near Eastern history at Princeton University)—suggested a radically new approach in their book *Hagarism: The Making of the Islamic World.*

Since there are no Arabic chronicles from the first century of Islam, the two looked at several non-Muslim, seventh-century accounts that suggested Muhammad was perceived not as the founder of a new religion but as a preacher in the Old Testament tradition, hailing the coming of a Messiah. Many of the early documents refer to the followers of Muhammad as "hagarenes," and the "tribe of Ishmael," in other words as descendants of Hagar, the servant girl that the Jewish patriarch Abraham used to father his son Ishmael.

In its earliest form, Ms. Crone and Mr. Cook argued, the followers of Muhammad may have seen themselves as retaking their place in the Holy Land alongside their Jewish cousins. (And many Jews appear to have welcomed the Arabs as liberators when they entered Jerusalem in 638.)

> *The Koran and the Islamic tradition present a fundamental paradox.*

The idea that Jewish messianism animated the early followers of the Prophet is not widely accepted in the field, but "Hagarism" is credited with opening up the field. "Crone and Cook came up with some very interesting revisionist ideas," says Fred M. Donner of the University of Chicago and author of the recent book *Narratives of Islamic Origins: The Beginnings of Islamic Historical Writing*. "I think in trying to reconstruct what happened, they went off the deep end, but they were asking the right questions."

The revisionist school of early Islam has quietly picked up momentum in the last few years as historians began to apply rational standards of proof to this material.

Mr. Cook and Ms. Crone have revised some of their early hypotheses while sticking to others. "We were certainly wrong about quite a lot of things," Ms. Crone said. "But I stick to the basic point we made: that Islamic history did not arise as the classic tradition says it does."

Ms. Crone insists that the Koran and the Islamic tradition present a fundamental paradox. The Koran is a text soaked in monotheistic thinking, filled with stories and references to Abraham, Isaac, Joseph and Jesus, and yet the official history insists that Muhammad, an illiterate camel merchant, received the revelation in Mecca, a remote, sparsely populated part of Arabia, far from the centers of monotheistic thought, in an environment of idol-worshiping Arab Bedouins. Unless one accepts the idea of the angel Gabriel, Ms. Crone says, historians must somehow explain how all these monotheistic stories and ideas found their way into the Koran.

"There are only two possibilities," Ms. Crone said. "Either there had to be substantial numbers of Jews and Christians in Mecca or the Koran had to have been composed somewhere else."

Indeed, many scholars who are not revisionists agree that Islam must be placed back into the wider historical context of the religions of the Middle East rather than seeing it as the spontaneous product of the pristine Arabian desert. "I think there is increasing acceptance, even on the part of many Muslims, that Islam emerged out of the wider monotheistic soup of the Middle East," says Roy Mottahedeh, a professor of Islamic history at Harvard University.

Scholars like Mr. Luxenberg and Gerd-R. Puin, who teaches at Saarland University in Germany, have returned to the earliest known copies of the Koran in order to grasp what it says about the document's origins and composition. Mr. Luxenberg explains these copies are written without vowels and diacritical dots that modern Arabic uses to make it clear what letter is intended. In the eighth and ninth centuries, more than a century after the death of Muhammad, Islamic commentators added diacritical marks to clear up the ambiguities of the text, giving precise meanings to passages based on what they considered to be their proper context. Mr. Luxenberg's radical theory is that many of the text's difficulties can be clarified when it is seen as closely related to Aramaic, the language group of most Middle Eastern Jews and Christians at the time.

For example, the famous passage about the virgins is based on the word *hur*, which is an adjective in the feminine plural meaning simply "white." Islamic tradition insists the term *hur* stands for "houri," which means virgin, but Mr. Luxenberg insists that this is a forced misreading of the text. In both ancient Aramaic and in at least one respected dictionary of early Arabic, *hur* means "white raisin."

Mr. Luxenberg has traced the passages dealing with paradise to a Christian text called *Hymns of Paradise* by a fourth-century author. Mr. Luxenberg said the word paradise was derived from the Aramaic word for garden and all the descriptions of paradise described it as a garden of flowing waters, abundant fruits and white raisins, a prized delicacy in the ancient Near East. In this context, white raisins, mentioned often as hur, Mr. Luxenberg said, makes more sense than a reward of sexual favors.

In many cases, the differences can be quite significant. Mr. Puin points out that in the early archaic copies of the Koran, it is impossible to distinguish between the words "to fight" and "to kill." In many cases, he said, Islamic exegetes added diacritical marks that yielded the harsher meaning, perhaps reflecting a period in which the Islamic Empire was often at war.

A return to the earliest Koran, Mr. Puin and others suggest, might lead to a more tolerant brand of Islam, as well as one that is more conscious of its close ties to both Judaism and Christianity.

"It is serious and exciting work," Ms. Crone said of Mr. Luxenberg's work. Jane McAuliffe, a professor of Islamic studies at Georgetown University, has asked Mr. Luxenberg to contribute an essay to the *Encyclopedia of the Koran*, which she is editing.

Mr. Puin would love to see a "critical edition" of the Koran produced, one based on recent philological work, but, he says, "the word critical is misunderstood in the Islamic world—it is seen as criticizing or attacking the text."

Some Muslim authors have begun to publish skeptical, revisionist work on the Koran as well. Several new volumes of revisionist scholarship, *The Origins of the Koran* and *The Quest for the Histor-*

ical Muhammad, have been edited by a former Muslim who writes under the pen name Ibn Warraq. Mr. Warraq, who heads a group called the Institute for the Secularization of Islamic Society, makes no bones about having a political agenda. "Biblical scholarship has made people less dogmatic, more open," he said, "and I hope that happens to Muslim society as well."

But many Muslims find the tone and claims of revisionism offensive. "I think the broader implications of some of the revisionist scholarship is to say that the Koran is not an authentic book, that it was fabricated 150 years later," says Ebrahim Moosa, a professor of religious studies at Duke University, as well as a Muslim cleric whose liberal theological leanings earned him the animosity of fundamentalists in South Africa, which he left after his house was firebombed.

Andrew Rippin, an Islamicist at the University of Victoria in British Columbia, Canada, says that freedom of speech in the Islamic world is more likely to evolve from within the Islamic interpretative tradition than from outside attacks on it. Approaches to the Koran that are now branded as heretical—interpreting the text metaphorically rather than literally—were widely practiced in mainstream Islam a thousand years ago.

"When I teach the history of the interpretation it is eye-opening to students the amount of independent thought and diversity of interpretation that existed in the early centuries of Islam," Mr. Rippin says. "It was only in more recent centuries that there was a need for limiting interpretation."

Islam in Russia

Notes of a Political Scientist[4]

By Aleksei Malashenko; translated by Michel Vale
Russian Social Science Review, November–December 2000

Sad as it may be, at the end of the nineties many Russians are developing a definite "Islamophobia," especially regarding the situation in the North Caucasus. The wars and conflicts in the North Caucasus, especially in Chechnya, are creating a certain aggressive image of the Muslim, which, one might add, is thoroughly supported by one segment of the mass media. On one hand, this is prompted by definite political calculation, while on the other, the motive is often to have "hot news." Such publications are "entertaining," and the reader reads all kinds of horrors about Muslim fundamentalism, terrorism, and so on with a mixture of interest and fear. It should be noted that our mass media, the electronic media included, show little, if any, competence in discussing Islam. Hence, to no mean degree a deliberately negative image of Islam is created, one that unfortunately is becoming increasingly entrenched.

At the same time, radical Muslims, at least the combatants, can certainly not be counted among the angels. Today, especially in the Caucasus, Islam enters politics specifically under the banner of radical slogans. The most important of these is the "holy war," the *jihad*, which in Chechnya became the ideological argument supporting its secession from Russia.

The war in Chechnya and the events of August–September 1999 in Dagestan have cemented in the minds of the Russian public the image of Islam as a driven religion aimed at expansion. Nonetheless, the situation must be assessed soberly and in a balanced, unprejudiced manner. It is especially important today to understand that "Islamophobia," the perception of Islam as an aggressive sociocultural religious system, will have an extremely negative impact on the country's stability and future.

Russia has been and will remain, at least for the foreseeable future, a multi-ethnic and multi-faith country. The number of Muslims will increase steadily. Whereas today they number approximately 20 million—including, of course, those in the North Caucasus—according to some calculations their number will reach 30 million in only fifteen to twenty years.

---

4. English-language translation copyright © 2000 by M.E. Sharpe, Inc. From *Russian Social Science Review*, vol. 41, no. 6 (November–December 2000), pp. 57–65. Reprinted with permission.

If we are to rid ourselves of the taint of "Islamophobia," it is crucial that we clarify the phenomena of which so many people write: fundamentalism, Islamism, and "Islamic terrorism." Does this last even exist? This is a task for the experts, the analysts, and the mass media, and it also interests the whole of society, including the political establishment.

What lies behind fundamentalism? Fundamentalism is an idealization of the past, an attempt to return to the seventh century, to the golden age of Islam, when the Prophet Muhammad founded the first Islamic state, when the four "true caliphs," who ruled in succession after his death, developed the principles of the Islamic state in which the factor of social justice played a tremendous role, according to Muslim ideologues. We know the importance attached in the Koran to helping the destitute, widows, orphans, and so forth. In addition to standards of social justice, much attention was devoted in early Islam to state-building problems.

Now let us examine the present situation. At the end of the twentieth century, the Soviet Union collapsed. All of us, including Russian Muslims, are experiencing a profound systemic crisis. Society exists in an atmosphere of disappointment—disappointment with Com-

---

Fundamentalism is an idealization of the past, an attempt to return to the seventh century, to the golden age of Islam.

---

munist and with democratic ideology—and is experiencing the negative impact of reform: various defects and distortions, impoverishment, a decline in social status, and so forth.

All these factors also affect the Muslim regions, including the North Caucasus, and perhaps there above all. Dagestan, for example, is one of the least economically developed Russian regions. In Dagestan, and in the North Caucasus in general, a considerable segment, perhaps even the bulk of the population, is disillusioned with the ethnic elite. They are also disillusioned because of the center's inability to help the Muslim regions emerge from their crisis. Under such conditions, some of the population is turning to Islam, seeing in their appeal some kind of "Islamic alternative." This is a utopian alternative, for it is impossible to create an Islamic state, especially on the foundations that existed at the time of Muhammad's prophesy. But one must also recognize that the present government and system are incapable of showing Muslims an appropriate means of escape from their present critical situation: declining living standards, crumbling traditions, a distortion of the mentality of society at large, especially among youth, and so forth.

This is the source of the phenomenon we call fundamentalism, the desire to return to the true faith. It is not necessary for all of Chechnya or any other Muslim society to believe this. What is important is that the tendency has appeared. According to various data, from 10 to 12 percent, perhaps more, of Dagestan's population (now I am not speaking of Chechnya) is genuinely convinced that a return to Islam is the way out of the crisis. Do people have a right to do this? Of course, and no one can take that right away from them.

However, one can be a fundamentalist and spend one's whole life dreaming about creating an Islamic state and introducing the Shariah but take no action to achieve this. Such a person becomes a "passive fundamentalist." After all, fundamentalism is first and foremost a type of consciousness, a way of thinking—if you will, an ideology. Not all experts and analysts, however, agree with this assessment.

There is another phenomenon as well: Islamism. I would call it the practical realization of the idea of fundamentalism. If you build an Islamic movement on a fundamentalist foundation, if you struggle within the framework set down by a state's constitution, in this case the Russian Constitution, for the establishment of an Islamic state, for the (partial) introduction of the Shariah or, as it is sometimes put in milder form, for enabling Muslims to pursue a Muslim lifestyle, if on the basis of these slogans you participate in a political struggle and in elections (and we have had this experience: the Union of Russian Muslims, the Nur Movement, and the Islamic Revival Party existed at one time; and today, on the eve of the [Duma] elections, Muslim sociopolitical associations are being formed), then you are an Islamist. There you have one more definition, one more term, used to frighten small children, as they say. But this is, after all, quite a normal phenomenon. If you acknowledge the existence of Muslims, a Muslim community, in society and in the state, then you must grant it the right to live in accordance with the laws and at least to make as much use as possible of those laws that correspond to religious values and norms—in this case, Islam. It is quite legal to have an Islamic party, to hold political rallies and meetings, and to participate in the struggle for seats in the State Duma.

Next come such terms as "Islamic terrorism," "Islamic radicals," and so forth. If someone takes up arms under fundamentalist slogans, goes into the mountains, and begins to resist the constitutional system—to fight for his goals by illegal means, including force of arms—no matter how noble these goals may seem from his standpoint, such a person becomes an Islamic terrorist. War is waged against such people, in Muslim states and everywhere else.

As we know, Islamism exists throughout the Muslim world. A percentage of society—let us say, 5 to 30 percent, depending on the country—also demands an Islamic state, the introduction of the Shariah, and the creation of a theocratic system in which the head of the community is also the secular ruler. In places where Islamists acquire the right to legitimate participation in sociopolitical struggle, they do not merely gain seats in representative bodies (parliaments, soviets) but sometimes enter the government as well.

One of the most recent examples of this is Turkey, where the Welfare Party led by N. Erbakan held power for part of 1997. In other words, Islamists won a wholly legal victory through parliamentary elections.

Another example is Algeria in 1990, where the Islamic Salvation Front gained roughly two-thirds of the votes in the first round of the parliamentary elections. The military responded with a coup d'etat. But the coup had the opposite effect, initiating a civil war that claimed hundreds of thousands of victims.

In any event, Islamism should be legitimate when it takes the form of a political current based on fundamentalism. We can and must reach an agreement with the Islamists. Life itself has shown that if pressure is exerted on them, if one allows what happened in Algeria, the consequences can be very severe.

In discussing the triad "fundamentalism, Islamism, and Islamic radicalism," one must also not leave out Wahhabism, especially since it has become quite popular in recent times. Wahhabism is a political movement that first appeared on the eighteenth-century Arabian Peninsula. Its founder was Muhammad ibn 'Abd al-Wahhāb, a famous ideologue and theologian of that time. Wahhabism, the ideology of consolidation of the Arab tribes, later became the ideology of Saudi Arabia. This has been explored in detail, for example, in the works of the Russian Arabic scholar A. Vasil'ev.

On one hand, Wahhabism has all the attributes of fundamentalism. It is an idealization of the past, based on the purification of Islam of medieval and all later innovations, plus—and this is very important—the removal of paganism from Islam. Despite the efforts of the Prophet Muhammad in the seventh century, despite the energetic struggle to Islamicize Arabia and the surrounding territories where Muslim states are now located, a pagan element persisted in these areas for quite a long time. Even today this element is sufficiently widespread throughout the Muslim world, including in the North Caucasus, where one can say that pre-Islamic beliefs exist.

In addition, Sufism, mystical Islam, is widespread in the North Caucasus, another current that is also not quite normal from the standpoint of classical Islam. It is based on the Muslim brotherhood, known as tarikats, and they have a very complicated relationship with the Wahhabites.

Wahhabites are against pre-Islamic beliefs and any philosophical interpretation of Islam; they favor pure Islam, a rigid monotheism.

Can one say that there are Wahhabites in Dagestan today? We should note that this term has become a kind of bogeyman in our country. Even in reference to the remarkable and recent formation of the settlements of Karamakhi and Shabamakhi, we must recall that the residents of this area were very unhappy because of the total license enjoyed by the local authorities, the corruption, and the narcotics mafia. We know that the residents destroyed several poppy plantations with their trucks. At the moment when the people's discontent reached its height, a preacher from Saudi Arabia appeared, introducing "Wahhabism" and declaring that their problems would be solved if they succeeded in living according to the laws of pure Islam, for which it was necessary to introduce the Shariah, and so forth. Were there radicals among the rank-and-file Wahhabites? Yes, but these people were preparing themselves not to attack but rather to resist. Prime Minister Sergei Stepashin of Russia, by the way, met them in early 1999 and for some reason did not see them as a threat to Russia's integrity.

There is another nuance to Wahhabism. It should be recalled that there are four theological-juridical currents in Islam: the Hanafi—the most widespread among Russian Muslims—the Shafii, the Malik, and the Hanbali. The strictest is Hanbalism, and the mildest Hanafism. Wahhabism, in a sense, grew out of Hanbalism. All these groups developed in the early Middle Ages. What distinguishes Wahhabism from the other groups, which in one way or other recognize one another, is that it recognizes none of them. For it, Islam has no sects; there is only one version, and that is

---

Despite all efforts to "domesticate" Islam,
it has established itself in Russia as an
integral sociocultural phenomenon.

Wahhabist.

There is one other major problem—the relationship between Islam and politics. We must emphasize here that Islam, unlike other monotheistic religions including Christianity, is all-embracing. This holism occurs because, as noted above, there is no division between spiritual and secular in Islam. It contains no precept comparable to Christianity's "Render unto Caesar the things that are Caesar's; and to God the things that are God's" [Matthew 22:21]; there is no division between these spheres. Hence the union of Islam and politics is organic. Of course, many people denounce this. Moreover, when Russian politicians speak out against the union of politics and Islam, they have a specific goal in mind, to promote what I might call a "domesticated," artificial Islam, one that will not interfere with their lives—an Islam without religious parties and movements. But experience shows that "restricting" Islam has never led anywhere: the greater the attempts to adapt it to one's own worldview or to any political system, the greater are the chances that radical elements will emerge.

It must be said that, despite all efforts to "domesticate" Islam, it has established itself in Russia as an integral sociocultural phenomenon. This also applies to its connection with politics. We have active Islamic political organizations. They frighten people, and it is said that they exist in defiance of the Constitution. I am not a lawyer, but if this is true, it means that we should find some reasonable compromise, especially since the Islamic organizations that already exist in the country are recognized. This is important.

These movements have an impact at the regional level. There is every reason to assume that their influence will grow. They are already participating in regional sociopolitical life—for example, in Tatarstan, Moscow, and the North Caucasus. Indeed, the Nur movement gained 0.69 percent of the votes in the previous State Duma elections. This is, at first glance, very few. Actually it is few, but it is a very important demonstration that such a movement exists. According to official data, the movement gained approximately 5 percent of the votes in Tatarstan and more than 20 percent in Ingushetia.

Now, at the end of 1999, a peculiar situation has developed. For whatever reason, strictly Islamic political parties and movements will not be represented in the upcoming parliamentary elections, at least to the extent that some Islamic politicians would like. The activism of 1995 and 1996 is no longer a factor. But this is offset by other interesting circumstances; specifically, in the summer and autumn of 1999, on the eve of the elections, Muslim politicians from the highest political levels in Russia became active. I have in mind above all President Mintimer Shaimiev of Tatarstan, President Murtaza Rakhimov of Bashkortostan, President Ruslan Aushev of Ingushetia, and certain others. Furthermore, the "Muslim factor"— in other words, the factor of Muslims in Russian society—was very important in the creation of the Fatherland–All Russia bloc; almost all the most important Muslim politicians, who enjoy considerable authority in their regions, supported Iurii Luzhkov (and Evgenii Primakov).

Of course, this does not necessarily mean that Luzhkov is an ardent champion of Islam. But it is to his credit that he takes the "Muslim factor" into account. We are now in a situation that requires us to recognize Islam's impact on politics. In the Russian political struggle this influence is exerted by Muslims in the country's highest political institutions. His recognition of this obvious fact gives more points to the Moscow mayor (Luzhkov). Indeed, Luzhkov in effect recognizes that Moscow is a multi-ethnic, cosmopolitan city. It is he who manifests a willingness to help Muslims establish a normal life in the capital. The mayor knows that Muslims in Moscow number about one million, and somewhat more if one includes the whole Moscow region. As a politician, he gives due consideration to the factor of multiple religions as it exists in Moscow and throughout Russia.

This is especially important now, as we witness the conflict in the North Caucasus, with consequences, including the prospect of terrorism becoming a permanent feature of the political scene, that so far bode nothing good.

But let us return to the theme of "Islamophobia." As an example of this phenomenon, one cannot fail to mention the demonstrations in Moscow in the early nineties against laying the cornerstone for an Islamic institute in Troparevo. When people tried to build a mosque in Murmansk, everything possible was done to prevent it; even the construction machines were wrecked. There were also problems in Vladivostok when the square set aside for a mosque placed it 300 meters higher than the Orthodox church, which provoked protests from the population. The authorities in Tiumen Oblast—Ialutorovsk in particular, as well as certain villages where at least half of the population was Muslim—obstructed the building of a mosque.

Certain questions naturally arise: What are general solutions to the present situation? What place and role does Islam play in relationship to Christianity? What is Islam's potential role in future Russian politics?

The most important step, in my opinion, is to support a constant dialogue between the religions—not a formal dialogue but one that takes place on various levels among the clergy and, even more important, among ordinary people. It is no secret that under the Soviet regime we were all the same. Our ethnic features were reduced to national songs and dances; and religious characteristics, generally speaking, did not exist, since officially religion was an opiate of the people destined, "fortunately," gradually to wither away. But now, however much one derides contemporary society, however one relates to the processes of democratization in the country, we are beginning to become aware of our own identities, including our religious identities. In a sense, we are beginning a dialogue with the representatives of other religions on a new basis. In other words, we must understand that our neighbors—whether they live next door, in the same town, or anywhere in the country—may be Muslims with their own tradition distinct from ours, and their own way of perceiving the world. We must understand one another and not be afraid because the Muslim worldview differs in some respects from the Christian worldview. This is the work of a generation, even a century. This is the most important result of dialogue—difficult but essential.

However, I would suggest that it is interesting, too, if your neighbors have value orientations that differ from yours. There is always an opportunity to discuss, to debate, to search for mutual understanding, and so forth. Communication among clergy is especially important, especially in the present conflict situation. Sometimes we hear: "Well, you think that a mufti has talked with a bishop, and they condemned religious extremism, conflict, and so forth. So what? Did that put an end to the conflict?" No, it did not. But there is another important point. A step, however small, was thereby made in the direction of settling the conflict. The most important point is that neither the bishop nor the mufti called for a religious war, nor did they begin to persuade their flock that they should be fighting Orthodox or Muslims. This is crucial. It is a point that we do not always notice and do not always evaluate at its true worth.

It is difficult even to imagine the nightmarish consequences that would ensue if most Muslim or Orthodox clerics adopted a position of religious intolerance. It would mean the spread of conflict, which would pit the Russian population of Stavropol and Krasnodar Krai against the Muslims of Dagestan, Ingushetia, and so forth. This, thank God, has not happened, for which we must give their due to the spiritual authorities who are formulating their positions clearly and not allowing the country to slide into religious conflict.

Of course, dialogue among clergy brings its own problems. Muslims are a minority in Russia, and their influence on politics is less significant than, say, the Orthodox hierarchy. Some Orthodox ideologues thus aspire to a monopoly on formulating Russia's national and state ideology. Evidently, no one has yet figured out how to solve the triangular problem of Orthodoxy, Islam, and the state in the common interest. This is a very serious problem: on one hand, most of Russia's population is Orthodox; and by tradition Orthodoxy, like Islam, actively interferes in secular, including political, issues. On the other, Muslims are afraid that the idea of creating an Orthodox Great Rus' will have a negative impact on the position of Muslims; and we might note that such considerations and fears have often been stated in the recent period.

It is clear that all these questions are subtle and delicate. They cannot be resolved by running roughshod over the sentiments of the faithful and without acknowledging the normality and naturalness of differences and the distinctive features of the various religions. And it is wholly unacceptable to succumb to various "phobias" merely because we often do not understand the nature of our differences and do not notice that, however great the differences between us may be, we are all united in one motherland and by one historical destiny.

Bibliography

Books

Abou El Fadl, Khaled. *The Place of Tolerance in Islam*. Boston: Beacon Press, c2002.

Afkhami, Mahnaz, ed. *Faith and Freedom: Women's Human Rights in the Muslim World*. Syracuse, NY: Syracuse University Press, 1995.

Ahmed, Akbar S. *Discovering Islam: Making Sense of Muslim History and Society*. New York: Routledge & K. Paul, 1988.

Ahmed, Leila. *Women and Gender in Islam: Historical Roots of a Modern Debate*. New Haven: Yale University Press, c1992.

Algar, Hamid. *Wahhabism: A Critical Essay*. Oneonta, NY: Islamic Publications International, 2002.

Ali, Abdullah Yusuf. *The Holy Qur'an: Text, Translation and Commentary*. Lahore, Pakistan: Sh. M. Ashraf, 1983.

An-Na'im, Abdullahi Ahmed. *Toward an Islamic Reformation: Civil Liberties, Human Rights, and International Law*. Syracuse, NY: Syracuse University Press, 1990.

Anway, Carol Anderson. *Daughters of Another Path: Experiences of American Women Choosing Islam*. Lee's Summit, MO: Yawna Publications, 1996.

Armour, Rollin S. *Islam, Christianity, and the West: A Troubled History*. Maryknoll, NY: Orbis Books, c2002.

Armstrong, Karen. *A History of God: The 4000-Year Quest of Judaism, Christianity, and Islam*. New York: A. A. Knopf, 1993.

———. *Islam: A Short History*. New York: Modern Library, 2000.

Baker, William W. *More in Common Than You Think: The Bridge Between Islam and Christianity*. Las Vegas, NV: Defenders Publications, 1998.

Ernst, Carl W. *The Shambhala Guide to Sufism*. Boston: Shambhala, 1997.

Esposito, John L. *The Islamic Threat: Myth or Reality?* New York: Oxford University Press, 1992.

Esposito, John L., ed. *The Oxford History of Islam*. New York: Oxford University Press, 1999.

———. *Unholy War: Terror in the Name of Islam*. New York: Oxford University Press, 2002.

Esposito, John L., and John O. Voll. *Islam and Democracy*. New York: Oxford University Press, 1996.

Hefner, Robert W. *Civil Islam: Muslims and Democratization in Indonesia*. Princeton: Princeton University Press, 2000.

Hixon, Lex. *Heart of the Koran*. Wheaton, IL: Theosophical Publishing House, 1988.

Huband, Mark. *Warriors of the Prophet: The Struggle for Islam*. Boulder, CO: Westview Press, 1998.

Kepel, Gilles. *Jihad: The Trail of Political Islam*. Translated by Anthony Roberts. London: I. B. Tauris, 2001.

Khalidi, Tarif, ed. and trans. *The Muslim Jesus: Sayings and Stories in Islamic Literature*. Cambridge: Harvard University Press, 2001.

Lang, Jeffery B. *Struggling to Surrender: Some Impressions of an American Convert to Islam*. Beltsville, MD: Amana Publications, 1994.

Lewis, Bernard. *Islam and the West*. New York: Oxford University Press, 1993.

Lewis, Bernard. *What Went Wrong?: Western Impact and Middle Eastern Response*. Oxford; New York: Oxford University Press, 2002.

Lunde, Paul. *Islam*. New York: DK Publishing., 2002.

Miller, John, and Aaron Kenedi, eds. *Inside Islam: The Faith, the People, and the Conflicts of the World's Fastest-Growing Religion*. New York: Marlowe, c2002.

Nasr, Seyyed Hossein. *The Heart of Islam: Enduring Values for Humanity*. San Francisco: HarperSanFrancisco, c2002.

———. *Islamic Science: An Illustrated Study*. Lahore, Pakistan: Kazi Publications, 1987.

Peters, F. E. *The Hajj: The Muslim Pilgrimage to Mecca and the Holy Places*. Princeton: Princeton University Press, 1994.

Robinson, Francis, ed. *The Cambridge Illustrated History of the Islamic World*. New York: Cambridge University Press, 1996.

Schwartz, Stephen. *The Two Faces of Islam: The House of Sa'ud from Tradition to Terror*. New York: Doubleday, 2003.

Shadid, Anthony. *Legacy of the Prophet: Despots, Democrats, and the New Politics of Islam*. Boulder, CO: Westview Press, 2001.

Smith, Jane I. *Islam in America*. New York: Columbia University Press, c1999.

Voll, John Obert. *Islam: Continuity and Change in the Modern World*. Boulder, CO: Westview Press, 1982.

Wadud, Amina. *Qur'an and Woman: Rereading the Sacred Text from a Woman's Perspective*. New York: Oxford University Press, 1999.

Warde, Ibrahim. *Islamic Finance in the Global Economy*. Edinburgh, Scotland: Edinburgh University Press, c2000.

Warraq, Ibn, ed. *The Origins of the Koran: Classic Essays on Islam's Holy Book*. Amherst, NY: Prometheus Books, 1998.

Additional Periodical Articles with Abstracts

More information on the Muslim world can be found in the following articles. Readers who require a more comprehensive selection are advised to consult *Readers' Guide to Periodical Literature, Readers' Guide Abstracts, Social Sciences Abstracts*, and other H. W. Wilson publications.

The Many Faces of Islamic Finance. Matthew Montagu Pollock and Chris Wright. *Asiamoney*, v. 13 pp31–7 August 2002.

The writers explain how Islamic finance divides opinion, with some people viewing it as a growing market of immense potential and others balking at the very concept. It is highly likely that Islamic finance will always be a minor sideline in revenue terms for international banks, although there are few more compelling reasons to embrace it than a Muslim population that now accounts for 20 percent of the world's population. The ways in which the Islamic banking system is trying to resolve such problems as liquidity management and the lack of an interbank market for Islamic institutions are discussed.

What Is the Koran? Toby Lester. *The Atlantic Monthly*, v. 283 pp43–6+ January 1999.

The writer discusses the largely secular effort to reinterpret the Koran, the Muslim holy scripture. In 1972, tens of thousands of pieces from almost a thousand different parchment codices of the Koran were discovered during the restoration of the Great Mosque of Sana'a in Yemen. Such textual evidence is fueling an effort by scholars, Muslims among them, to place the Koran in history, providing a spark for a kind of Islamic revival. The writer covers, among other topics, the Yemeni fragments, the Koran as a literary text, the history of Islam, and revisionism within the Islamic world.

Bin Laden's Reasons: Interpreting Islamic Tradition.   John   Kelsay. *Christian Century*, v. 119 pp26–9 February 27–March 6, 2002.

Kelsey relates how, in 1998, Osama bin Laden and a number of other militant leaders who called themselves the World Islamic Front produced a statement entitled the "Declaration on Jihad against Jews and Crusaders." This document is pertinent to the discussion on whether true Islam has anything to do with the killing of innocent people or is a militant faith that at times requires its adherents to make war on non-Muslims. The document is worth studying for anyone who wants to understand the reasons and motives of those responsible for the September 11 terrorist attacks and others influenced by their ideas. The formation of the World Islamic Front is a sign that at least the leaders of the groups perceive themselves as pursuing a common set of Islamic goals, and that they aim to address the conscience of "all Muslims." The writer discusses the declaration in detail.

Women in Islam: Clothes and Convictions. Jane I. Smith. *Christian Century*, v. 119 pp26–9 January 30–February 6, 2002.

According to Smith, in most Muslim societies, no discussion is more pressing than that concerning the roles of women. Relegated and sometimes confined to the home, women in Muslim societies have practiced their religion in private and have been subject to the dictates of the males of their families. Scholars are increasingly convinced that the prophet Muhammad did not support the bifurcation of the sexes into private and public spheres. Women were clearly in evidence in the first Islamic communities, and Muhammad's wives stand as models for the Muslim women of today who want to legitimize female activity in all areas of society. The increasingly acute problem that Muslims face is that they must rediscover what their religious texts truly say about women's rights and responsibilities and address those cultural practices that are not in accord with the teachings of the Koran and the practices of Muhammad.

Islam and Christianity Face to Face. John L. Esposito. *Commonweal*, v. 124 pp11–16 January 31, 1997.

Esposito writes that the current period is an exceptionally dynamic and fluid one in Muslim history. Diverse voices in the Muslim world are struggling with issues ranging from scriptural criticism and exegesis, modernism, democracy, and pluralism to women's rights and family values. The fundamental issue for Muslims today, however, which also affects Muslim-Christian relations, is the direction of Islamic revival or reform. It remains to be seen whether it will be merely a process of restoration of classical law or a process of reformation. The writer discusses the history of conflict and misunderstanding between Muslims and Christians, the remarkable growth of Islam in the West, and the challenges posed by contemporary Islam on a number of fronts.

Bin Laden, the Arab "Street," and the Middle East's Democracy Deficit. Dale F. Eickelman. *Current History*, v. 101 pp36–9 January 2002.

In future years, Eickleman says, public diplomacy and open communications will have an increasingly important role in countering the image that Osama bin Laden and Al Qaeda assert for themselves as guardians of Islamic values. Video is bin Laden's main vehicle of communication, with mass education and technologies enabling large numbers of Arabs to hear and see Al Qaeda's message directly. Al Qaeda is reaching at least part of the Arab "street," which was described by American policymakers as a new phenomenon of public accountability. The Middle East in general has a democracy deficit, which makes it easier for terrorists, asserting that they act in the name of religion, to hijack the Arab street. For the West, the immediate response is to learn to speak directly to the street, a task that has already started.

Iran's Liberal Revolution? Bahman Baktiari and Haleh Vaziri. *Current History*, v. 101 pp17–21 January 2002.

The writers explain that during presidential election campaigns in 1997 and 2001, Mohammad Khatami appealed to four constituencies that formed the core of Iran's reformist movement. His 1997 victory revealed Iranians' hopes that he would ease the Islamic Republic's restrictions on cultural and social freedoms in the name of religion, execute the rule of law consistently, and strengthen civil society. The groups he appealed to included youths hungry for an easing of cultural and social restrictions and in need of higher education and jobs. Reformists in government have been unable to fully implement their platform, however, including amending restrictions on the press. Arguably, the reform movement has stumbled at three obstacles. These include the dualism of executive power between a secular and religious leader, which renders gridlock more likely in policy making.

The Attractions of Sharia. *The Economist*, v. 364 p44 September 7, 2002.

This article reports that, since 2000, 12 predominantly Muslim states in northern Nigeria have adopted versions of sharia, or Islamic law, for criminal cases, and most of Nigeria's Muslims support the law partly because they believe it reflects the will of God and partly because Nigeria's civil courts are so awful. Supporters of sharia argue that harsh punishments deter violent crime, but Nigeria's Christian leaders argue that northern politicians are exploiting "sharia" to strengthen their power base.

The Case for Islamic Law. John McBeth. *Far Eastern Economic Review*, v. 165 pp12–15 August 22, 2002.

McBeth writes that in Indonesia an increasing number of moderate Muslims, who are concerned about corruption and a collapse of moral values, seem to think of Islamic law, sharia, as a kind of remedy for the country's economic and social problems. Sharia already operates to a degree, although it is largely limited to rituals and social issues that are dealt with through a network of courts that adjudicate on marriage, inheritance, and other domestic disputes. The short-term future could see alcohol becoming a scarcity, head scarves becoming regulation for women, gambling being driven further underground, and women and men possibly being separated at public gatherings.

Sufism and the Indonesian Islamic Revival. Julia Day Howell. *The Journal of Asian Studies*, v. 60 pp701–29 August 2001.

Looking at Indonesian Islam since the 1970s, the writer argues that Sufism has survived and even prospered in the midst of the Islamic revival that has taken place in Indonesia since the 1970s. Indeed, Sufism is being enthusiastically pursued in country and city and has captured the interest of members of the elite and people who are educated. Sufism has attracted people of both sexes who are still fully engaged in their careers, including some in positions of power. These aficionados are reinterpreting Sufi thought as a source of inspiration for contemporary religious practice, and there exists a complex interplay between old and new forms of Sufi devotion.

Jesus and Muhammad: A Historian's Reflections. F. E. Peters. *Muslim World*, v. 86 pp334–41 July/October 1996.

Peters explores some of the reasons why Jesus research is so different from Muhammad research. Among the topics discussed are the sorts of testimony available in both cases, the absence of "neutral" sources on Muhammad, the importance of Henri Lammens's portrait of Mecca for Muhammad's biography, the importance of Josephus in Jesus research, the separation of the "historical Jesus" from the "Jesus of history," and Muhammad's relations with Jews and Christians.

Lessons in Islam from India. Akeel Bilgrami. *The Nation*, v. 273 pp31–2 December 24, 2001.

Bilgraimi examines how Muslim religious life in India has been marked by two inclinations, which are preserved in a fragile balance by the continual tension between them. On the one hand, at the level of ritual, ceremony, and a wide selection of other everyday practices, there is a great deal of retention of local elements that are quite continuous with numerous aspects of Hindu life and cultural practice. On the other hand, there is the spiritual, transcendental, and normative aspect characterized by a deferential look that goes beyond the local toward the Arab lands in which classical doctrine began. The tense dialectic formed by this double movement of form and root has endured in India through the centuries. The writer discusses what the Muslim experience in India reveals about wider realities.

The World of Islam. Don Belt. *National Geographic*, v. 201 pp76–85 January 2002.

Belt reports that about 1.3 billion people embrace Islam, the fastest-growing and possibly most misunderstood religion on Earth. Many non-Muslims' perceptions of the faith have been skewed by terrorists, whose unspeakable acts in the name of Islam have been condemned by leaders everywhere. Islam traces its lineage to the prophet Abrahim, with whom God made covenants that became the foundation of Judaism, Christianity, and Islam. Muslims revere the Prophet Muhammad as their ultimate messenger. They believe that Muhammad was visited by the archangel Gabriel, who began reciting to him the Word of God. Muhammad passed along these revelations to a growing band of followers, and soon after his death the verses were compiled and became the Koran. The writer explains how this book is subject to distortion, and radicals use Muhammad's armed struggle against his enemies as a pretext for waging a holy war against nonbelievers. Such interpretations cannot be overruled because there is no established hierarchy in Islam.

Islam in Action. David Pryce Jones. *National Review*, v. 53 pp20–4 December 3, 2001.

According to Jones, the strongest of distinctions must be drawn between Islam and the terrorism carried out in its name. President Bush is just one of the leaders repeating the mantra that Islam is peaceful and tolerant. There is no quarrel with the religion as such, but only a just war against Osama bin Laden and the Taliban regime behind him. The Muslim world has, however, long been immersed in tyranny, corruption, and poverty. Political extremism is the dominant expression of Islam. What is currently at stake is the role that peace and tolerance will play in the Islam of the future.

Islam and Scientific Fundamentalism. Munawar Ahmad Anees. *New Perspectives Quarterly*, v. 19 pp96–101 Winter 2002.

The writer discusses the philosophy of knowledge in Islam. Post-scientific society faces the difficulty of reestablishing a spiritual identity. Muslims consider soul-searching even more important in light of the cultural relativism and plurality vindicated by postmodernism. The solution lies not in clinging to the vanishing phantom of scientific fundamentalism but in creating new cognitive niches without abandoning substantive knowledge.

When Galileo Meets Allah. Farida Faouzia Charfi. *New Perspectives Quarterly*, v. 19 pp89–95 Winter 2002.

Charfi writes that conservative traditionalists have seized on the lack of economic progress in the Arab-Islamic world as a perceived betrayal in order to disseminate their fundamentalist ideology by force. Fundamentalists do not lay claim to the entire Islamic heritage—in particular, to the rationalist philosophy espoused in the 12th century by Ibn Rochd (known as Averroes by the Latins), whose philosophical work contributed to the separation of faith and knowledge, of religion and philosophy. The writer asserts that it is now time to rehabilitate Ibn Rochd in order to open up Islam to modern scientific thought. The world will advance further and further ahead of Islam if Islam cannot manage in this era to separate knowledge from belief.

Mohamed Khatami, President of Iran. Christopher Dickey and Maziar Bahari. *Newsweek*, v. 139 pp74–5 December 31, 2001–January 7, 2002.

The writers say that Iranian president Mohamed Khatami could be the best hope the rest of the Muslim world has, at least in 2002, for a leader who is able to reconcile modern democracy with Islamic culture. When he first stood for the post of president in 1997, Khatami called for a "civil society" that accepted Islam as the foundation of government but rejected brutality in the name of God—and went on to win by a landslide. If he gets his way now, the nation that started the modern fundamentalist state could offer the most promising way out of Islamic extremism, which is the United States' No. 1 enemy.

The Great Koran Con Trick. Martin Bright. *New Statesman*, v. 130 pp25–7 December 10, 2001.

According to Bright, the conclusions by the so-called "new historians" of Islam about the origins of the religion, the Koran, and the life of the Muslim Prophet Muhammad are deeply provocative and have caused much offense in Muslim circles. Their conclusions include claims that almost nothing is known about the life of Muhammad; that the rapid rise of Islam can be in part attributed to the attraction of conquest and jihad; that the Koran was compiled or written long after Muhammad's death; and that the religion may best be understood as a heretical branch of rabbinical Judaism. According to Francis Robinson, editor of *The Cambridge Illustrated History of the Islamic World*, this new history remains in obscurity because there is not yet one figure who can bring its revolutionary ideas together in an accessible way.

Faces of American Islam. Daniel Pipes and Khalid Dur'an. *Policy Review*, v. 114 pp49–60 August/September 2002.

The writers discuss Muslim immigrants living in the West. They estimate the numbers of Muslims resident in the United States and where in the country they tend to congregate. They outline the history of Muslim immigration to the United States and explain why Muslims have made the move. The writers also explain religious and educational practices particular to Muslim society and discuss the tensions within the Muslim community, the pressures on Muslim children growing up in Western society, and some of the Muslim institutions founded and operating in the United States.

Islam and Democracy. Hugh Goodard. *The Political Quarterly*, v. 73 pp3–9 January/March 2002.

The writer discusses the diversity of opinion among 20th-century Muslims regarding the relationship between Islam and democracy. He argues that four distinct perspectives can be identified as particularly influential in the bid to formulate an Islamic response to democracy. He outlines these points of view—namely, that Islam and democracy are in fundamental opposition, Islam is incompatible with democracy, Islam and democracy are compatible, and democracy is essential for Islam.

Women's Political Rights: Islam, Status and Networks in Kuwait. *Sociology*, v. 36 pp639–62 August 2002.

The article reports that during the last decade there have been signs of increased democratization in the Middle East, yet women's political rights remain limited. This article focuses on Kuwait, a country representative of how citizenship rights have been gendered in the Middle East. Some Kuwaiti women's groups support expanding women's political rights. This article seeks to determine if they have potential allies in the general population. Using survey data from 1,500 Kuwaiti citizens in 1994, potential advocates for extending women's rights are identified by examining social status, social networks, religious identity, and Gulf War experiences. Organized women's groups are found to have potential allies in Sunni young people and men who belong to voluntary organizations, Shia young men, older women, and those who backed Islamic movements abroad. These, groups form a basis for developing a broad base of popular support for expanding the citizenship rights of women.

Public Islam and the Problem of Democratization. Robert W. Hefner. *Sociology of Religion*. v 62 pp491–514 Winter 2001.

Hefner explains that, as in much of the late modern world, Muslim societies in recent years have seen an unprecedented resurgence of religious issues and organizations into public affairs. The resurgence has given special urgency to the question of whether this revitalized Islam is compatible with democracy and civic pluralism. Drawing on comparative materials and an in-depth discussion of recent events in Indonesia, the world's largest majority-Muslim country, this article presents a preliminary analysis of the relationship of Islam to democratization. Hefner argues that most Muslims continue to look to their religion for principles of public order as well as for personal spirituality. The political ideals Muslims derive from their tradition, however, are not immutable but vary in a manner that reflects competing views as to how Muslims should respond to the challenges of the late modern world. Some Muslim activists invoke the idea of Islam as "religion and state" to justify harshly coercive policies and the fusion of state and society into an unchecked monolith. But there is also in the Muslim world an emerging democratic or civil-pluralist tradition that seeks to recover and amplify Islam's democratic endowments. Its supporters argue that, by concentrating vast power in rulers' hands, the "Islamic" state only increases the likelihood that the religion's high ideals will be subordinated to authoritarian intrigues. As events in Indonesia illustrate, this "clash of cultures" between promoters of a Muslim civil society and democracy and supporters of an anti-pluralist "Islamic" state is likely to remain a key feature of Muslim politics for some time to come.

The Legacy of Abraham. David Van Biema. *Time*, v. 160 pp.64–70+ September 30, 2002.

Biema writes that, aside from God, Abraham is the only biblical figure acclaimed by Jews, Christians, and Muslims, but his value as a unifier is negligible. The events of September 11, 2001, and the ensuing tensions between the West and Islam led many to seek to use Abraham as an interfaith unifier, but the reality is that, although Jews and Muslims both see him as their father, they disagree on almost everything else. Indeed, a disagreement over whether Abraham's covenant with God entitles Israelites to sole property of the Holy Land has resulted in the settler movement and the current conflict with Palestine.

Why Jerusalem Was Central to Muhammad. Karen Armstrong. *Time*, v. 157 pp50–1 April 16, 2001.

Armstrong relates how Jerusalem has been central to the spiritual identity of Muslims since the early days of their faith. When, according to the earliest biographers, the Prophet Muhammad first started preaching in Mecca, in approximately 612, he had his converts prostrate themselves in prayer facing jerusalem. They were symbolically reaching out toward the Jewish and Christian God; Muhammad was convinced that he was simply bringing the old religion of one God to the Arabs. As a result, the Koran worships the great prophets of the Judeo-Christian tradition. The writer discusses the way in which the story of Muhammad's mystical night journey to Jerusalem shows the centrality of the city in Muslim faith.

Is the Face of Islam Changing? Farid Esack. *U.S. Catholic*, v. 67 pp12–7 January 2002.

In the wake of September 11, South African scholar and progressive Muslim theologian Farid Esack has become one of the most sought-after interpreters of Islamic thought in the United States. In an interview, Esack, who is currently a visiting scholar at Union Theological Seminary in New York, discusses such topics as the size of the progressive Islam movement, what the movement offers in the present crisis, what ordinary people can do to improve Christian-Muslim relations, and the specific role of the United States in today's interconnected world.

Defender of the Faith. Jay Tolson. *U.S. News and World Report*, v. 132 pp36–8 April 15, 2002.

According to Tolson, UCLA law professor Khaled Abou El Fadl has become a thorn in the side of reactionary Muslims wolrdwide. He maintains that sharia, the basis of the Islamic legal system, is a moral vision broader than any single set of injunctions or prohibitions and can therefore support something far more promising than crude attempts to impose primitive customs on modern societies. Throughout the 1990s, Abou El Fadl was subjected to verbal and physical attacks at numerous American mosques and Islamic centers where he had gone to speak or simply worship. During the summer of 2001, he began to receive a well-orchestrated barrage of death threats from a group of disgruntled zealots.

Muslim in America. Jeffery L. Sheler. *U.S. News and World Report*, v. 131 pp50 October 29, 2001.

Sheler writes that American Islam is characterized by wide-ranging diversity. Although it is the nation's fastest-growing faith, it remains widely misunderstood in the United States. The religion of over 20 percent of the world's population is seen by many Americans as foreign, mysterious, and even threatening, despite the fact that it shares common roots with Christianity and Judaism and has been present in North America for centuries. The way in which Muslim beliefs can conflict with the dominant culture of a country is examined.

Wahhabis in America: A Saudi Export We Could Do Without. Stephen Schwartz. *Weekly Standard*, v. 7 pp15–7 November 5, 2001.

According to Schwartz, the main public critics of America in Saudi Arabia are the Islamofascist imams and muftis of the Wahhabi sect, the ideological arm of the Saudi royal dictatorship. The Wahhabi-Saudi establishment also subsidizes terrorism and seeks to control Muslim religious institutions and activities across the globe. In 1999, Sheikh Hisham Kabbani of the Islamic Supreme Council of America stated that 80 percent of mosques in America are subject to Wahhabi manipulation through financial subsidies. Schwartz claims that the Council on American Islamic Relations, which is only a minor line item in the Wahhabi budget, is the most obnoxious front for terrorist apologetics to be found in America; even since September 11, it has tried, on the pretext of promoting "sensitivity," to dictate how Islam may be discussed in American media.

Islamic Banking. World Link, v. 13 pp66–68 September/October 2000.

The article reports that Islamic banking has emerged as an increasingly important financial industry, and Bahrain is poised to become a leading center. Islamic financial institutions offer Muslims an ethical way to invest with potentially attractive returns, and the FTSE World Index reveals that Islamic investment is growing by 12–15 percent a year. Moreover, more than half of the region's Islamic financial institutions are based in Bahrain, and Al Baraka Banking Group recently decided to bring nine of its subsidiaries into a new structure regulated by the Bahrain Monetary Agency. The origins and development of Islamic banking are discussed, and charts depict the locations of the 182 Islamic banks worldwide and the projected growth of the Muslim population in relation to the rest of the world.

The Lineaments of Islamic Democracy. Ray Takeyh. *World Policy Journal*, v. 18 pp59–67 Winter 2001/2002.

The writer discusses whether an Islamic Middle East is capable of producing populaces and governments that are prepared to adopt international modes of conduct. He notes that Western commentators have long contended that Middle Eastern culture, particularly the effect of Islamic religious doctrine, is the primary obstacle to democratization. However, he contends that throughout the Middle East a new generation of Islamic thinkers is hoping to blend Islam's precepts with democracy's imperatives. He concludes that a global war against poverty is the most effective way to combat extremist ideologies.

Index